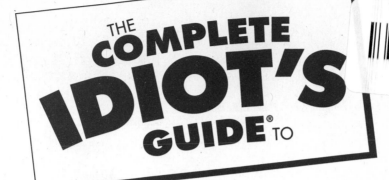

THE **COMPLETE IDIOT'S GUIDE®** TO

Green Building and Remodeling

by John Barrows and Lisa Iannucci

ALPHA

A member of Penguin Group (USA) Inc.

 Printed on recycled paper

ALPHA BOOKS

Published by the Penguin Group

Penguin Group (USA) Inc., 375 Hudson Street, New York, New York 10014, USA

Penguin Group (Canada), 90 Eglinton Avenue East, Suite 700, Toronto, Ontario M4P 2Y3, Canada (a division of Pearson Penguin Canada Inc.)

Penguin Books Ltd., 80 Strand, London WC2R 0RL, England

Penguin Ireland, 25 St. Stephen's Green, Dublin 2, Ireland (a division of Penguin Books Ltd.)

Penguin Group (Australia), 250 Camberwell Road, Camberwell, Victoria 3124, Australia (a division of Pearson Australia Group Pty. Ltd.)

Penguin Books India Pvt. Ltd., 11 Community Centre, Panchsheel Park, New Delhi—110 017, India

Penguin Group (NZ), 67 Apollo Drive, Rosedale, North Shore, Auckland 1311, New Zealand (a division of Pearson New Zealand Ltd.)

Penguin Books (South Africa) (Pty.) Ltd., 24 Sturdee Avenue, Rosebank, Johannesburg 2196, South Africa

Penguin Books Ltd., Registered Offices: 80 Strand, London WC2R 0RL, England

International Standard Book Number: 978-1-59257-828-3
Library of Congress Catalog Card Number: 2008931270

11   10   09   8   7   6   5   4   3   2   1

Interpretation of the printing code: The rightmost number of the first series of numbers is the year of the book's printing; the rightmost number of the second series of numbers is the number of the book's printing. For example, a printing code of 09-1 shows that the first printing occurred in 2009.

Printed in the United States of America

Note: This publication contains the opinions and ideas of its authors. It is intended to provide helpful and informative material on the subject matter covered. It is sold with the understanding that the authors and publisher are not engaged in rendering professional services in the book. If the reader requires personal assistance or advice, a competent professional should be consulted.

The authors and publisher specifically disclaim any responsibility for any liability, loss, or risk, personal or otherwise, which is incurred as a consequence, directly or indirectly, of the use and application of any of the contents of this book.

Most Alpha books are available at special quantity discounts for bulk purchases for sales promotions, premiums, fund-raising, or educational use. Special books, or book excerpts, can also be created to fit specific needs.

For details, write: Special Markets, Alpha Books, 375 Hudson Street, New York, NY 10014.

Publisher: *Marie Butler-Knight*
Editorial Director: *Mike Sanders*
Senior Managing Editor: *Billy Fields*
Acquisitions Editor: *Tom Stevens*
Development Editor: *Jennifer Moore*
Production Editor: *Kayla Dugger*
Copy Editor: *Megan Wade*

Cartoonist: *Steve Barr*
Cover Designer: *Bill Thomas*
Book Designer: *Trina Wurst*
Indexer: *Heather McNeill*
Layout: *Chad Dressler*
Proofreader: *Laura Caddell*

Contents at a Glance

Part 1:   **Green Home Basics**   1

   1 Why Green Homes Matter   3
*What exactly is a green home, and why does it matter that
you have one? Learn about the problems with the environment and how the choices you make in your home can make a
positive impact on your family and the environment.*

   2 It *Is* Easy Being Green   19
*Just go green, experts say, but what exactly does that mean
and how do you get there? Learn how to integrate green
features into your current home, understand the differences
between building a traditional home versus a green home, and
get a handle on what it means to have your home certified.*

   3 Planning Your Green Home   29
*Here is where you start evaluating and prioritizing your
remodeling or building project. Should you build a new home
or remodel your current one?*

   4 Dollars and Sense   45
*Learn how much it is going to cost you to remodel or build a
green home. Uncover tax and utility breaks for getting money
back. Find out about new energy-efficient mortgages.*

   5 A Material World   55
*What makes a product sustainable? Repeat your new mantra:
reduce, reuse, recycle. Learn creative approaches to finding
building materials for free.*

   6 Home Sweet Home   65
*Select the best sites to build your home. Consider avoiding cer-
tain types of land.*

Part 2:   **Your Home's Structure**   77

   7 Homebuilding Techniques   79
*Start with a strong foundation. Learn options for framing
your house and choices of eco-friendly insulation.*

   8 Windows and Doors   93
*Select energy-efficient windows. Choose the right front door
and skylights, and make the right skylight selections.*

  9 Roofing and Siding   105
     *Decide on roofing material and consider options for exterior
     materials. Learn about surface choices based on your location.*

 10 Floors and Walls   117
     *Select flooring for each room. Choose from the traditional to
     the exotic and decide on wall coverings and budget consider-
     ations.*

Part 3:   Energy   129

 11 Heating and Cooling   131
     *Learn about solar heating, wind power, biofuels, geothermal,
     and other mechanical systems, as well as selections of water
     heaters.*

 12 Water Heating   143
     *Learn about preserving water and reducing the energy needed
     to heat your water. Go behind the walls and install environ-
     mentally favorable piping.*

 13 Appliances and Countertops   151
     *Choose ENERGY STAR dishwashers, stoves, refrigerators,
     washers, and dryers. Pick a countertop and cabinets, from
     stone to tile to bamboo and wood.*

 14 Light and Power   165
     *Install your lighting system. Select automated systems, solar
     panels, net metering, and more.*

Part 4:   Water and Air   175

 15 Water Preservation and Conservation   177
     *Learn about water quality and water scarcity. Find out how
     to reuse water, control contamination, and irrigate your back-
     yard.*

 16 Faucets and Fixtures   187
     *Study the benefits of a low-flow toilet. Design a water-efficient
     shower and learn some facts on shower and toilet fixtures.*

 17 Air Quality   195
     *Improve indoor air quality by letting the house breathe.
     Prevent offgassing contamination.*

Part 5:   Outdoors   **207**

  18 The Great Outdoors   209
      *Eliminate invasive plants and plant edible yards. Design your
      yard wisely to maximize its environmental benefits. Get quick
      tips on mulching and getting rid of pests.*

  19 Shade and Sun   219
      *Protect yourself and your house from the sun and heat. Choose
      deciduous trees, evergreens, canopies, and shutters.*

  20 Let It Rain!   227
      *The benefits of rain, capturing and reusing rain, and perma-
      nent erosion controls. Consider xeriscaping as a landscaping
      option.*

  21 Pools, Hot Tubs, Fencing, and More   235
      *Consider greening your pools and hot tubs. Get the facts on
      environmentally friendly fencing. And find out which wood
      you should choose for your deck.*

  22 It Can Be Done   247
      *Get motivated and inspired by reading stories of other home-
      owners and communities that have successfully built and
      remodeled green.*

Appendixes

   A Glossary   259

   B Green Building Resources   267

   C The NAHB National Green Building Program   281

   D LEED Rating System List   297

      Index   303

Contents

Part 1: Green Home Basics 1

1 Why Green Homes Matter 3

Why Green Homes Matter 5

    Shrink Your Carbon Footprint 6

    Reduce Your Energy Use 8

    Save Money 9

    A Healthy Home 10

    High Air and Water Quality 11

    Good for the Environment 12

    Help Your Local Economy 12

    Increase the Value of Your Home 12

    You Get a Good, Good Feeling 13

The Green Home Movement 13

What a Green Building Is *Not* 15

Environmental Stewardship 16

It Can Be Done 17

2 It *Is* Easy Being Green 19

Deciphering Facts and Myths 20

    Myth: Green buildings are funny-looking and made out
    of hay bales, old tires, and other bizarre materials. 21

    Myth: I can't afford to go green and install high-priced
    technologies like solar roof panels. 22

    Myth: Builders don't want to build green. 23

    Myth: To be green, we have to replace everything in our home! 24

    Myth: There's too much to learn. 24

    Myth: Green building materials don't last longer than
    traditional building materials. 24

    Myth: It seems like every business makes some claim to
    being "green" these days. I can't decipher the truth from
    hogwash, so it's not worth it. 25

    Myth: Historic homes can't be greened. 25

National Homebuilder Mainstream GreenHome 26

3 Planning Your Green Home 29

Brainstorm Your Wants and Needs 30

    Designing Byte by Byte 30

Everything Old Is New (and Green) Again 31
Buying Resale 31
   Location, Location, Location 32
   Resale Value 32
   Affordability 32
   Foreclosures 33
   Handyman Specials 34
Evaluating 35
   Integration Not Separation 35
Prioritizing 36
   Climate 36
   Local Requirements 37
   Budget 37
   No Job Too Small 38
Building an Eco-Friendly Home 39
   Evaluating and Prioritizing 39
   Land 39
   McMansions' Major Footprint 40
   Smaller Footprints 40
Other Alternatives: Granny Flats and Green Communities 41
It Can Be Done 42
   LivingHomes LEED Platinum Rating 42
Certification 43

4   Dollars and Sense   45

Energy Efficient Mortgages 46
Tax Credits 47
Your Green Dream Team 49
   Builder and Remodeler Basics 49
   Drawing It Up 50
   Landscaping Your Site 51
Sign on the Dotted Line 52
Insurance Coverage 53

5   A Material World   55

LEED Standards for Green Materials 56
Sustainable Versus Unsustainable 56
Locating Suppliers 58
   Think Local 58
   Reduce 58

Reuse: One Man's Trash 59
Deconstruction 62
Construction and Demolition 63

6   Home Sweet Home   65

Smart Growth 66
Site Planning 67
Infill Development 67
Adaptive Reuse 69
Brownfields Are Green Again 69
Greyfields 71
Sites to Avoid 71
Wetlands 71
Floodplains 72
Farmland 72
Build Some, Save Some 73
It Can Be Done: An Infill and a Brownfield 73

Part 2:   Your Home's Structure   77

7   Homebuilding Techniques   79

Foundations 80
Framing 81
Structural Insulated Panels (SIP) 81
Steel 81
Advanced Framing Techniques 82
Novel Framing Techniques: Earthships and Yurts 83
Straw Bale Homes 84
Heat and Moisture 101 84
Conduction 84
Convection 84
Radiation 85
Moisture Movement 85
Get It Under Control 86
Insulation 87
Which Insulation Is Right for You? 88
Loose-Fill Insulation 89
Batt Insulation 91
Open-Cell Foam 91
Denim, Cotton, and Soy 92

8 Windows and Doors   **93**

The Importance of Efficient Windows 94
Window Design 95
   Glazing *97*
   Low-E *97*
   U-Value *98*
   The Solar Heat Gain Coefficient (SHGC) *98*
Frames and Sashes 99
Window Placement and Size 99
Skylights 100
Low-Budget Upgrades 101
   Storm Windows *101*
   Window Film *101*
   Caulking and Weatherstripping *102*
   Smart Windows *103*
Doors 103
   Garage Doors *104*
   Sliding Glass Doors *104*
   Interior Doors *104*

9 Roofing and Siding   **105**

Roofing Styles 106
Climate Control 107
Types of Roofing 107
   Shingles and Shakes *108*
   Tile *109*
   Concrete *109*
   Slate *110*
   Metal Roofs *111*
   Adobe *111*
Green Roofs 111
   Cool Roofs *112*
Siding 113
   Wood *113*
   Cement and Brick *113*
   Vinyl *114*
   Aluminum Siding *114*
Exterior Paint Job 114
It Can Be Done: Alys Beach, Florida 115

10 Floors and Walls   **117**

The Facts on Flooring 118
The Wonders of Wood 119
   Reclaimed Wood..*120*
   Laminated Wood..*120*
   Plantation-Grown Wood *120*
   Bamboo...*120*
   Stone *121*
   Ceramic Tile..*122*
   Cork *122*
   Linoleum *123*
   Concrete *123*
   Leather, Coconut, and Other Exotics....................................*124*
   Carpeting *125*
Paints 125
   The ABCs of VOCs...*126*
   Get the Lead Out! *126*
Wallpaper..127

Part 3: Energy   **129**

11 Heating and Cooling   **131**

Warming Trends...132
   Forced Hot Water *132*
   Forced Air *133*
   Floor Heating *133*
   Heat Pump *134*
Warmth from the Hearth 134
   Pellet Stoves...*135*
   Wood Stoves...*135*
Bigger Is Not Necessarily Better 135
Green Heat..137
   Solar Heating...*137*
   Geothermal Energy..*138*
Fuel Efficiency Standards for Your Home 139
Cooling Down: Air Conditioners and Fans 139
   Room Air Conditioners *140*
   Central Air Conditioning..*140*
Facts About Fans 141
Passive Cooling 141

12 Water Heating   **143**

Water Heaters 144

  On-Demand Hot Water Heaters.. 144

  Indirect Heaters 145

  Solar Water Heaters 145

  Drain Water Recovery Systems 146

Piping.. 146

  Good-Bye PVC 146

  Hello PEX.. 147

Insulation 148

Water Temperature 149

13 Appliances and Countertops   **151**

When to Upgrade Your Old Appliances 152

  Stoves and Ovens.. 154

  Refrigerators and Freezers 155

  Washing Machines and Dryers.. 156

  Dishwashers.. 157

Disposing of Old Appliances 158

Countertops.. 158

  Countertops to Reconsider 158

  Paper Composite 159

  Recycled Glass 159

  Concrete 160

  Recycled Ceramic Tiles 160

  Glass Tiles 161

  Recycled Plastic 161

  Terrazzo.. 161

  Other Countertop Options.. 162

Kitchen and Bathroom Cabinets 162

  Holding Them Up 163

14 Light and Power   **165**

Education on Electricity 166

  Lighting.. 166

  Compact Florescent Lights 167

  Halogens.. 169

  Light-Emitting Diode (LED) 169

Design for Your Lighting Needs 169
Artificial vs. Daylight 170
Lighting Controls 171
Power! 171
   Solar Power! *172*
   Wind Power! *172*

Part 4:   **Water and Air**   **175**

15   **Water Preservation and Conservation**   **177**
Building Green Protects and Preserves Our Water 178
Water Quality 178
   Make Changes *179*
Use Rain Barrels 180
Reuse Greywater 182
Create Rain Gardens 184

16   **Faucets and Fixtures**   **187**
Toilets 188
   Toiletry 101 .... *188*
   Low-Flow Toilets *189*
Showerheads 191
Faucets 192
   Aerators *193*
   Sensors *193*

17   **Air Quality**   **195**
Know Your Home's Air Pollutants 196
   VOCs *197*
   Radon *198*
Know Your Moisture 198
Ventilation 200
   Air Quality Tests *202*
   Combustion Venting *203*
   A Few Words About Humidifiers *203*
Filtration 203
Garage Exhaust 204
Duct Cleaning 205

Part 5: Outdoors 207

18 The Great Outdoors 209

Design Your Yard Wisely 210
Invasive Plants 211
Pesticides 212
   The Good Bugs 213
   Integrated Pest Management 214
   Natural and Organic Pest Remedies 215
Green Fertilizers 215
   Compost 216
   Buying Bugs 216
Grow Your Own 216

19 Shade and Sun 219

Trees 220
   Deciduous Trees 220
   Evergreens 221
Windbreaks 221
Canopies, Shutters, and Awnings 222
   Canopies 222
   Shutters 224
Roof Gardens 224
   What's Your Climate Zone? 225

20 Let It Rain! 227

Protecting the Watershed 228
Permeable Pavements 228
Xeriscaping Made Simple 230
Irrigation Information 230
Wasteful Watering Habits 231
Go with the Flow 232
Erosion 232

21 Pools, Hot Tubs, Fencing, and More 235

Pools and Hot Tubs 236
   Eco-Friendly Pumping and Filtering 237
   Heating and Filtering 237
   More Energy- and Water-Saving Tips 238
   Chemical-Free Zone 239

Fencing 240
    Living Walls 241
Step Up to Your Deck 242
Light the Way: Outdoor Lighting 243
The ABCs of BBQs 243
Play Structures 245
A Few Extras: Keeping Warm 245

22 It Can Be Done   247

Green Communities 248
    Raleigh's Chavis Heights Community 248
    DC's Jefferson at Half Street 248
    Oakland Park, Florida 249
    From Tragedy to Triumph: Greensburg, Kansas 249
    Cherry Hill, New Jersey 250
Ed Begley Jr. and the $100 Thermostat 251
Matthew Linden, ConsciousBuild 252
A Green Interior and Exterior in Louisville, KY 253
Bryan Roberts's Florida Earthship 254
Platinum Living 255
Take the Next Steps 256
That's Not All Folks! 256

Appendixes

  A Glossary   259

  B Green Building Resources   267

  C The NAHB National Green Building Program   281

  D LEED Rating System List   297

  Index   303

Foreword

When it comes to addressing most of the challenges we face as a society, it is often said that change begins at home. This is an exciting prospect—that we can make a difference around the world by changing the way we live our daily lives—and nowhere is it truer than in our efforts to improve the health of our planet, our communities, and our families. A greener home is the ideal place to start as we work toward a greener world.

According to the U.S. Department of Energy, buildings' energy use accounts for 39 percent of the United States' carbon emissions, and the typical American family pays upward of $1,500 a year in energy costs. Buildings' designs often fail to make the most efficient use of water, an increasingly scarce and valuable resource. The materials used to build them are often harvested and transported in ways that are detrimental to the environment, and those same materials can release toxic chemicals that damage the health of building occupants. Americans spend roughly 90 percent of their day indoors, breathing air that is affected by the chemicals and products that fill our buildings.

This all may sound like bad news at first blush. In reality, the opportunity to make real change by building and renovating greener homes is great news. Families can save money, live in greater comfort and health, enjoy the durability of longer-lasting homes, and help in the fight against climate change and environmental degradation all at once. A truly green home makes efficient use of energy and water, is built with responsibly harvested and produced materials, has a healthy indoor environment, minimizes its impact on the land it sits on, and is inhabited by people who know how to live as green as possible. All kinds of homes can be green, from single-family detached homes to high-density apartments, and from luxury condominiums and townhouses to affordable housing projects. Green homes can be built green, or they can be renovated to be green. But green building and renovation are more than just the sum of a handful of green features. A green home is the result of a holistic, integrated plan where green features, systems, designs, and products complement each other and work as a sustainable whole.

If all this sounds like a lot of work, don't worry. There are a host of tools out there to help you make the wisest green decisions in building or renovating a green home. The U.S. Green Building Council's LEED® for Homes rating system is like a nutrition label for green homes. LEED-certified homes have been inspected and rated by third-party experts, and they are given a score based on all the factors that go into making a home green. USGBC also offers The Green Home Guide at www.thegreenhomeguide.org, which provides more information on green homes, profiles of LEED-certified homes, and the free-to-download REGREEN Residential

Remodeling Guidelines, which will guide you in detail through any type of green home remodeling project. And by buying this book from the folks at *Complete Idiot's Guide*, you are demonstrating the vital foundation for successful green building projects: a desire to be educated, to learn to do it the right way.

Now is a great time to build green. The 2007 McGraw-Hill Construction SmartMarket Report showed a rapidly growing market for green homes, with truly green homes valued nationwide at almost $2 billion in 2005. The report predicted that market will grow to $20 billion by 2010. Experts say green homes are certain to outpace their conventional counterparts in resell value, with some predicting that within 10 years, homebuilders who aren't building green won't be building at all.

Good luck as you work to make your home part of the solution—for yourself, your family, your community, and our planet.

Rick Fedrizzi

CEO, President, and Founding Chairman of the U.S. Green Building Council

Introduction

Ever since the green movement took off, there has been an abundance of material written on the subject, from greening your life, your car, and of course your home. But like any subject that you are delving into for the first time and want to learn more about, the amount of information can be overwhelming. So you want to build a green home, but how do you start? How does each system in your home connect to one another? Whom do you contact? How much is it going to cost you?

If you already own a home, you may be wondering how you can make it more energy efficient. Where do you start? What do you upgrade first? What will bring you the most payback in terms of energy efficiency and cost?

This book is going to give you a step-by-step process to learning about green building and remodeling. Most important, this book is going to show you how to integrate your systems to one another. For example, if you are remodeling your home, it isn't logical to invest in a solar heating system if you haven't fixed the air leaks in your home. If you want an on-demand water heater, that's great, but how about starting with a low-flow toilet and faucet fixtures first? This book will show you how making even the smallest green building upgrades will improve your energy efficiency and heating and cooling costs almost immediately. This book will also show you how you can take one green step at a time, work within your budget, and make the transition happen.

What this book isn't going to do is give you extreme "out there" suggestions for greening your home. It's more about the mainstream, traditional methods of building and remodeling your home, but made better. Although we mention earthships and yurts, we believe that most readers won't give up their current digs and move to a small home made of tires and earth. Although earthships are a great idea and certainly meet the criteria of a green home, we're going to talk more about traditional styles of building with some earth-friendly alternatives to choose from.

Once you're done with this book, you might have more questions about your specific home. That means it's time to talk to your builder about your specific needs in your specific geographic location. As much as we can generalize to talk about all different locations, we can't possibly cover everything on green building in one book, so it's important to have this very vital conversation with your builder.

As we write this book, the building industry is still learning about the green industry. Builders who have spent decades building homes the same way are suddenly being inundated with questions on greener materials and other alternatives. They are learning at the same time we are. Some are more ahead of the curve than others, so it's important to find a builder that's qualified to have these discussions with you. And remember that to have a successful green home, you need to know about the industry, too. Stay on top of the information that's out there, so you know the options that are available.

It's often said that making a difference starts at home—this time it just so happens that it's *with* your home.

Although it's best to read this book from the beginning, feel free to skip around to find exactly what you're looking for. Here's how the book is structured:

Part 1, "Green Home Basics," lays the groundwork for green building and remodeling. Start by taking a tour of the environmental issues that face us today and learn how you can make all the difference. Find out how you'll save money and live a healthier, cleaner life. Finally, start planning your green home, from its size, the location, your dream team, and the materials you'll choose.

Part 2, "Your Home's Structure," demonstrates the importance of creating a strong foundation for your home. You'll learn about the various framing techniques that keep your home tighter and the many environmentally friendly styles of roofs, windows, doors, floors, and walls. Finally, find out how to keep your home from being too hot or too cold with the right kind of insulation.

So many new green heating and cooling systems are available today. **Part 3, "Energy,"** covers various "green" heating and cooling systems and helps you determine which one is right for you. You'll also learn how to efficiently heat and cool your home and water. Finally, you'll learn how to choose an efficient appliance, sustainable countertops, and toxic-free cabinets and light the way with an energy-efficient lighting system.

Part 4, "Water and Air," begins by pointing out how easy it is to reuse rainwater for many of your daily chores. It also helps you choose water-efficient piping and bathroom fixtures for your home and covers the ins and outs of adequate ventilation and indoor air quality.

In **Part 5, "Outdoors,"** you'll learn how to "go green" on the outside of your home. You'll find out how to utilize your landscape for shade and sun and choose the best fencing and driveway material. Finally, you'll put the finishing touches on your green home with an eco-friendly pool and energy-efficient outdoor lighting, as well as other features that will make your house a home.

You'll also find four appendixes: a comprehensive glossary of green building and remodeling terms; a list of helpful organizations, websites, and other green building and remodeling resources available to you; information on the NAHB National Green Building Program; and a partial list for LEED certification.

We've also developed some little helpers you'll find throughout the book:

def•i•ni•tion

Here you'll find meanings to words you might not understand.

Tips & Tools

Here you'll find interesting tidbits about green living and tools to get you started.

Hard Hat Area

Here you'll find warnings for potential obstacles that could hinder your green building plans.

Green Facts

Here you'll find statistics and interesting information on the nation's and your carbon footprint.

Acknowledgments

One of my favorite parts about writing a book is the acknowledgments because, as all writers know, books like this don't get written without a little help from our friends:

To Patricia Quaglieri, who worked for hours looking up as much information on green building and remodeling as she could possibly find.

To David Stenger of Creekview Homes in Hopewell Junction, New York, for putting me in touch with my co-author John Barrows and for being there for me professionally every time a project comes about.

To John Barrows, who has an incredible wealth of knowledge on the green building industry and was willing to share it with me for this book.

To my agent Marilyn Allen of the Allen O'Shea literary, who had faith in me for this project.

To my editor Tom Stevens at Alpha Books, who made this book possible and gave me a wealth of guidance and advice.

To one of my favorite writers, Bobbi Dempsey, whose professional advice helped me write this book; and to Lori Hall Steele, an incredible writer whose strength and determination I admire tremendously.

To my children, Nicole, Travis, and Samantha. You understood what commitment it took to write this book, and you all took on additional responsibilities so I could meet the deadline. I love you and you're all awesome! —Lisa Iannucci

I would like to acknowledge my parents, John and Carol Barrows, for instilling a life-long appreciation and wonder for the environment and the belief that even the small steps have a long-lasting impact.

—John Barrows

Trademarks

All terms mentioned in this book that are known to be or are suspected of being trademarks or service marks have been appropriately capitalized. Alpha Books and Penguin Group (USA) Inc. cannot attest to the accuracy of this information. Use of a term in this book should not be regarded as affecting the validity of any trademark or service mark.

Part 1

Green Home Basics

Traditional methods of building or remodeling a home use a tremendous amount of materials—many of them nonrenewable and toxic—and pay little attention to the impact the home's site has on the landscape.

In this part, you will learn how greening your home will not only allow you to tread more lightly on the environment, but will also make your home healthier and more energy efficient, which will save you money in the long run.

This part also walks you through the process of choosing a piece of property or existing structure that helps you minimize your impact on—or perhaps even improve!—the environment. Along the way, you'll read inspiring stories of others who have chosen to "go green."

Why Green Homes Matter

In This Chapter

- ◆ You and your home can make a difference
- ◆ Reduce your carbon footprint
- ◆ Save green by going green
- ◆ What a green building *isn't*

"It's time to go green!" "Make your home eco-friendly!" "Live a green life!" "Protect the environment!" It seems as though every magazine and talk show these days is talking about how to live a more earth-friendly existence and protect the environment. And for good reason. After all, there is a serious crisis occurring in our environment—it's called global warming.

Global warming is an increase in the earth's temperature due to an excessive amount of greenhouse gases in the atmosphere. Although many greenhouses gases are naturally occurring, other gases end up in the atmosphere due to the burning of fossil fuels—the coal from power plants, the heat from the oil or gas in our homes, and the gas in our cars. The gases get trapped in the air, making the atmosphere slowly heat up.

The consequences of global warming can be extreme. Temperatures will continue to warm, so some locations may experience more hot days and fewer cool days, while other areas experience less snow or excessive rain while some dry areas receive even less rain. This intense warming can have detrimental effects, leading to melting ice caps and glaciers, which in turn cause sea levels to rise. As a result, some animals, such as the polar bears, are facing extinction, while other animals and insects are moving out of their natural habitats. This insect relocation, combined with warmer temperatures, is creating an influx of bugs that are destroying trees and vegetation. According to the National Research Defense Council, global warming is also causing excessive wildfires, severe dust storms, and flood damage in many parts of the United States.

Simply put, scientists have discovered that global warming is caused by humans. It is our fault that Earth's temperature is rising due to the cars we drive, the material goods we own, and the houses we live in. And we need to make changes now.

In addition to global warming, we are running through the world's resources at an alarming rate. We must learn to rely on sustainable, or renewable, resources to build our homes. According to Greenpeace, half of the world's forests have disappeared—only 20 percent remain relatively undisturbed and intact—and the remaining forests are shrinking at an alarming rate due to both legal and illegal logging. Every second, an area of forest equal to the area of a football stadium is destroyed—that's over 23 million acres a year.

Understandably, you want your dream home, and that dream home can be everything your family, the environment, and future generations need it to be by making simple changes in your design choices. These changes will save you money over the course of living in the home, *and* you will be living in a healthier home that is not detrimental to the environment. You probably already recycle and reuse everyday products in your home; now you're ready to take that bigger step and build a green home or remodel the home you have now. Congratulations! Change truly does start at home.

Green building is not a passing trend. However, there is so much information right now on green building that the concept can seem daunting. It doesn't have to be. This book will take you step-by-step through choosing the right products and processes for making your home an environmentally friendly place to live.

In this chapter, you will learn more about why converting your current home to a green home, or building a green home from the ground up, is the right decision for you, your family, and the environment.

Why Green Homes Matter

Does having a green home really matter to the environment? In a word, *yes*.

More than a million single-family homes are built in the United States every year. Over the last 30 years, the square footage of these homes has gotten bigger and bigger. Think of all the wood, metal, and fuel that are used when building one single-family home. Or the fact that the construction of an average 2,000-square-foot home also creates more than a ton of construction waste—waste that is rarely reused or recycled. Now multiply that by more than a million homes. When you do the math, you can see that building a home consumes a great deal of natural resources and energy. And after the home is built, it requires energy to run the appliances, air conditioning, lights, and all the electronic gadgets we can't seem to live without.

Not only does building a green home help reduce the amount of materials and energy used in the construction of the structure, but it also helps reduce water waste from showers, baths, dishwashers, washing machines, pools, spas, toilets, and more.

Green Facts
The United States tops the list among other large nations in the amount of pollution it contributes to global warming.

According to GreenBuilding.com, in homes that have not been "greened" yet:

◆ Toilets use 3.7 to 7 gallons per flush.

◆ Dishwashers use 8 to 14 gallons per cycle.

◆ Top-loading washers use 45 gallons per load.

◆ A dripping faucet wastes 15 to 21 gallons per day.

◆ Americans withdraw enough water to fill a line of Olympic-size swimming pools reaching around the world every day (300 billion gallons).

Then, there are other problems with our homes:

◆ The Environmental Protection Agency (EPA) ranks indoor air pollution among the top-five environmental risks. Unhealthy air is found in up to 30 percent of new and renovated buildings that haven't been greened.

◆ The World Health Organization (WHO) reports that indoor air pollution causes 14 times more deaths than outdoor air pollution (2.8 million lives).

◆ Twenty percent of all housing in the United States has lead dust or chippings, which cause kidney and red blood cell damage, impair mental and physical development, and may increase high blood pressure.

◆ The *volatile organic compounds* (including pesticides), commonly referred to as VOCs, found indoors are believed to cause 3,000 cases of cancer a year in the United States.

def•i•ni•tion

Volatile organic compounds (VOCs) are emitted as gases from certain solids or liquids and include a variety of chemicals, which can have short- and long-term adverse health effects. When shopping for products such as paint and carpeting, look for low- or no-VOC labels.

That's scary stuff, but you already know the remedy. Building or remodeling your home to be as green as possible can actually help to offset many of these problems. Most importantly, a truly green home includes all aspects of construction—you can green the inside, the outside, and even the landscape!

Take a look at what a green home looks like on the following page.

Now let's break down the benefits of owning a green home even more.

Shrink Your Carbon Footprint

For many of us, a typical day is as follows: get out of bed in your heated or air-conditioned home, flip on switches to turn on the lights, start your morning cup of joe and heat your oatmeal, take a long hot shower, blow-dry your hair, drive to work, work for several hours, drive back home, cook dinner, run your ancient dishwasher and washing machine, drive to the gym and make several stops along the way to pick up the kids, head back home, and start the whole process again tomorrow.

Green Facts

Want to know your carbon footprint? Check out www.nature.org/initiatives/climatechange/calculator/. Answer questions and find out your carbon footprint score. Then learn more steps you can take to reduce your score even more.

Have you ever really stopped to think about the impact of your daily routine on the environment? You might want to check your carbon footprint.

A carbon footprint is a description of how much carbon dioxide (CO_2) each one of us is responsible for putting into the environment on a daily basis. Many of the things we do—driving a car, hopping a plane, heating our home, turning on the television—require fossil fuels such as gas, oil, and coal to work. Burning these fossil fuels sends CO_2 and other greenhouse gases into the air.

ENERGY INNOVATION
How Homes Become Green

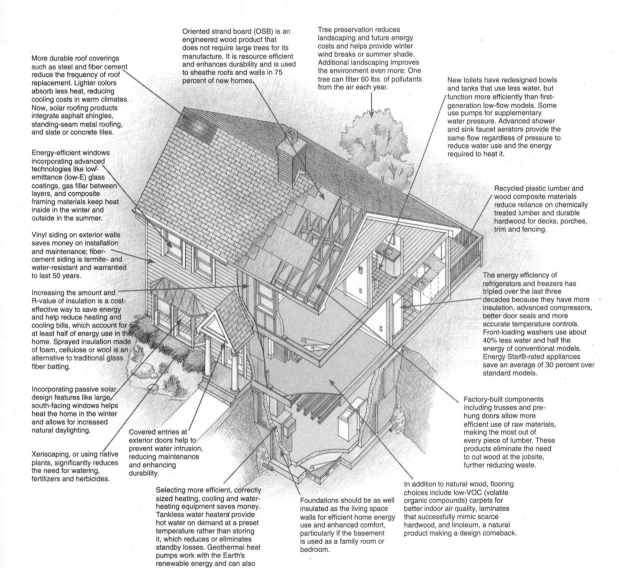

Oriented strand board (OSB) is an engineered wood product that does not require large trees for its manufacture. It is resource efficient and enhances durability and is used to sheathe roofs and walls in 75 percent of new homes.

Tree preservation reduces landscaping and future energy costs and helps provide winter wind breaks or summer shade. Additional landscaping improves the environment even more: One tree can filter 60 lbs. of pollutants from the air each year.

More durable roof coverings such as steel and fiber cement reduce the frequency of roof replacement. Lighter colors absorb less heat, reducing cooling costs in warm climates. Now, solar roofing products integrate asphalt shingles, standing-seam metal roofing, and slate or concrete tiles.

New toilets have redesigned bowls and tanks that use less water, but function more efficiently than first-generation low-flow models. Some use pumps for supplementary water pressure. Advanced shower and sink faucet aerators provide the same flow regardless of pressure to reduce water use and the energy required to heat it.

Energy-efficient windows incorporating advanced technologies like low-emittance (low-E) glass coatings, gas filler between layers, and composite framing materials keep heat inside in the winter and outside in the summer.

Recycled plastic lumber and wood composite materials reduce reliance on chemically treated lumber and durable hardwood for decks, porches, trim and fencing.

Vinyl siding on exterior walls saves money on installation and maintenance; fiber-cement siding is termite- and water-resistant and warrantied to last 50 years.

The energy efficiency of refrigerators and freezers has tripled over the last three decades because they have more insulation, advanced compressors, better door seals and more accurate temperature controls. Front-loading washers use about 40% less water and half the energy of conventional models. Energy Star®-rated appliances save an average of 30 percent over standard models.

Increasing the amount and R-value of insulation is a cost-effective way to save energy and help reduce heating and cooling bills, which account for at least half of energy use in the home. Sprayed insulation made of foam, cellulose or wool is an alternative to traditional glass fiber batting.

Incorporating passive solar design features like large, south-facing windows helps heat the home in the winter and allows for increased natural daylighting.

Covered entries at exterior doors help to prevent water intrusion, reducing maintenance and enhancing durability.

Factory-built components including trusses and pre-hung doors allow more efficient use of raw materials, making the most out of every piece of lumber. These products eliminate the need to cut wood at the jobsite, further reducing waste.

Xeriscaping, or using native plants, significantly reduces the need for watering, fertilizers and herbicides.

Selecting more efficient, correctly sized heating, cooling and water-heating equipment saves money. Tankless water heaters provide hot water on demand at a preset temperature rather than storing it, which reduces or eliminates standby losses. Geothermal heat pumps work with the Earth's renewable energy and can also heat water.

Foundations should be as well insulated as the living space walls for efficient home energy use and enhanced comfort, particularly if the basement is used as a family room or bedroom.

In addition to natural wood, flooring choices include low-VOC (volatile organic compounds) carpets for better indoor air quality, laminates that successfully mimic scarce hardwood, and linoleum, a natural product making a design comeback.

(The National Association of Home Builders; artist, Rick Vitullo)

There are two types of carbon footprints—a primary footprint, which measures the emissions from these fossil fuels, and a secondary footprint, which measures the CO_2 emissions products give off when they break down. The average American generates about 15,000 pounds of carbon dioxide per year from both primary and secondary uses!

By building or remodeling your home to become more efficient, you will reduce your carbon footprint. A truly green home has been built or remodeled with materials that have been reused, can be replenished, are not harmful to the environment or to our health, and make efficient use of energy and water. Your morning cup of coffee, the lights, and your blow dryer can be powered using a solar electricity system. Your dishwasher can be upgraded to an energy-efficient appliance to use less water *and* energy. You can buy products closer to home. There's so much that you can do!

Reduce Your Energy Use

Do you have drafty windows? Are your doors allowing air to escape out of the bottoms or sides? Leaky doors and windows mean higher energy costs and energy use. Your heating and cooling systems will require more energy if the air is leaking out of the house. As a result, your systems—which run on fossil fuels—are adding even more carbon dioxide to the atmosphere.

This pie chart shows the breakdown of energy use in your home.

(U.S. Department of Energy)

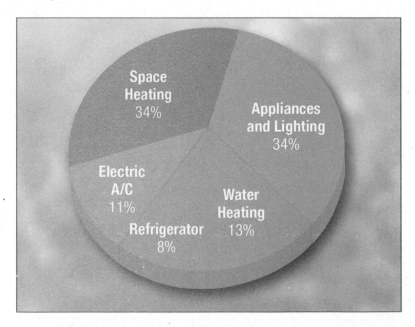

There are other sources of energy loss in your home, including poor insulation in your attic, basement, or crawl space. Old, outdated appliances also use massive amounts of energy, and electricity generated by fossil fuels to run your computers, appliances, televisions, and other devices puts more carbon dioxide into the air than two average cars. Even when your appliances are on "sleep mode," they are still using electricity.

Making energy-saving changes such as upgrading to newer energy-saving appliances; plugging up leaks in doors and windows; and properly insulating your attic, basement, and crawl space will create a home that is energy efficient and environmentally sound.

Save Money

Building a green home—especially one equipped with a solar electricity system—once had a sully reputation of being extremely overpriced. Why? Because certain features of a green home are costly to install. For example, solar panels can cost $25,000 or more to install, and it can take several years before you actually see a financial return on your investment. Energy-efficient washing machines, dishwashers, and dryers can also cost more upfront than traditional machines.

But things are looking up. Several factors are starting to drive down the prices in the green building industry. First, there is more competition—more businesses, products, and sustainable materials coming on the market—and businesses are beginning to drop their prices to compete with each other. Second, as more businesses enter the green market, the costs of developing and manufacturing green technologies is going down.

On the flip side, some green building materials may actually cost significantly less than traditional materials. For example, using materials from a *deconstructed* barn or building or from salvage yards can cost you next to nothing.

All things equal, today a green-built home will cost anywhere from 2 to 20 percent more than the same house built with non-sustainable materials. Of course, the actual cost depends on several factors, including your location, the size of the home, and the products and systems you decide to install. The good news is that you will continue to

def•i•ni•tion _____

Deconstruction means taking apart or removing some home components with the primary goal of reusing them.

reap the benefits of your investment for years to come. Some efforts—such as installing proper insulation and efficient windows, air sealing, and appliances—will begin to save you money almost immediately on your monthly electric and water bills.

More good news is that an energy-efficient home is less costly to own, operate, and maintain. It is practically guaranteed to stop you from throwing money out your drafty, energy-wasting windows and, instead, lets you put it where it belongs—right into *your* own pocket year after year!

For example, statistics show that the most efficient new appliances typically use 50 percent less energy than the most wasteful models. As a result, you could save up to 30 percent on your household energy bills by implementing energy-efficiency improvements.

In addition to pocketing some extra cash, homes that meet green building standards might also qualify for special mortgages, known as Energy Efficient Mortgages (EEMs) and Energy Improvement Mortgages (EIMs) that offer better interest rates and additional purchasing power. The changes you make in your home can also qualify for various federal and state tax credits, depending on which state you live in. (See Chapter 4 for more information on these programs.)

According to a survey conducted for the National Association of Home Builders (NAHB), a builder's trade association that helps to promote the policies that make housing a national priority, homeowners are ready to pay a little more for a green-built home because they recognize they'll get more out of the home than they put into it.

A Healthy Home

No one wants to think their home can make them sick. Unfortunately, many of the materials used to build and decorate your home could be making you and your family to suffer from allergies, shortness of breath, ear infections, migraines, skin reactions, birth defects, cancers, and more.

Modern building materials can come with a host of problems, including the following:

◆ Homes built before 1978 might have been painted with **lead-based paint,** which, when breathed in or ingested, could lead to nervous system and kidney damage, learning disabilities, muscular problems, hearing loss, and speech and other language disorders, especially in children.

◆ Older homes might have been built with products that contain **asbestos,** such as pipe and furnace insulation materials, roofing shingles, millboard, textured paints, and floor tiles. Asbestos can cause serious lung disease that can lead to disability and death.

◆ Pressed wood can include **formaldehyde,** a colorless, pungent-smelling gas that can cause watery eyes, burning sensations in the eyes and throat, asthma attacks, nausea, and difficulty breathing. The World Health Organization (WHO) labeled formaldehyde as a human carcinogen (cancer-causing) in 2004.

◆ Vinyl flooring and certain carpeting have also been linked with **volatile organic compounds (VOCs)** that worsen respiratory problems like asthma.

◆ **Polyvinyl chloride,** otherwise known as PVC and found in piping and even in shower curtains, has been linked to cancer, kidney and liver damage, growth problems, and other serious health problems.

In addition, if a home is poorly ventilated, outdoor pollutants such as pesticides and pollution can seep into the home through cracks in the structure and affect your health. A green home helps protect you and your family from these and other maladies. The building materials in a green home are free of lead, asbestos, formaldehyde, PVC, VOCs, or other chemicals that can be detrimental to your health.

> **Green Facts**
>
> When David Bach, author of the best-selling *Automatic Millionaire* book series, moved into his apartment at The Solaire, an environmentally progressive New York City apartment building, he said the air filtration system eliminated his allergies and winter asthma.

High Air and Water Quality

The EPA lists poor indoor air quality as one of the top-five most urgent public health risks in the United States. This means that the level of air pollution inside your home can actually be higher than outside of your home!

Without proper ventilation, mold and mildew can form in any home—even one built using environmentally friendly materials. You can find mold and mildew where there have been water leaks or in walls where moist air condenses on cool surfaces. This growth can contribute to a host of medical problems, including skin rashes, runny noses, eye irritation, coughs, nasal congestion and aggravation of asthma, difficulty breathing, flulike symptoms, and infections.

Building your home with low-toxic materials and installing proper ventilation systems creates a healthier atmosphere for you and your family.

Good for the Environment

Building a green home isn't just about doing what is right for you and your family. It's also about recognizing the impact the choices you make today have on the environment tomorrow. It is about *sustainability*. It is about evaluating the effect that a particular product has on the environment from the time it is created to the end of its life span.

def•i•ni•tion

Sustainability means meeting human needs today and in the future while preserving the natural environment.

The farther a product—let's say a slab of stone that you absolutely must have for your kitchen countertop—is shipped, the less green it can be considered, due to fuel used to extract, manufacture/refine, package, and ship the product. Too many steps = too much possible negative impact on the environment. Making choices to reduce your energy and water waste; improve your carbon footprint; and use natural, renewable, and local resources protects and nurtures the environment and our precious resources.

Help Your Local Economy

People often overlook the fact that it is vital to purchase as many of your green building materials as possible from within your community. In addition to reducing the impact on the environment and your energy use, using local products and materials actually helps to stimulate your neighborhood economy. And by using goods gathered from a nearby salvage yard or recycling plant, you can keep products out of your local landfills.

Increase the Value of Your Home

Of course, you will want to live in and enjoy your wonderful green home, but there might come a day when you decide to sell it. In 2008, the real estate market suffered—sales were down a whopping 40 percent from a few years ago, when they were at their peak. Homes that were once selling within days or weeks of being listed are now sitting on the market for more than a year before an offer is even made.

By making green renovations, you offer potential buyers a home with cleaner air, reduced water usage, and lower energy bills. In other words, you're adding value to your home. And as the price of fuel continues to rise, that real estate value continues to increase as well, and current research shows that green-built homes are selling at a much better rate than nongreen homes.

def•i•ni•tion

Making a home **adaptable** means to build it for your future needs. For example, wider doorways to accommodate wheelchairs, kitchen features that allow you to reach things easily, and levers instead of doorknobs.

If your plan is to stay in this home for your entire life, you'll want to make it *adaptable* to your possible future needs. It's a smart strategy that prevents the need to renovate again later.

You Get a Good, Good Feeling

You wouldn't have picked up this book if you didn't know that building or remodeling your home to be more environmentally friendly is the right thing to do. And doing the right thing makes you feel good. You are taking a socially responsible step to do your part in saving the environment.

The Green Home Movement

Although saving the environment and building green have taken on new urgency with the release of former Vice President Al Gore's best-selling book and movie *An Inconvenient Truth*, they really aren't new concepts. According to the EPA, advocates have been using natural resources to build and run homes—and have been urging others to do the same—for a long time.

The EPA says that some practices, such as passive solar design or using renewable materials in home construction, date back millennia. For instance, ancient Greeks built entire cities so that all the homes received solar heat in the winter.

The contemporary green building movement arose out of the need and desire for

Green Facts

In 2006, consumer awareness and interest in green building and living catapulted when former Vice President Al Gore released the documentary film and book *An Inconvenient Truth*. It won multiple awards, including an Academy Award, and became the fourth highest-grossing documentary in U.S. history. Gore received the Nobel Peace Prize for his efforts to combat global warming.

more energy-efficient and environmentally friendly building practices. The oil price increases of the 1970s spurred significant research and activity to improve energy efficiency and find renewable energy sources. This, combined with the environmental movement of the 1960s and 1970s, led to the earliest experiments with contemporary green building.

In the 1990s, the green building industry began to come together with the launching of various organizations, including the following:

- ◆ The American Institute of Architects (www.aia.org) formed a **Committee on the Environment** in 1989, which works to educate the trade and the public on green building design. This organization also helps consumers locate qualified architects and provides resources on choosing an architect and building a home.

- ◆ In 1992, the **ENERGY STAR** Program (www.energystar.com) became a joint program of the U.S. EPA and the U.S. Department of Energy. The ENERGY STAR Program is dedicated to helping consumers save money and protect the environment by guiding consumers to purchase products that have met its strict energy-efficient guidelines.

- ◆ In 1993, the nonprofit **U.S. Green Building Council** (**USGBC;** www.usbgc. org) was launched with the aim of expanding sustainable building practices. USGBC comprises more than 13,500 organizations from across the building industry that are working to advance structures that are environmentally responsible, profitable, and healthy places to live and work. Members include building owners and end users, real estate developers, facility managers, architects, designers, engineers, general contractors, subcontractors, product and building system manufacturers, government agencies, and nonprofits.

- ◆ In 1998, the USGBC launched its **Leadership in Energy and Environmental Design** program, which is almost always referred to simply as LEED. LEED is a third-party certification program and a nationally accepted benchmark for the design, construction, and operation of high-performance green buildings. LEED promotes a whole-building approach to sustainability by recognizing performance in five key areas of human and environmental health: sustainable site development, water savings, energy efficiency, materials selection, and indoor environmental quality. LEED certifies buildings that meet its strict green standards and classifies the structures according to certified, silver, gold, and platinum ratings.

In 2006, NAHB, the International Code Council (ICC), and the NAHB Research Center initiated a process for the development of a voluntary green home building standard that can be adopted by local green home building programs.

We are finally starting to see a difference. In 2007, Americans saved enough energy to avoid greenhouse gas emissions equivalent to those from 27 million cars, while at the same time saving $16 billion on their utility bills. In 2006, more than 172,000 new ENERGY STAR–qualified homes were built nationwide, accounting for more than 12 percent of all new site-built, single-family homes permitted.

And according to NAHB, as much as 10 percent of all housing starts are expected to include environmentally friendly construction by 2010—up from 2 percent of starts in 2007.

And there is more good news on the horizon. Entire green residential communities are now being built throughout the country, and consumers like you are starting to demand more green products and services in their homes and their lives.

There are still many obstacles to overcome, however. At the time of writing this book, the real estate and building industries were suffering from serious setbacks. As a result, some construction companies that were eager to add green building to their business during boom times are now holding off, especially because some of the upfront costs are a little higher than standard building materials and many businesses are doing their best to cut expenses. Hopefully, builders will continue to educate themselves on the financial benefits of green building and learn that, with a little creative ingenuity, the up-front costs can be reduced to compete with traditional building construction.

What a Green Building Is *Not*

Decades ago, a green home was thought of as a habitat that only die-hard "tree huggers" and environmentalists built because they were on a mission to "save the planet." What did *you* have in mind when you pictured a green home? Perhaps you thought it would look like something that the three little pigs would build? You know, a plain—okay, unsightly—home, made of piles of straw bales or old tires? It's a myth that having a green home equals having an ugly, tiny, or even space-saucer–shaped home. Green-built homes can look just like any other conventional home, no matter what style—ranch, colonial, southwest, whatever—you choose to build or remodel. It will look the same on the inside, too.

Actually, from a building perspective, the three little pigs had the right idea, but they really didn't know how to execute it. Straw bale homes really can withstand big bad wolf winds, and houses made of sustainable wood really can last much longer than standard homes. And most importantly, no matter what style you choose, your home will be beautiful because of the richness of the renewable materials that you have used and the care and thoughtfulness that you have put into it.

Environmental Stewardship

Buying this book means you have taken a major step to do your part and make changes both in and out of your home that will positively affect the environment. *Environmental stewardship* is the term used to reflect the responsibility shared by all those whose actions affect the environment.

To fix the problems, it's important to understand how the problems were started in the first place. To do so, you must educate yourself on environmental issues and how decisions humans make today can have a significant impact on the environment tomorrow and for generations to come. You can stay educated by regularly visiting the websites mentioned in this book for updates. Many colleges are now offering courses on environmental stewardship. You can also volunteer for organizations such as the Natural Resources Defense Council (www.nrdc.org) and work hands-on for various projects, learn how to write your congressman to stop or pass legislation that can affect the environment, or raise funds so organizations can do their part to save the environment.

Tips & Tools

Visit the EPA's website (www.epa.gov) and search for "environmental stewardship." After entering your state and selecting an environmental issue, a list of opportunities will display. It's up to you to volunteer your time, money, or talents to one or more causes.

Making these changes and becoming involved isn't just to benefit you and your family—it's to benefit future generations as well. Former president Jimmy Carter was once quoted as saying, "It is good to realize that if love and peace can prevail on earth, and if we can teach our children to honor nature's gifts, the joys and beauties of the outdoors will be here forever."

It Can Be Done

When you're learning something new, it's always helpful to see how others have done it. Green building is no exception. If you have the opportunity, visit the home of a family member or friend who has incorporated green building techniques and see how the systems work up close. Or visit one of the many "show" homes green builders across the country have built to be used as educational tools and selling points for potential customers. Throughout this book, we'll be providing real-life examples of green homes to show you that it can be done.

Sharon Patterson converted a 540-square-foot, pre-1948 house and preserved as much of it as possible while adding 730 square feet to the structure. The vision for the project was to incorporate OM, a yoga chant that represents consciousness and having a connection with all that exists, into the design. It was a priority of Patterson's to achieve a sense of balance, beauty, and harmony between the myriad of "green" choices: nontoxic/healthy materials, preservation, reused and recycled materials, energy efficiency, working with nature (solar, natural ventilation), water conservation, durability, affordability, waste reduction, and an adaptable design.

This home was renovated with a variety of green building features.

(Sharon Patterson, LEED, OmYourHome.com)

The renovated home.

(Sharon Patterson, LEED, OmYourHome.com)

A few of the features include stairs built from old wood reclaimed from a barn; countertops made of recycled paper; native, drought-tolerant landscaping with drip irrigation; pre-plumbing for a solar hot water system; recycled denim wall insulation and soy-based spray-foam insulation in the attic; window placement to capture the sun from the south in the winter (with overhangs) as well as capture prevailing winds from the northwest in the summer; no-VOC paint; no mechanical air conditioning; windows laid out to encourage cross-ventilation with a whole-house fan; a closed-loop system of composting; and rainwater capture and edible gardening.

According to Patterson, "The goal was to be realistic about a budget and produce a beautiful and sustainable home that the average person could relate to and be inspired by."

The Least You Need to Know

- ◆ To help save on rising fuel costs and reduce the damage to the environment, a green home really is the best option.

- ◆ A green home can be an attractive home built to fit any lifestyle.

- ◆ Although the green home movement has been around for a long time, it has grown significantly in recent years.

- ◆ Today, there are numerous organizations and websites available to help consumers build a green home.

It *Is* Easy Being Green

In This Chapter

- ◆ Shattering myths about green building
- ◆ Facts on greenwashing
- ◆ Visiting a green home
- ◆ Greening a historical home

For years, the lovable, adorable Muppet, Kermit the Frog, has told us in song that it's not easy being green. Of course, he's not singing about green building and remodeling; he's pouring his heart out about being an amphibian. Unfortunately, however, many humans out there share Kermit's cry of woe when it comes to learning about, and trying to be, green—especially when it comes to making sense of green building technologies. Many make an energetic attempt, but their lack of knowledge causes them to fall short and exclaim in frustration, "It's not easy being green!"

The truth is that green building and remodeling is easier than you think. You don't need to be as knowledgeable as a builder or contractor, but like anything new, there's bound to be a learning curve. Think back to when you bought a car—before you headed off to the showroom, you researched the type of car you wanted, decided on the features you wanted, and then armed with this knowledge you bought your new car. The automotive industry has its own jargon, but you took time to learn how to speak the language.

Like the automotive industry, green building and remodeling comes with a lingo all its own, but it's pretty easy to understand and doesn't take long to learn. Right now if you were to read about a homeowner who installed a heat recovery ventilator, geothermal heating system, window film, and blown-in insulation, and who designed a living wall in his backyard, you might shake your head, close the book, and wonder why you even tried. In some respects you *are* learning a new language. But by the time you're done with this book, you'll know what each of these green features means and you'll even be able to determine what features you want and don't want for your own home. Then, armed with your new knowledge, you can design and build or remodel your dream green home.

Deciphering Facts and Myths

Over the last decade, the green building and remodeling industry has erupted with new products and technologies, and everybody seems to be calling themselves green specialists. Flip through the phone book or stroll the aisles of your local home show, and you'll encounter green builders, environmentally friendly remodelers, and even realtors who specialize in helping you to buy green homes. Add to this the number of magazine articles and books on the subject, and the amount of information that's out there can be overwhelming!

Although you're ready to begin this amazing transformation to build or remodel the green home of your dreams, perhaps you've come into this process wondering about everything you've been told and read about.

- ◆ Can green building and remodeling really be easy to understand and affordable no matter what budget you are on?

- ◆ Is green building and remodeling only for those die-hard environmentalists who have dedicated their lives to environmental and political awareness?

- ◆ Does living in a green home mean living in a cramped house packed under the earth, run solely on the sun's rays, and lacking today's modern conveniences?

Actually, these are all misconceptions about today's green building movement.

But don't worry, you are not the only one—and certainly won't be the last one—trying to sort out all of this information. Everybody is leaping into unfamiliar territory when it comes to the green industry. Even builders are immersed in the subject, taking classes on green building techniques and becoming certified as green builders. Some builders have even gone so far as to build green homes for themselves so they can learn, hands-on, how it all works. At the same time, local, state, and federal governments are now designing programs to assist communities and individuals who are interested in becoming more energy efficient and doing their part to help the environment.

Why are more and more consumers finally recognizing the benefits of green building?

◆ **There is more guidance available.** Organizations and departments such as USGBC's LEED, ENERGY STAR, the EPA, the American National Standards Institute (ANSI) Green Building Standards, the NAHB, and more are providing resources and guidance as to how the performance of your home can be measured.

◆ **Consumers are becoming more aware of the financial benefits of green building and remodeling.** A benefit from the tremendous amount of media attention on green building is that consumers are learning more about the cost-saving features of having a greener, more energy-efficient home. For example, energy-efficient appliances and systems will allow you to run your home for less money. In addition, you might be eligible for tax breaks for buying and installing these appliances and systems and upgrading other areas of your home with green features. (This topic is covered in more detail in Chapter 4.)

◆ **Green materials and furnishings are now only slightly more expensive than traditional materials.** In some cases, they are even less expensive than their nongreen counterparts.

So let's get to the truth and debunk Kermit's notion that it's not easy being green, as well as any preexisting ideas you might have—about green building anyway. Sorry, we can't comment on what it's like to an amphibian.

Myth: Green buildings are funny-looking and made out of hay bales, old tires, and other bizarre materials.

Fact: It's true that green building used to be associated with granola-eating, Birkenstock-wearing environmentalists whose primary mission was to save the planet by cutting back on their damage to Earth. They lived in yurts (circular homes covered in earth) or homes made out of straw bales or even recycled tires and at the time, these homes were considered pretty darn peculiar by mainstream folks.

Well, we've now learned that the environmentalists were on to something. The environment does need protecting. It's vital to conserve our precious resources, and living in yurts is one way of doing so. However, many homeowners don't want to live in yurts. Instead, they want a Victorian, colonial, Tudor, or other traditional-style home.

Fortunately, today's green building industry can make any home a green home. You'll see pictures of various styles of green homes throughout this book. Some of them are built with straw bales, tires, and even denim, but they are extremely well-designed and even look like other, nongreen, homes.

Myth: I can't afford to go green and install high-priced technologies like solar roof panels.

Fact: It's a big misconception that you must purchase expensive technologies such as geothermal heating systems or solar panels to be green. You can make green changes in your home no matter what your budget. The cost of your project depends on three things:

◆ What level of green you are striving for.

◆ What green practices your builder/remodeler uses.

◆ Whether you are incorporating green practices into an existing structure or a newly designed home. It's often more costly to incorporate green technologies into an existing structure than it is to go green from the ground up.

If you are on a budget, don't worry. Done right, green remodeling won't blow your budget out of the water. If you can't afford to completely remodel your home in one shot, you can do it on a project-by-project basis or you can start small and pick what we call the "low-hanging fruit." For example, insulating your crawl spaces and attic, sealing the house for air leaks, orienting your house to make the most of natural conditions, and choosing materials that are environmentally safe are all choices that can be accomplished without making a big dent in your wallet. In turn, they might even start to save you some money.

For instance, if you have a $1,000 budget, you might use that money to pay for an energy audit of your home. During an energy audit, a professional energy auditor comes to your home to evaluate how much electricity you use and where you are losing energy in your home. The audit will also identify ways that you can reduce your energy use through simple repairs and the installation of energy-efficient systems. You can also conduct this energy audit yourself by looking for air leaks throughout the house and ways to improve your insulation and home heating and cooling systems. Conserving energy is the most effective way to go green, and you can start to do so without the pricey technologies.

If your budget is a little higher, let's say $5,000, you have the funds to consider upgrading any older, leaky windows or doors in addition to completing the energy audit and installing the insulation. After these projects are complete, you should begin to see a reduction in your heating and cooling bills. You can then take *that* extra money and·put it toward your next green remodeling project!

Tips & Tools

One homeowner we know wanted to replace his old windows to save energy and cut down on oil consumption, but an energy audit showed that the windows didn't need to be replaced. Instead, the home-owner beefed up the insulation in his house's attic and replaced the century-old furnace.

Green Facts

Planet Green is the first and only 24-hour eco-lifestyle television network and it also has a robust online presence and community. Launched in 2008, Planet Green includes expert advice from on-air personalities such as Sara Snow, Annabelle Gurwitch, Emeril Lagasse, and Steve Thomas. Check with your local cable or satellite television provider to find out whether Planet Green is available in your area.

Myth: Builders don't want to build green.

Fact: Over the last decade or so, the building industry has recognized the benefits of green building and is embracing this concept. Just as there are more resources available to consumers today, more training and resources are available to builders as well.

The U.S. Green Building Council developed the Leadership in Energy and Environmental Design (LEED) Green Building Rating System that encourages sustainable green building. The organization also offers training courses for industry members to increase their knowledge of the green building industry. The National Association of Home Builders sponsors the annual NAHB National Green Building Conference and the NAHB National Green Building Awards and provides information for builders on how to use sustainable design to build homes that use renewable materials prudently to conserve energy and environmental resources. In February 2008, NAHB unveiled the NAHB National Green Building Program and the University of Housing Certified Green Professional designation for builders and remodelers.

Myth: To be green, we have to replace everything in our home!

Fact: Don't throw out that old air conditioner just yet! Although it's true that you might need to replace some items immediately, don't start ripping out all the old to bring in all the new just yet. Green building is about sustainability, which means you should use what you have until it's no longer functioning. For example, if your old refrigerator or dishwasher is still functioning well, don't send them to the landfill just so you can replace them with more energy-efficient models. The same thing goes for your floors. Don't rip up your old wooden floors for the sole purpose of laying down a sustainable bamboo floor. Instead, your remodeling goal should be to wait until these items need replacing and then make better greener choices when choosing new ones.

Myth: There's too much to learn.

Fact: Do you own a high-definition television, a DVD player, surround sound speakers, and TiVo? I bet you do, and I also bet you figured out pretty quickly how to install them and use them in conjunction with one another. It's the same thing with green technology. Of course, there is a learning curve for understanding green technology. Sure, it'll take some time and you won't need to know as much as your builder knows, but it's essential to have a basic understanding of how your dual-flush toilet works or how the geothermal heating system and solar panels work in case of maintenance and repair issues. All of these things are really no more difficult than setting up your home entertainment system.

Also keep in mind that the actual process of building or remodeling a green home is really no different from building a traditional home. First, you will either remodel the home you own now or you will purchase a home or piece of property to build on. Then, you hire the necessary players to help you construct or modify your dream home and you choose the features you want to include. Your house will then be built or remodeled, and you're done. Some of the systems you have installed are obviously different, but for the most part (unless you're changing from a traditional home to a home completely made of tires and other nontraditional materials), not much has changed.

Myth: Green building materials don't last longer than traditional building materials.

Fact: Most sustainable building materials are as durable as traditional building materials. In addition, unlike many traditional products, green products do not emit toxins and can often be recycled. So even if an alternative product doesn't last as long as its traditional counterpart, it's still the better choice for the environment.

Myth: It seems like every business makes some claim to being "green" these days. I can't decipher the truth from hogwash, so it's not worth it.

Fact: Just because a product or system is labeled "green," "biodegradable," "eco-friendly," or "environmentally friendly" doesn't mean it is, and just because a business calls itself green doesn't mean it follows green practices. Businesses are slapping the green label on everything these days because green sells. For example, when interviewed, one developer said he is a green builder because he installs ENERGY STAR–rated appliances in his condos. He doesn't include any other green features, but it doesn't matter because, he says, most people don't have a clue what green building practices really are. Although installing energy-efficient appliances is a start, this developer really didn't understand the green philosophy and was just using the green label to gain sales.

Unfortunately, the green industry has already seen its share of *greenwashing* by businesses that claim that their company features "green" business practices or that their products are good for the environment. They prey on innocent people who are willing to pay for a product or service they believe will help the environment.

With all the false advertising out there, how can you tell whether a product or service is really green?

One way is to check with reputable organizations that monitor businesses, services, and products. For example, the nonprofit Green Seal, based in Washington, D.C., has been identifying products and services that protect the environment from toxic chemicals, noxious fumes, and wasted resources since 1989. If the product meets Green Seal's standards, it is awarded a Green Seal that may be used on the product or in any advertising or promotional materials. Check them out at www.greenseal.org.

def•i•ni•tion

Greenwashing is the practice of falsely advertising your product or company as green or sustainable.

Myth: Historic homes can't be greened.

Fact: Many homes are located in historic districts, and there are often building and remodeling limitations on these homes. But just because your home is in a historic district doesn't mean you're prohibited from greening it. It all depends on your community and its restrictions. Take Ron Gompertz and his wife, who wanted to do what he called an "extreme green renovation" on their Bozeman, Montana, home, but there was one big glitch: It was a century-old home in the historic district. Because homes in this historic district must follow very specific guidelines about what can and cannot be changed, it presented more of a challenge for a green remodel.

The couple first had to have their blueprints approved by the City of Bozeman Historic Preservation Division. Most historic districts have policies that prioritize the restoration of the original building materials over any energy-efficient and "green" materials. Gompertz said the challenge was to balance these two, often conflicting, priorities.

The couple's approach was to camouflage as much of the green technology as possible and to integrate the visible green elements in such a way that respected the integrity of the house's original design. Their home had undergone updates and remodels over the years, so they researched the history of the house and found old photographs of what the house originally looked like. With this information in hand, the couple was able to locate green materials that worked nicely with the original historic features of the home.

Then, they installed photovoltaic panels and solar water heater panels on a new roof that they built facing the southern sky. They preserved the street side perspective of the building, adding on to the backyard-facing side instead. They kept all of the original size window openings, but replaced the old single-pane glass with more energy-efficient double-glazed windows. The entire renovation took almost a year.

If you're interested in doing a green renovation on a historic home, first discuss your plans with the local building department and then, if possible, with your neighbors, who might be concerned about the impact your renovation will have on the neighborhood. If you have a historic home, consider discussing your plans with your local historic preservation committee.

National Homebuilder Mainstream GreenHome

The National Homebuilder Mainstream GreenHome in Raleigh, North Carolina, was specifically built to incorporate green and sustainable features without sacrificing traditional design or comfort. The home serves as an educational tool for builders and homeowners. As you can see, it's a beautiful traditional-style home!

The National Homebuilder Mainstream GreenHome in Raleigh, North Carolina.

(National Homebuilder Mainstream)

Many of the green features of the home might sound foreign to you right now, but by the end of the book you'll understand all of them.

The GreenHome features a geothermal heat pump, which uses the earth's relatively constant temperature to heat the home during the winter and cool it in the summer. Solar panels, shaped like roofing shingles, give the illusion of a traditional roof. In addition, a plethora of low- and zero-VOC products help create healthy indoor air quality. A sustainable closet system manufactured outside the home prevents toxins from entering.

The furniture in the GreenHome is made from recycled materials and is itself completely recyclable. Floors were manufactured from salvaged wood taken from the bottom of the Cape Fear River. In addition, all the carpets in the home are made from recycled nylon; the carpet is indoor air quality-friendly and can be sent back to the manufacturer to be reused.

The Least You Need to Know

◆ Don't believe everything you hear about green building. Find out facts from reliable sources.

◆ Building and remodeling the green way can be for everyone at every budget, no matter how small.

- There are plenty of resources and organizations to help you step-by-step.

- Watch television shows and visit homes where green building and remodeling is showcased. You'll see that it can be done!

- Don't be quick to spend your money for a new "green" product or service that claims to be eco-friendly. Not all products with a green label are truly green.

Planning Your Green Home

In This Chapter

- ◆ Brainstorming your ideas
- ◆ Setting goals and priorities
- ◆ Buying a green home
- ◆ Finding creative ways to build and/or remodel green

Planning for your green home is similar to planning for a great vacation getaway. For most successful trips, you need a plan of action. Do you have a map and an itinerary? Have you set a budget? Do you know where you want to go? How to get there? What you're going to pack?

When you are remodeling a home or building one from scratch, you also need a plan of action. Brainstorming whether you want to build or remodel, knowing what you can afford, and deciding which features you want will help you get focused and prioritized. Then you can watch your dream come true. Let's get started!

Brainstorm Your Wants and Needs

Have you ever gone grocery shopping without a list when you're hungry? Before you know it, your cart is overflowing with items you don't need because everything looks good, and you end up spending way more than you planned to. Don't let the same thing happen when you're building or remodeling your home.

Brainstorming a list of must-haves and don't-wants in your remodel (the remainder of the book offers explanations of many green features that are now available) will help the building and remodeling process go smoothly and help you stay on budget. Your contractor will probably present you with an overload of options, makes, and models that are all going to look and sound wonderful, but by brainstorming your goals and preferences, you will be able to hone in on exactly what products are right for you and your budget.

For example, suppose you are remodeling because you need to expand the size of your home to accommodate your growing family. Ask yourself the following questions:

- How many rooms do I need?
- How big do I need them to be?
- What will their purpose be?
- Am I adding another level?
- Do I need a new roof?
- Do I need a new hot water heater?
- Have I always dreamed about having skylights?

Think about your project and write down all your wishes. Bring this list to your meeting with your general contractor.

Designing Byte by Byte

Need help envisioning your new home or remodeling project? Traditionally, the planning phase of a building and remodeling project has involved working with an architect or contractor, who provides sketches and blueprints for the homeowner to review. The homeowner suggests changes, the architect makes the changes to the blueprints, and the process is repeated until the plans are finally approved by both homeowner and local town building departments. Although many people still follow this pattern, things have changed somewhat. Today, architects use computer-aided design programs (called CAD for short) to help homeowners visualize the final project in both three dimensions and color.

Professional CAD programs are much too expensive for do-it-yourselfers. Less expensive software programs are now available, however. These programs are a great way of getting a visual idea of how your home is going to look before you start. You can use these programs to lay out a floor plan, arrange furniture, choose paint color, shrink or enlarge existing space, and even tour the final product. Landscaping programs feature many styles of plants and flowers and the tools to combine the right landscape for your style home and size of yard.

Hard Hat Area

Even if you decide to design your own building or remodeling plans, almost all plans must be approved by a local building inspector, town zoning boards, and, if pertinent, homeowners' associations. Depending on your city or town, they might require that the plans come from a professional, licensed architect.

Although these programs aren't yet geared toward green building and remodeling, designing your own floor plans allows you to have a starting point for a conversation with your contractors when you are searching for bids.

Everything Old Is New (and Green) Again

You really don't need to build a brand-new home to be greener and healthier. You don't even have to pack up and move to a green home that has already been built. Actually, if you own a home, remodeling—and even expanding—it instead of building new is considered a greener choice for the environment because you're using existing resources. And, if your home is more than a few decades old, most likely it either needs or is going to need home improvements now or in the near future. If that's the case, this is the perfect opportunity to invest in your future by upgrading anything that is outdated or broken to a healthier green alternative.

Buying Resale

If you are buying a resale home to remodel with the newest in green technologies, there are a few important issues to consider.

Location, Location, Location

What that hackneyed real estate expression means is that the location of your green home is very important. Obviously, you want to pick a location that you like and that will increase your home's potential *resale value*, but you also want to live somewhere that's close to where you work and shop and that's near public transportation and other amenities. That way, you can walk, ride a bike, or take a bus or train to many of your destinations, which reduces your carbon emissions and helps you lower your overall carbon footprint. Buying a home quite a distance away and having to commute adds to the greenhouse gas emissions.

def•i•ni•tion

Resale value is the future value of a piece of property. This value depends on many factors, including the economy, what other neighborhood homes are selling for, the success of local schools, and so on.

Resale Value

When considering the resale value of your green home, you want to buy one that will appeal to the needs of a large number of potential homebuyers when you're ready to sell. For instance, buying a home that's too far from next-door neighbors as well as basic amenities might be a deterrent to potential buyers.

At the same time, buying a home in a run-down neighborhood because you heard that the area might be up for revitalization sounds like a good idea, but confirm your information with local town or city officials to make certain there is further economic investment planned for that area. Otherwise, you might not be able to sell the home when you're ready to move.

You'll also want to purchase a home in a good school district, even if you don't have children. Good school districts boost property values and attract buyers when it comes time to sell.

Affordability

Owning any home comes with unexpected costs and repairs—even green systems that are more energy efficient can sometimes break down—and maxing out your spending potential will not leave money to pay for these financial surprises. Consider what you can afford: you want a home you can pay for—and add green upgrades to—without breaking the bank.

The rule of thumb when buying a home is that your housing costs should not exceed more than two-and-a-half times your annual salary. What you can afford to buy will depend on several factors, including your income, *credit rating*, monthly expenses, and the size of down payment you put on the home.

def•i•ni•tion

A **credit rating** is a rating given by the major credit bureaus (Trans Union, Experian, and Equifax) based on how you've managed your credit in the past. Factored into your credit rating are your payment history for credit cards, loans, and previous mortgages. The higher your credit score, the lower your interest rates on various loans.

To help reduce the cost of your home, think outside of the box in your home search. There are homes with great potential at affordable prices, including foreclosures and handyman specials, that can give you more home for less money. You can then use those savings to upgrade.

Tips & Tools

Order a copy of your credit report as soon as possible. Work on fixing any potential issues that might stand in the way of financing your home. At AnnualCreditReport. com, you can request a free annual credit report. The website was created by the three nationwide consumer credit reporting companies—Equifax, Experian, and TransUnion.

Foreclosures

One person's loss can be your gain. A foreclosure means the homeowner has defaulted on his or her mortgage and the mortgage lender has reclaimed the home. The home is then put up for sale, sometimes at a discount compared to market value. The Mortgage Bankers Association says that 1 out of every 200 homes will be foreclosed on, so now is the time to start searching.

You can buy a foreclosure directly from a distressed owner before the actual process of foreclosure takes place, or you can buy at the foreclosure auction itself. You can also find foreclosure opportunities with government agencies or lenders who have taken over a foreclosed property.

What do you get when you buy a foreclosure? It depends. Some foreclosures have been neglected by their owners and are in desperate need of repairs and upgrades.

Hard Hat Area

Beware of advertisements urging buyers to call for foreclosure information. These ads claim that for a set fee you can obtain a listing of foreclosure properties. All foreclosure information can be obtained through your local real estate professional or lending institution.

Others are in great shape but might just benefit from a better heating or cooling system, the addition of solar panels, or an upgrade in appliances. Some are luxury properties with amenities that may or may not be green already. To find a foreclosure, ask your local real estate professional to access a listing of foreclosures in the Multiple Listing Services, or go directly to area banks.

Buying a foreclosure is very competitive, so offer your best bid up front. Remember that he who hesitates, loses.

Handyman Specials

Think of a handyman special, also known as a "fixer-upper," as a diamond in the rough. With a little elbow grease, underneath that worn first impression could be the charming green home you have been dreaming about. They differ from foreclosures because while foreclosures might or might not need some degree of work, all handyman specials are in desperate need of repairs and upgrades, which makes them ideal candidates for a green conversion. The listing prices of fixer-uppers are far below market value for similar-style homes in good condition.

To get the best value for your money, purchase a fixer-upper in a good community because the resale value will be greater in a better area. Keep in mind that your lender may have special mortgages and mortgage requirements for fixer-uppers (see Chapter 4 for information on green mortgages), including financing through the Federal Housing Administration (FHA) or through Fannie Mae's HomeStyle Renovation Mortgage, which combines home purchase or refinance with home improvement financing in one loan with one closing. In addition, some private lenders offer their own mortgage products geared toward buyers of fixer-uppers. Make sure you tell the lender that you plan on "greening" the property. You may be able to finance the green improvements as part of the mortgage.

Tips & Tools

Try to get records of any systems that the previous homeowner has already installed (furnaces, A/C units, central air, etc.), especially if they have installed any green systems or products.

Foreclosures and handyman specials are mostly sold "as is," so have a home inspector and an experienced green remodeling contractor look at the property to give you an idea of how much it will cost to add energy-efficient features and other green upgrades to it and to identify any obstacles that you might encounter in the reconstruction process.

To find a home inspector near you, visit the American Society of Home Inspectors website at www.ashi.org and search by your zip code.

Evaluating

Once you're settled in a home, or you're remodeling your current home, it's time to decide which green projects you want to accomplish and in what order. You can choose to remodel one project at a time or, if your budget allows, you can hire a green remodeling contractor to complete an entire makeover all at once.

The thought process behind green remodeling is to "think green" every time you need to repair or replace something in your home. Need a new heater? Buy tankless. Need new flooring? Consider cork or bamboo. Painting a room? Buy no-VOC paint. Planting for the spring? Choose flowers that need little or no irrigation. Once you start to make changes, choosing a green alternative will become second nature to you. Before you make any changes, however, think about what it means to the whole house.

Integration Not Separation

When you are green building and remodeling, we want you to look at your home from a whole-house perspective. For every system you install and every repair you make, we want you to think about the interaction between you, your building site, your climate, and the other elements or components of your home—such as the furnace, roof, and lighting. For example, when you install solar panels, consider where those solar panels are going to be installed—front or back of your building site?—and which other repairs you need to have made before you install them. For instance, you wouldn't install solar panels before upgrading or improving your windows, so that element of your home needs to be done first.

Here's another way of looking at it: let's say you own a conventional, yet drafty, 1970s home and are ready to add some eco-friendly systems in order to reduce your heating and cooling costs. You read a magazine article about geothermal heating (an underground heating system; see Chapter 11) and think that would be a perfect addition to your home. You pick up the phone to make an appointment with a geothermal heating expert for an estimate. STOP! Your home isn't ready for a geothermal unit just yet.

Why? Before installing a high-end unit like that, you need to know what other home repairs and upgrades you need to do first in order for a geothermal system to be effective. Air that leaks through old windows, poorly insulated attics, and under doors and windows can be responsible for up to 25 percent of your home's heat loss, especially in an older home. If you don't upgrade your windows to more energy-efficient models, add insulation in your attic, or repair air leaks under the doors and around air conditioners (if these upgrades and repairs need to be done), you're going to continue to lose money and energy regardless of how efficient your pricey new geothermal heating system is. The bottom line is that you shouldn't install a geothermal system without integrating it with other energy-efficient features in your home. By prioritizing and thinking of your home as a whole, you'll know exactly what steps to take next.

Prioritizing

Once you have a list of wants and needs, it's time to prioritize. What repair or upgrade needs to be done first? You want to start with any repairs or upgrades that need to be done for safety or functionality. For example, if your windows are broken or if your furnace isn't working properly, start with those. You can still think green when repairing these items—upgrading with energy-efficient windows, for example—and continue your remodel once this has been completed. Other factors you need to consider when prioritizing your remodel include your area's climate, local requirements, and, of course, your budget.

Climate

When you prioritize your remodeling jobs, you need to consider your local climate.

The climate zone will dictate how certain green systems are designed in your home. For instance, in the hotter southern states, cooling is the predominant concern, and you must take special care to prevent moisture from entering the home. Residents of colder northern climates need to be concerned with the affects of freezing and thawing as well as preventing warm moist air from escaping the home.

The middle states (or transitional zones) have a unique problem in that heating and cooling share equal importance in the design of the home. In this case, you need to pay extra attention to the makeup of the wall cavity to handle the flow of moisture in both directions.

Your climate will also determine the type of energy-saving coatings you choose for your windows. Those living in warmer climates will want the window to reflect the exterior heat, while those living in cooler climates will want to allow the heat from the sun's rays to enter the home (more on this in Chapter 8).

Local Requirements

In some communities, you need special permits from your local town board to install certain green technologies, such as wind turbines, geothermal systems, or solar panels. These special permits can determine which features may or may not be installed in or around your home. Permits for green features might fall under "conditional" or "special use rules," so check with your local county planning department for your town's zoning rules while you're in the planning stages.

Budget

As we talked about briefly in Chapter 2, what you can accomplish depends in large part on your budget, but homeowners of every budget can do a little something to make their homes more environmentally friendly.

For example, with a budget of $1,000 you should be able to insulate your attic and crawl spaces and make some minor repairs around your home. If you have a budget of $10,000, your money might best be spent upgrading your furnace or water heater or making other small changes to your home that will improve heat loss.

If you have $20,000, you might be able to do all of the previously mentioned upgrades as well as install new energy-efficient windows; upgrade broken appliances to new ENERGY STAR models; and replace old, rusted water fixtures with new low-flow fixtures.

If you have a $30,000 budget, you can probably complete all of the above as well as add additional features, including adding a permeable driveway or walkway, or adding solar panels to your roof.

Do you have an even bigger budget? Perhaps you can afford to do all of the above as well as install a geothermal heating system!

> **Hard Hat Area**
>
> The costs of building materials and labor often vary significantly throughout the country, so where the prices might differ, we don't include prices and instead suggest that you check with your local builder/contractor to find out the cost in your area. Some products, such as low-flow toilets, do not differ so much in price, so we include these prices when appropriate.

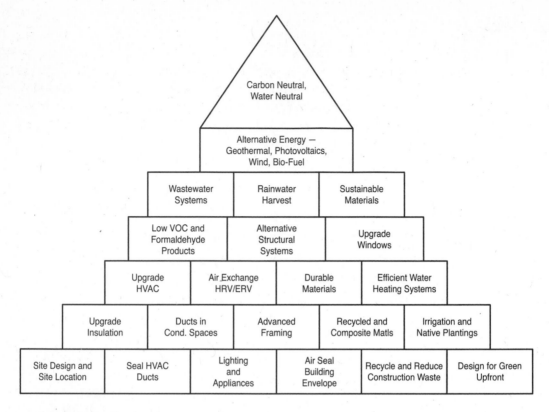

This *"Green Pyramid" shows the order in which you should tackle your green remodeling projects. Starting on the bottom row, which begins with site design and site location, these are the projects that will take the least amount of effort and cost. Some projects require no cost at all (for example, site design and location and recycling and reusing). As you move up the chart, the projects begin to require some financial investment, but you will start to gain more financial and environmental rewards as well. After you begin to combine various projects—such as upgrading insulation with upgrading HVAC, for example—you will see even greater returns. It's important to note that what you do first also depends on several factors and needs unique to each homeowner.*

No Job Too Small

No job is too small when it comes to making changes that can better the environment and your health. The important thing is to get started! Making small changes now adds up to big changes later.

For example, let's say your washing machine breaks down and replacing it with an ENERGY STAR model will cost you $600. It's a small investment, but once you use this new energy-efficient model, you should see a slight savings on your electric bill.

Or perhaps you decide to invest $500 to add insulating window film to your windows. Doing so will reduce air leaks and minimize the amount of heat and sun penetrating into your home. What's the domino effect here? If you live in a cold climate, your home will now be a little warmer in the winter. Consequently, you should be able to turn the heat down, even just a little, thereby saving you more money and energy. See how this works? So don't think you need a lot of money in order to make a difference.

Building an Eco-Friendly Home

Have you always dreamed of building a home from the ground up, so you can have everything created to your specifications? And what if those specifications include sustainability and energy efficiency?

A new home has the added benefit that it is easier to incorporate green features into the project. Including these features at the planning stage will achieve the greatest cost efficiencies.

Evaluating and Prioritizing

When you daydream about your dream home, what do you imagine? Which features do you absolutely want or need? How many bedrooms and bathrooms? Do you need a home office? What will your home look like? As you make your list, refer to the Green Pyramid for ideas and tips for a list of green techniques that should be incorporated in the design of your home to help reduce the cost of installing these systems later.

Just as with remodeling, what you build will depend on several factors, including the size of the land, the size of the home, and your budget.

Land

Where do you want to build your new house? A home in the woods with solar panels and a geothermal heating system might sound great, but if that plot of land requires building a road, chopping down trees, installing utility wires and piping, your location isn't so environmentally friendly anymore. You might want to consider a piece of land that is already filled with *infrastructure*—roads, sewer, electricity, water, etc.—or one that had a previous use. Chapter 6 delves into more detail about where you should and shouldn't buy your land.

def•i•ni•tion

Infrastructure refers to whatever public works are needed for a home or community to function, such as roads, bridges, rail lines, electricity, sewers, and cable and telephone lines.

McMansions' Major Footprint

Lately, it seems that everyone wants things supersized—bigger cars, bigger meals, bigger televisions, and, of course, bigger homes. Some homes are so big that the term "McMansions" was coined by an environmentalist to describe cookie-cutter architectural style homes, often found in newer subdivisions, that are so much larger than a typical home. According to the NAHB, the average size of newly built houses has continued to rise from just over 1,600 square feet in the late 1970s to nearly 2,300 square feet now, with some being as large as 5,000 square feet. But is a bigger home a larger environmental risk than a smaller home?

It depends on how they are being compared. If you are comparing the two dwellings on the amount of land they occupy and building materials used, then obviously the smaller house has less of an environmental impact than the larger one. However, if you are comparing which home uses less energy, it gets a little trickier. In this case, the smaller house isn't necessarily more energy efficient. Before determining an answer, you need to consider a number of factors: is the smaller home an older home that has creaky, leaky windows and a roof and furnace that are in desperate need of upgrading? If the McMansion is equipped with green features such as solar panels, a green roof, proper shading, and a rainwater collection system, it might be more energy efficient and environmentally friendly than the smaller home that doesn't have these features installed.

Smaller Footprints

An NAHB study also determined that 60 percent of potential home buyers would rather have a smaller house with more amenities than a larger home with fewer amenities, so smaller homes may be making a comeback. They are also ideal for those looking for a smaller environmental footprint.

If you're unsure about the benefits, functionality, and attractiveness that small homes offer, simply pick up a book by author Sarah Susanka. Her widely acclaimed and best-selling first book, *The Not So Big House*, created a movement that's changing the way Americans think about the size of their homes. According to her later book, *Creating the Not So Big House*, many consumers make the wrong decisions about their homes that create oversized rooms and cold, impersonal spaces. Susanka's books provide readers with advice for how to make smaller, energy-efficient spaces work, minimizing the home's environmental footprint on the world.

When thinking green and thinking smaller, Susanka recommends incorporating the following innovative design concepts to make a smaller home seem even bigger:

- **Framed openings** allow you to create the illusion of more space while also clearly separating one room from another. Because a framed opening is wider than a normal doorway, it doesn't obstruct your view, but it does indicate that you are entering a new area as you move through it.

- **Spatial layering** takes the concept of framed openings one step further. By using a series of openings and surfaces to subtly break the perceived space into segments, it both is more comprehensible to the eye and encourages you to explore around each edge and corner. Successive layers also give the impression that an area is larger than it actually is.

- **Visual weight** can lend a greater sense of shelter to a room, particularly one with a high ceiling. By darkening a ceiling, by adding texture, or doing both, you can manipulate the sense of scale, making it seem heavier, and therefore not as tall.

Other Alternatives: Granny Flats and Green Communities

If it's extra space you need for aging parents or adult children, why not consider building a granny flat—also called an in-law apartment or an accessory apartment—instead of building a new home? Back in the 1950s, when extended families tended to live together more frequently, accessory apartments were more common than they are today. Building a second level or unit onto your home can provide accommodations and are a great way to protect land and allow more residents to share the same resources.

There is also an increasing number of green communities. In these communities, a builder custom builds your home with green features. In addition, there are additional neighboring amenities, including retail stores, restaurants, and other entertainment right in your own community. These "mixed-use" communities help to reduce the development's overall carbon footprint because residents can walk to access basic necessities. A local realtor can tell you about where these communities are located in your area.

Hard Hat Area

Some neighborhoods don't allow granny flats, so check with your town's zoning commission before making any plans.

It Can Be Done

Colette Brooks and her husband Eric Cadora had the opportunity to build a 11,000-square-foot McMansion on their 5-acre property, but they wanted to preserve the original envelope of their 1,400-square-foot, mid-century block structure while adding several green features. The eco-chic couple expanded their home to just over 2,800 square feet and included renewable, recycled, and/or nontoxic materials for the structure itself, as well as for all surfaces and finishes. Some of the other green features include a solar hot water collector, cork flooring on all newly constructed floors, plywood that has been certified by The Forest Stewardship Council. Recycled glass tile flooring was installed in the bathroom, rubber flooring in the kitchen, and sustainable wheat stalk panels were used for kitchen cabinet boxes. The homeowners installed a tankless water heater, a waterless urinal in the master bathroom, hemp countertops in the kitchen and bathroom, double pane low-E windows throughout the house, naturally colored decomposed granite for a new driveway in lieu of asphalt, a garage door made from 86 percent recovered and recycled content, cool metal roofing technology made from 25 percent recycled steel, and ENERGY STAR appliances throughout the house.

LivingHomes LEED Platinum Rating

LivingHomes (www.LivingHomes.us), a developer of modern *prefab* homes, received a platinum rating from the USGBC's LEED for Homes rating system, making it the first residential project in the country to achieve such a standard in sustainable construction. The LivingHomes model home is a zero-energy, zero-water, zero-waste, zero-carbon, and zero-emissions residence, proving that less is indeed more. The LivingHomes model home, designed by southern California architect Ray Kappe, FAIA, was awarded a total of 91 LEED points out of a possible 108.

def•i•ni•tion

A **prefab** home is manufactured on other property in advance and shipped in sections to the building site. The home is then put together and finished onsite.

The model home incorporates a unique blend of materials and innovative environmental systems. The home's anticipated energy use is 80 percent more efficient than a conventional residence of similar size, which qualifies the home as an ENERGY STAR home. The green features include the following:

◆ The majority of the home's energy is produced by onsite photovoltaic, or solar, energy. It also has solar water heating and radiant floors heating.

♦ Water for irrigation is reclaimed and reused for other purposes. An integrated stormwater management system includes subsurface irrigation, a 3,500-gallon cistern, and a greywater recycling system to divert sink and shower water for irrigation.

♦ Most of the materials in the home are reused or have been sustainably created.

♦ The home was produced with 75 percent less construction waste compared to traditional home construction.

♦ The home includes super resource-efficient ENERGY STAR appliances and LED lights that use a fraction of the power of conventional lights.

♦ Exhaust fans, a whole-house fan, and a fan in the garage remove carbon monoxide.

LivingHomes also uses low-E glazing on the doors and windows, which saves energy.

LivingHomes, a leading developer of modern prefab homes designed by world-class architects, has received the highest rating possible from the U.S. Green Building Council's LEED for Homes rating system, making it the first residential project in the country to attain a platinum rating and setting a new national standard in sustainable construction.

Certification

More than once throughout this book we've mentioned that homes can be "certified" as green. The only way to ensure that your home is truly green is to get it independently verified through an organization, such as the USGBC or NAHB. Such certification, however, is not required. You can complete all of our suggestions for building, upgrading, and improving your home to be green without having it certified.

Many people who want to register their homes or commercial buildings go through the USGBC LEED program. This certification verifies that your home is sustainable and green. It can help you to achieve certain tax deductions and can increase the home's resale value when you decide to sell. Certification through LEED costs approximately $300.

The LEED certification process awards your home points for each green building system and technique that you have implemented. For example, energy-efficient windows, green roofs, low-VOC paint, and ENERGY STAR appliances all earn points. The more systems and technologies you implement, the more points you will receive. The total number of points determines your home's level of certification. For the "certified" level, a score of 45 to 59 is required (out of a possible 136 points); silver is 60 to 74; gold is 75 to 89; and platinum (the highest to date) is 90 to 136.

The number of points for each certification level is adjusted for smaller-than-average and larger-than-average homes using a mechanism called the Home Size Adjustment.

To participate in the LEED program, contact the USGBC to join the program, build the home according to their designations, and then have it certified by a LEED certifier.

The Least You Need to Know

◆ Planning is everything when it comes to building green.

◆ Keep a close eye on, and prioritize, your budget.

◆ Consider creative alternatives such as adding on to your existing home or buying a fixer-upper.

◆ Good things—including environmentally friendly houses—come in small packages!

Chapter 4

Dollars and Sense

In This Chapter

- How to pay for it all
- The lowdown on green mortgages
- Tax breaks for going green
- Builder and remodeler basics
- How to insure your new green home

Let's get down to brass tacks—well, dollars and cents really. We've already discussed several variables you need to consider when determining exactly how much your green home is going to cost to build or remodel, but some important questions remain: How will you pay for it? Who is going to do the work? And precisely what are those tax breaks that you keep hearing about, and are you eligible to receive them?

You might have some money put aside for some basic remodeling projects and upgrades, but most of us don't have tens of thousands of dollars lying around, so unless you can plunk down the entire payment in one lump sum, you are going to have to take out some sort of a loan to build or remodel your home.

def•i•ni•tion

A **home equity loan** is a fixed or adjustable-rate loan secured by the equity in your home. The interest you pay is usually tax-deductible. A **home equity line of credit** uses your home as collateral. You can borrow from the line of credit until you have reached your maximum credit limit.

Typically, when you build, buy, or remodel a home, you can either apply for a conventional mortgage, refinance your current mortgage to provide extra money for projects, or apply for a *home equity loan* or *home equity line of credit*.

And there are even mortgages specifically designed to encourage homeowners or homebuyers to upgrade their home with energy-efficient features. Called Energy Efficient Mortgages (EEMs) and Energy Improvement Mortgages (EIMs), these lending options let you finance greening your home as part of your mortgage payment each month. Let's look at each a little more closely.

Energy Efficient Mortgages

An EEM comes with just one caveat—you can apply for one only if you have had a Home Energy Rating Systems report performed on your home. A trained Home Energy Rating Systems (HERS) evaluator, whom you can find through the Residential Energy Services Network (www.resnet.us/directory/raters.aspx), will come to your home and determine whether it will benefit from cost-effective energy upgrades. The rater will then provide you and potential lenders with estimates of recommended upgrade costs and potential savings. If the home qualifies for energy improvements and you qualify for the loan, the lender will put the home improvement funds into an account to be used after you have moved in and are ready to begin the remodeling work.

The three types of EEMs are conventional, Federal Housing Administration (FHA), and Veteran's Administration (VA). Conventional EEMs are for Fannie Mae and Freddie Mac loans. FHA EEMs allow lenders to add 100 percent of the cost of improvements to an already-approved loan. VA EEMs are for qualified military personnel, including reservists and veterans. Some loans have caps on the costs of energy improvements that can be included, so be sure to verify the requirements before beginning the application. An EEM can be used for one-unit, single-family, owner-occupied principal residences, and condominiums.

One of the primary benefits of an EEM is that it increases the amount of money you can borrow. Your estimated energy savings are added to your income for the purpose of calculating how much money you qualify to borrow. This enables you to include the cost of the improvements into the total mortgage amount. After the home is improved, the overall value of your home will increase and you will also benefit from the tax-deductible interest on your mortgage payments. In addition, with the green improvements, you will benefit from lower electric and heating/cooling costs.

According to Energy Rated Homes of Vermont, on a $75,000 VA 30-year mortgage at 7.5 percent interest, a homeowner is likely to reduce his monthly housing costs by $32, or almost $400 a year, by adding in energy-efficiency improvements, as shown in the following table:

Monthly Costs	With $4,000 in Energy Improvements	Without Energy Improvements
Mortgage payment	$552.38	$524.42
Energy expenses	$90	$150
Total monthly cost	$642.38	$674.42

Tax Credits

In 2005, President George W. Bush signed the Energy Policy Act, a national law that provided federal tax credits for homeowners who make specified energy-efficiency upgrades to their homes. From January 2006 to December 2007, tax credits of up to $500 were available for such improvements as insulation, replacement windows, and certain high-efficiency heating and cooling equipment. Unfortunately, this tax credit was not extended, but there are other federal and state tax breaks you might still qualify for.

For example, homeowners who install qualified solar water heating and photovoltaic (solar electric) systems between January 1, 2006, and December 31, 2008, may qualify for a federal tax credit of 30 percent of the cost of the system up to $2,000. If you install both systems, you may receive a credit up to $4,000.

Tips & Tools

Need an updated list of tax credits for your state? Visit the Alliance to Save Energy (www.ase.org) for a full listing of the nation's energy-efficient policies.

The credits and incentives available at the state level vary considerably, and some states offer no credits or programs at all. The following list identifies some state and metropolitan programs:

def•i•ni•tion

A **megawatt** is a measurement of electricity. One megawatt equals 1 million watts, which is enough electricity to power roughly 1 million homes.

◆ **California** residents can benefit from the Million Solar Roofs Plan, which was signed into California law in 2006, with a goal of providing 3,000 *megawatts* of additional clean energy and reducing the output of greenhouse gases. Homeowners who install solar electric systems can sell excess energy back to the power companies for credit on their monthly bills. This credit is a key incentive for consumers to install solar panels.

◆ In **Seattle, Washington,** Seattle City Light offers its customers an energy production incentive. Customers who generate electricity from alternative energy sources—such as wind and solar—may qualify for an annual incentive payment based on the amount of electricity they produce. The program runs through June 30, 2014. To qualify for the program, the renewable energy system has to be certified by the Department of Revenue.

Seattle also offers the WashWise Rebate Program, which offers rebates for the purchase and installation of a qualified energy- and water-saving clothes washer. The more energy and water you save, the higher the rebate. And Seattle's HomeWise Program offers low-interest loans to residents who insulate, weatherize, repair, and otherwise retrofit their homes.

◆ **New York, New Jersey,** and **Connecticut** will pay their residents up to 50 percent of the installed cost for solar electric systems. New York also covers 25 percent of the cost of installing solar domestic hot water systems; this may be in addition to the federal tax credits.

◆ **South Carolina** taxpayers can apply for a solar heating and cooling tax credit of 25 percent of the costs of installing a solar energy heating or cooling system, or both.

Check with your state to see what tax breaks they offer and to find out more about the ones mentioned here. In addition, check with your utility company to see what incentives they offer. Most utilities offer incentives that, when coupled with the tax credits, mortgages, and other programs, generate much quicker paybacks for your investment.

Your Green Dream Team

If you're particularly handy and have the time, you might want to consider building your home or installing your green technology on your own. However, for most people it's best to rely on the experience of a general contractor or builder.

Word of mouth is a great way to get recommendations for any members of your green building dream team. If other neighbors or friends have gone green, check out their properties and see what they have done. What did they like and not like about the contractors they used? But remember, just because your best friend really liked her contractor doesn't necessarily mean he is the right one for you. You can also find a remodeling contractor or builder in your area through the websites of the national building trade organizations mentioned in this chapter as well as the websites of their local chapters.

Once you've narrowed down your list of potential contractors to one or two, ask for recommendations from past clients, schedule a consultation, and review portfolios of the company's previous work.

When talking to a contractor's previous customers, ask them whether they would hire the contractor again, whether the job was finished on schedule, whether the company was responsive to phone calls, and whether the homeowner was kept informed about the progress of the project. Finally, ask yourself if you would be comfortable having this contractor and his employees in your home and around your family for the life of the project.

Talk to and get bids from several businesses before deciding on one to work with. Even though everybody wants a job done for the least amount of money, don't automatically accept the lowest bid.

> **Hard Hat Area**
>
> If a contractor's bid is more than 20 percent lower than the other estimates, ask yourself why. Make sure it's not because the contractor is desperate for your business and deposit in order to finish another job. Otherwise, you're going to get what you pay for.

Builder and Remodeler Basics

It's important to select a contractor or builder who has been trained in green building or remodeling. Several national organizations have programs that educate, train, or certify builders and remodelers as experts in green building.

Launched in 2001, the United States Green Building Council's (USGBC) **LEED Professional Accreditation program** certifies that building professionals have the knowledge and skills to successfully steward the LEED certification process, which provides independent, third-party verification that a building project meets the highest green building and performance measures. LEED-accredited professionals have demonstrated a thorough understanding of green building practices and principles and the LEED Rating System (see Chapter 3).

The National Association of Home Builders (NAHB) has a **Certified Green Professional (CGP)** designation. The builder/remodeler must complete 24 hours of technical and business management training and commit to a Code of Ethics to achieve the CGP designation. Additionally, individual homes may be certified green with an independent, third-party verification.

The National Association of the Remodeling Industry (NARI) is a national organization of 800,000 companies and individuals in the United States identifying themselves as professional remodelers. NARI offers a **Green Certified Professional (GCP)** training course and certification and a GreenHomeGuide, a directory of green-certified professionals. To attain certification through NARI, the remodeler must have been a full-time remodeler for at least five years; have conducted remodeling projects using green principles, practices, or products for at least three years; have at least 16 hours of green or sustainable remodeling-related continuing education; and pass a comprehensive examination.

Drawing It Up

When you think about your dream home, do you already have a vision in mind? If you're unsure of what you want, take a look through plan books—you can find them in your local bookstores—for ideas on the style of home you are interested in building. Do you want a Cape Cod? Victorian? Georgian style? Split level? Two-family? There are so many options to choose from.

For remodeling ideas, visit magazine stands and look for remodeling publications. You can also surf the Internet for ideas. Once you have one or more ideas of what you like, an architect can help you put the ideas to paper. An architect prepares sketches of the home on the site, conducts elevation studies, proposes a list of materials, and sometimes even offers a three-dimensional model to show you exactly how the house will look.

Tips & Tools

The American Institute of Architects (AIA) offers resources for their members and the public on green building techniques and other important green issues. They provide a list of 20 questions that you can ask your architect. Their website (www.aia.org) also offers an architect finder feature. Simply enter your zip code and you can choose from a list of architects in your area and visit their websites. Ask them what green properties they have completed in your area and, if possible, visit the property and see for yourself.

Landscaping Your Site

Whether you're planting trees for shading, capturing rainwater, or *xeriscaping*, the landscape is a vital part of building and remodeling your green home. Consider adding a landscape architect to your dream team. These landscape professionals know how the sunlight falls in your location and where to plant flowers and trees to reap the sun's maximum benefits. She'll know what plants and flowers grow best in your area and will be able to coordinate the installation of drip irrigation systems with your general contractor or builder so your plants and lawn are kept watered with as little water waste as possible.

Keep in mind that a landscape architect is not the same as a landscaper or gardener. A landscape architect is, in most states, licensed with a degree in landscape architecture from an accredited school, has work experience, and has passed the Landscape Architect Registration Exam.

def•i•ni•tion

Xeriscaping is an environmentally friendly form of landscaping that uses a variety of native and drought-tolerant plants, shrubs, and ground cover.

After you've chosen a landscape architect, he or she will study your project and come up with a design that factors in the budget, climate, soil, slope of the land, drainage, vegetation, sunlight and existing buildings, roads, walkways, and utilities. If it is an undeveloped site, the landscape architect will work with the home architect or builder to examine the topography, solar gain, trees, and so on. He or she will also take into account any local, state, or federal regulations, such as those protecting wetlands or historic resources.

Tips & Tools _____

A great place to start looking for a landscape architect is the American Society of Landscape Architects (www.asla.org). It was founded in 1899 and is the national professional association representing landscape architects.

Sign on the Dotted Line

It's almost time to sign on the dotted line and get your project started, but before you do so, it's important to do a little more homework on any company you want to hire.

First, those who claim to be green building specialists from any organization should be able to supply proof. You should also make sure that any subcontractors the contractor hires are experienced.

Tips & Tools _____

Think local! It's best to hire your dream team from local recommendations.

Second, check for complaints against the company by calling your local Better Business Bureau and state attorney general's office; they should be able to tell you whether any letters or complaints have been registered against the contractor. Your local builder's association can also help you to steer clear of scam artist contractors facing criminal charges. To find your local builders' association, visit the NAHB website (www.nahb.org) and click on your state.

Third, call the contractor's bank and ask whether their account is stable. Some banks might tell you only if there is an account and how long that account has been open. Others might provide more detailed information. This will determine the stability of the contractor.

Fourth, check the contractor's license—if licenses are required in your state—and insurance policies to confirm that they are up-to-date. Contractors should be able to supply a copy of their insurance certificate, although most homeowners don't ask for it. Don't take your contractor's word for it; ask to see each policy. Note the policy numbers; the dates the policy is in effect; and the names, addresses, and phone numbers of the insurance companies. Then call the companies to make sure the policies are still current. If you learn of any problems, find someone else to do the work. Insurance is very important in case there are major problems with a job or damage to the house.

After you choose a builder or contractor, get *everything* in writing and avoid signing anything until all the terms are agreed upon. Before you pay, make sure you are getting everything that was listed in the contract, all the way down to what products, systems, and materials will be used, which will protect you from the contractor substituting

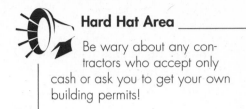

Hard Hat Area

Be wary about any contractors who accept only cash or ask you to get your own building permits!

inferior-quality products. Check out any warranties on systems and products that have been installed, too. Will the contractor or builder give you a complete description of any warranties covering the installation portion of the project? Has the company been in business long enough to honor those warranties? Keep a file of paperwork during the job, and include copies of signed contracts, change orders, plans and specifications, cancelled checks, and any other correspondence.

Insurance Coverage

You have researched green-friendly tax breaks and mortgages and your dream team is in place. It's time to ensure that you adequately protect your most important investment.

Traditionally, homeowners' insurance covers your home in case of damage or catastrophe, but not all homeowners' insurance companies cover all green building products or systems.

At the time this book was being written, Fireman's Fund offered a credit for LEED-certified homes and an endorsement for green homeowners' coverage. If a home is LEED-certified, homeowners receive a 5 percent discount on their policies. If a homeowner is interested in upgrading to green in the event of a loss, Fireman's Fund offers an upgrade-to-green endorsement, in which it replaces items involved in a loss with green technologies such as ENERGY STAR appliances, HVAC systems, energy- and water-efficient systems, and ENERGY STAR roofs. Fireman's Fund will replace old paint with low-VOC paints and flooring and will pay the extra cost of recycling debris from the loss rather than sending it to the landfill. In the event of a covered total loss, it will pay to rebuild the home to LEED Bronze standards and for the cost of the LEED certification as well as for a

Tips & Tools

For more information on Fireman's Fund, visit their website at www.firemansfund.com or call 1-800-227-1700.

LEED-accredited professional to participate in the design and construction of the rebuild.

The insurance industry is beginning to respond to an increased demand for coverage for green building products and other initiatives. We should begin to see more options on the horizon.

The Least You Need to Know

- ◆ There are new kinds of mortgages on the market that are specifically designed for green building and remodeling; check them out and see if you are eligible.

- ◆ Check the credentials of the architect, builder, landscape architect, and anyone else involved in the design and construction of your home, especially if they claim to be green building experts.

- ◆ Call your current home insurance carrier and see whether it will cover your green home features or your green building upgrades.

- ◆ Make sure your home is insured properly once your project is complete.

Chapter 5

A Material World

- ◆ The practice of sustainability
- ◆ Demolition, deconstruction, and salvation
- ◆ Going once, going twice, sold!
- ◆ Click a mouse, build a house

To build or remodel a green home, you need to use green building materials, which are composed of renewable, rather than nonrenewable, resources. What materials you choose will affect the environment, the economy, and the health of those who live there. For example, studies show that the occupants of a building are exposed to much higher levels of volatile organic compounds (VOCs) and formaldehyde in the first 6 to 12 months after construction or renovation than at any other time, due to the wide range of high-emission materials (paints, adhesives, sealants, carpets, wood-based panels, furniture, and so on) used in construction. Choosing low-VOC materials reduces exposure to these toxic emissions.

LEED Standards for Green Materials

According to Leadership in Energy and Environmental Design (LEED), for a material to qualify as "green," it must …

- Meet or exceed performance requirements.

- Have sufficient, predictable strength, durability, or stability.

- Be resistant to moisture, decay, or biocontamination.

- Be nontoxic or nonhazardous to occupants and installers.

- Be comparable in cost (labor + materials + equipment + other) to traditional materials.

- Be able to be harvested sustainably and installed efficiently.

- Be rapidly renewable or abundant.

- Be a closed-loop material, which means it can be recycled again and again.

- Involve minimal direct/indirect use of nonrenewables.

- Be adaptable, reusable, or recyclable.

One of the most fundamental principles in successful green building is to increase the amount of recycled and reusable—yet still sustainable—materials used to construct your home. This includes everything from the walls to roofs, floors, insulation, landscape, and more. To do so, you and your contractor should work on incorporating the three r's—reduce, reuse, recycle—right at the beginning of your planning and design stages. Doing so will maximize the environmental and financial benefits of your project.

Fortunately, there are more sustainable materials and products available for green building and remodeling than ever before. Most have guidelines in place to ensure you have chosen properly. For example, the Sustainable Forestry Initiative (SFI) certifies new wood that can be purchased as sustainable flooring, while ENERGY STAR certifies various new appliances as being energy efficient.

Sustainable Versus Unsustainable

As noted previously, *sustainable* means meeting the needs of the present without compromising the ability of future generations to meet their needs. When determining the sustainability of any product or material, the green building industry performs what's called a "life-cycle analysis." This analysis examines the effect that the product has on the environment from the time it is created to the time that it is disposed of and, sometimes, beyond. The product with the life cycle that has the least damaging effects on the environment is considered a better building option.

For example, Product A might require mining to produce, plastic for packaging, fuel to transport the product from a distant location, and final disposal in a landfill. Compare that to Product B, an item that is manufactured closer to your home from recycled materials using minimal energy. Because it uses fewer resources, Product B is a better environmental choice.

Not all building materials or products are truly green, even if they claim to be. To determine whether they really are green, you need to look at the entire life cycle of the product. How is the product manufactured? Is it produced in a factory in another country? Does that factory release pollution into the environment? What is the product made of? Does it contain recycled content or renewable materials? How much *embodied energy* or water consumption does it take to create the product? And, finally, is the product biodegradable or recyclable once you are done with it?

Manufacturers are continually finding more ways to reuse building materials. For instance, according to the Concrete Materials Recycling Association (CMRA), more than 140 millions tons of concrete are recycled each year, and the new aggregate made from recycled content is of equal quality to its nonrecycled counterpart, is lighter (which means it will save on project costs), and reduces landfill waste.

def•i•ni•tion

Embodied energy is the total amount of energy used to create any product—including energy expended in extracting raw materials, processing, manufacturing, and transportation.

Engineered wood products are also made using recycled building materials. These wood products are actually made with waste wood, making efficient use of available resources. According to the Engineered Wood Association, engineered wood can be manufactured from fast-growing, underutilized, and less expensive wood species grown in privately managed forests. There are even recycled paint options now, in which old paint is added to new paint and resold.

Green Facts

Chuck Leavell, a musician for such legendary acts as The Rolling Stones, Gov't Mule, Eric Clapton, and George Harrison, is also a conservationist and tree farmer. He and his wife own the Charlane Plantation in Dry Branch, Georgia, and have been recognized by several conservation organizations. Leavell is also the only two-time recipient of the Georgia Tree Farmer of the Year award.

Locating Suppliers

In the past, to obtain green building materials you had to order them from specialized companies and have them shipped to you, but the building industry is catching up to the times. Today more green building materials can be purchased in traditional home improvement stores, and more online stores now offer green building materials as well. There are also several nontraditional routes to finding environmentally friendly building materials.

Think Local

Hopefully your local business community already encourages you to buy from area vendors to help boost your city's economy, but that's not the only reason you should buy building materials from your neighborhood stores.

Suppose you live in California and purchase a wood product that is made from trees grown in Brazil. That wood has traveled a long way to be used in your home. Let's suppose it was shipped from Brazil to a warehouse in New York. A retailer near your city in California places an order to have that product shipped to its San Diego branch. The product must then be shipped using a cross-country trucking service. After the product has been delivered to the store, you—the consumer—drive to the branch and select the product you want to use in your home. In this example, your product has made at least four stops before it ends up in your hands (although some products make many more), adding more greenhouse gas emissions to the environment during every stage of the process. Tracking the product's history to its original point is called the *chain of custody*. By shopping closer to home and knowing a product's chain of custody, you can reduce the carbon emissions on the environment. It might take a little bit of effort and research on your part, but it's worth it.

def•i•ni•tion

Chain of custody is a process of tracking how products (especially wood products) are distributed from their origin to their end-use (which would be you).

Reduce

Building a sustainable home does not have to be more complicated than building a traditional home. As a matter of fact, a green home can be built with even less material than a traditional home *without* sacrificing the home's quality or structural integrity. For example, one building technique, advanced house framing (also called optimum value engineering [OVE]) is a framing method that minimizes the amount of lumber and materials used in the structure of the home by replacing it with insulation. As a result, fewer building materials are used and the house actually becomes more energy efficient thanks to the extra insulation material.

Tips & Tools

Purchase nails, screws, and other hardware in bulk to minimize the amount of packaging you use.

Reuse: One Man's Trash ...

You know the old expression, "One man's trash is another man's treasure?" When it comes to recycling and reusing, there couldn't be a better way to green your home than using what another homeowner or builder doesn't need anymore. By reusing materials, you are limiting the amount of waste that would otherwise end up in landfills, reducing the consumption of new resources, reducing your own construction costs, and even contributing to local job opportunities with new reuse and recycling businesses opening up in local communities.

There are many ways to find these hidden treasures—from searching at local salvage yards to logging in on the computer and surfing popular online sites such as Craigslist (www.craigslist.com), Freecycle (www.freecycle.org), and eBay (www.ebay.com). There is also the old standby—garage sales.

Online Auctions and Classified Listings

Think of online communities as neighborhood garage sales without the need to traipse from home to home—which wastes gas and increases emissions, by the way—looking at things you really don't need. And it doesn't cost anything to join or post on either Freecycle or Craigslist (there are nominal fees for posting on eBay).

In 1995, Craigslist was started as an e-mail list of San Francisco events by Craig Newmark. Today hundreds of cities have their own Craigslists featuring free classified advertisements for jobs, housing, personals, services, and so much more. You can find

Hard Hat Area

Be sure to ascertain that the items are environmentally sound. Even a free purchase is not a smart purchase if it's not meeting your sustainable, healthy, and energy-efficient goals. For example, do not accept paint if it is not a low- or no-VOC paint, even if it is free.

items on sale, for barter, and even for free on this list. Today, the site generates more than 10 billion page views per month.

Freecycle is another online network, made up of more than 4,300 groups with more than 5 million members who literally give stuff away for free.

To access these sites, simply log on to either Craigslist.com or Freecycle.com and search for your city and state (or one only a short driving distance away) to minimize your travel time and environmental impact. On Craigslist, select the category you are interested in—for sale, barter, or free.

When you sign up to use Freecycle, you are taken to a message board page where you can choose to browse through the listings at your own pace (they are not categorized to make searching easier) or have them e-mailed to you either as they are posted (a little overwhelming) or in a condensed digest once a day (although you stand a good chance of being too late to snag highly sought after items).

On Craigslist, you must search for items; the site doesn't e-mail listings. You can find virtually anything on these sites, including extra drywall, windows, doors, flooring, and even excess paint. Examples of listings have included someone who deconstructed a fireplace and gave away bricks. All you need to do is be the first person to contact the lister and arrange to pick the item up. Another homeowner purchased a cast-iron pedestal sink in good condition at a deeply discounted price. By using these sites, you can get some great deals and have the satisfaction of knowing you are reusing materials that would have otherwise been tossed in the landfill.

New posts to both Craigslist and Freecycle are added every day, all day, so be sure to check the sites frequently. When you find something you want, send an e-mail (or call if the person has listed a phone number) immediately. Keep in mind that the competition on all of these sites is intense, so you need to know what you want and act on it when you first see it. Free items are usually given away on a first-come, first-serve basis, so don't hesitate. After you have made arrangements with the seller to buy an item, be ready to purchase it when you meet. Make sure you have cash on hand and a car or truck large enough to haul the item or items away.

Hard Hat Area

Never feel pressured from a seller or a store if the item you want is not as described. You are not obligated to purchase any items you're not happy with. Also, if you are giving away or selling items of your own, be careful about buyers who try to change the terms of the deal.

EBay, a huge online auction community, is another valuable site for finding reusable, sustainable materials. You don't have to register to see what's available for sale on eBay, but you do need to register if you want to buy (or decide to sell). When you find an item you like, you must bid on it. (In some cases, sellers offer a "Buy-It-Now" option, where you can purchase an item for a set price.) At the end of the auction, the person with the highest bid wins the item. The bidding can often go down to the last second. You make arrangements with the seller for shipping and payment after the auction ends. To keep your environmental footprint to a minimum, try to find a local eBay dealer or purchase multiple items from the same seller to eliminate shipping multiple times.

Salvage Yards and Reuse Stores

Green-educated consumers have uncovered the value in searching for items at salvage yards, also called *reuse stores* or *materials exchanges*. No matter what you call these second-hand havens, the concept is the same. These stores stock used architectural gems or everyday necessities that might just be the perfect fit to complete your green remodeling or building project.

Don't worry, though. Gone are the days when you pulled up your sleeves, hunkered down, and searched for hours through piles of junk, hoping you would find a hidden treasure. Today, many salvage yards have been converted into well-organized warehouses where you can shop 'til your heart's content for reusable and sustainable materials.

Some facilities even specialize in particular materials. For example, the Historic Albany Foundation in Albany, New York, works to preserve historic buildings and their materials and accepts donations of salvaged parts. They stockpile doors and windows, decorative iron work and stained glass, lighting fixtures, claw foot and other tubs, plumbing accessories, sinks and toilets, mantels and fireplaces, radiators and heating, spindles, stair rails, newel posts, moldings, woodwork, flooring, and other miscellaneous items. The foundation then resells these parts. Another site, Second Use Building Materials in Seattle, Washington, has more than 20,000 square feet of shopping space and a changing inventory of vintage architectural pieces and contemporary building materials.

Tips & Tools

Although not a common practice, it is possible to move an entire home that is slated for demolition to save the materials. Often, the home is sold for the paltry sum of $1, although the actual excavating and moving costs can run into the tens of thousands of dollars. However, it might still be a savings when compared to the construction costs of a new home.

Material exchanges—also known as solid waste reduction programs—are another free service designed to help find new markets for nonhazardous materials. These exchanges are usually done through your state or county. Type your state name and "materials exchanges" in an Internet search engine and you should be able to find a listing for your area's exchange. Some states have multiple exchange lists.

Reuse stores, where you can buy surplus building materials at a lower cost, might sell only to low-income customers or nonprofit organizations. Others, such as Habitat for Humanity's Habitat ReStores, have no restrictions.

Deconstruction

Traditionally, when a builder demolishes or tears down a home or building, it is bulldozed and pulled apart as quickly as possible (sometimes in one shot!). The materials are then thrown into dumpsters and carted off to a local landfill. This practice is becoming less and less common these days. Now when a home or other property is deconstructed, it's often taken apart piece by piece—think of building a home, but backward. The industry then reuses and recycles as much of the material as possible.

For example, when a New York homeowner needed wood to use in his remodel, he actually purchased an old barn that was made from American chestnut—a tree that was wiped out in the early 1900s by bacteria. After he had used as much material as he needed, he sold off the surplus of this highly desirable wood to recoup his reconstruction costs.

If you're looking to buy demolition waste materials, check out a demolition auction. These fast-paced sales are becoming more popular as a means of disbursing used building materials.

The EPA says that much of this construction waste can be salvaged from one job and reused. Here are some building materials that can be reused:

- Concrete
- Wood
- Asphalt
- Gypsum (main ingredient in drywall)
- Metals
- Bricks

- Glass

- Plastics

- Salvaged building components such as doors, windows, and plumbing features

- Trees, stumps, earth, and rock from clearing sites

Similar to a classic auction, everything from a demolition or deconstruction—including fixtures, appliances, flooring, landscaping, walls, and materials—are for sale and go to the highest bidder. Some auctions require that the bidders tour the house before the auction, bid on the items, and bring their own removal teams. So, for example, if you want to buy hardwood flooring, you would bring a team and tools to remove and transport the flooring on your own.

Construction and Demolition

Statistics show that building the average 2,000-square-foot house yields about 8,000 to 12,000 tons of construction waste. Think about the cardboard boxes your appliances, cabinets, and siding are delivered in. Add in the waste from wood and drywall and other building materials as well. An incredible amount of material ends up in landfills. Even with builders getting smarter about recycling construction waste, there is still going to be some waste by the end of any construction project.

No matter how hard you try to limit waste, you're still going to end up with some left-over construction materials. Decide what to do with this excess before you even begin. Find out who accepts what materials, and make arrangements ahead of time to have the materials removed properly. Arrange to have recycling containers on the property, clearly labeled and monitored.

 Tips & Tools _____

Donating excess materials to nonprofit organizations can earn you a tax deduction.

Here are some guidelines to follow:

- Set waste reduction goals at the beginning of the project.

- Search for reusable materials before ordering new ones.

- Choose the most efficient products and try not to order too much.

- Make certain to cover materials so they don't get damaged by weather.

Hard Hat Area

Green builders know better, but contractors and even property owners can be fined thousands of dollars for illegal disposal of materials, so make sure you know exactly how to dispose of those materials you cannot reuse or recycle.

◆ Determine where salvaged items are going and contact salvage companies or nonprofit agencies that accept these materials ahead of time so you can follow their guidelines.

◆ If you have extra materials at the end of the project, consider using Freecycle, Craigslist, newspaper ads, or other sites to offer them to the public.

◆ Allow the construction crew to take excess materials (this should not be announced until the entire job is complete).

The Least You Need to Know

◆ Think outside of the box when finding materials for your project.

◆ Discuss with your contractor the types of sustainable products you want to use in the construction/remodel of your home.

◆ Reusing, reducing, and recycling can help the environment and your bottom line.

◆ Follow your local recycling guidelines and make arrangements ahead of time for pickup and disposal of construction waste.

Chapter 6

Home Sweet Home

In This Chapter

- ◆ Preserve land through smart growth
- ◆ Consider the green features of any potential home site
- ◆ Building on brownfields and infills
- ◆ Where *not* to build

Homeownership is considered a large part of the American dream, and you probably want to build that dream on a perfect little piece of property that you picked out, right? Perhaps you always wanted to own a home in a rural area or deep in the woods so you can enjoy some solitude and nature. Where you choose to build your home is one of the most important green building decisions you will make. The wrong choice can have a serious negative impact on the environment.

Smart Growth

Over the years, studies have shown that the amount of available land on which to build homes is shrinking, but at the same time, our population is growing. Land is a precious resource that needs to be conserved, but developers need land to build houses and commercial properties to accommodate the increasing number of people who want their own homes.

Recognizing this tension between conservation needs and development needs, local municipalities and national organizations, such as the National Association of Home Builders (NAHB) and the Environmental Protection Agency (EPA), are working together to create ways to preserve land. Collectively, these preservation techniques are known as *smart growth*. Smart growth is also a means of protecting valuable, and sometimes historic, *open space*. Failure to protect these open spaces also means a failure to protect wildlife and plants, some of which are already endangered or threatened because they are simply running out of habitats.

def•i•ni•tion

Smart growth is the process of developing creative methods of using land efficiently so it vitalizes already existing communities.

Open space is a portion of a site that is permanently set aside for public or private use and will not be developed. The space might be used for passive or active recreation or be reserved to protect or buffer natural areas.

According to the EPA, one means of helping to preserve open space is to build homes and communities closer together so they can share the same amenities, resources, and infrastructure. This reduces the impact of new construction on the environment than if the same number of homes were built farther apart from one another. For example, the EPA reported on a 2000 study that found that compact development in New Jersey would produce 40 percent less water pollution than more dispersed development patterns. In Seattle, a 2005 study determined that in neighborhoods where land uses were mixed (half residential and half commercial), streets were better connected (making nonauto travel easier and more convenient) and residents traveled 26 percent fewer miles in their vehicles than residents of neighborhoods that weren't so close together. This significantly reduces a neighborhood's environmental impact.

Studies have also shown that preserving open space actually costs less money than developing it. Why? When building homes or developments on new land, there are the additional costs to cover the needed infrastructure, as well as community services (emergency services, schools, etc.) for new residents. Protecting these lands costs much less.

Once undeveloped land is developed, the landscape is forever changed, and it reduces the amount of open land available for recreation, wildlife, wetlands, and so on. So when you're thinking about buying land, look for a plot of land that is a better choice for the environment. You'll be protecting our treasured open spaces.

So is there any land left that you can build your home on? Of course there is! There are still plenty of great sites you can build on. It's all a matter of site planning.

Site Planning

Site planning is the process of considering all the features of your selected plot of land before making a final decision. You want to ensure that the site maximizes your green building techniques and philosophy and minimizes the impact on the environment. Here are some key criteria to look for in the ideal plot of land:

- It already has that much-needed infrastructure, especially a good water supply and a good drainage system.

- It is suitable for solar access and/or wind power.

- Building on the site won't damage trees, vegetation, or wetlands.

- It is on a greyfield or brownfield (see next section).

- It has natural features that will help with your goals of green building. For example, there are trees that can provide natural shade and keep your home cooler or can be used as windbreaks.

- It is bound by existing sites that have been developed for more than five years (called "infill development").

Infill Development

Think of infill development as "filling in" available plots of land where the infrastructure and public services already exist. If there is an empty lot between two homes or buildings, that could be the perfect spot to build your home.

When considering an infill development, you should first find out why that particular site wasn't already built on. Did the original design call for the space to be left vacant?

Is there an environmental problem with the land? You can find out by going to the town or city building department and talking to someone who is knowledgeable about the background of the land and area surrounding it.

Hard Hat Area

Depending on the location of the infill, it can come with its own set of challenges. The Urban Land Institute, a nonprofit organization that focuses on the use of land in order to enhance the total environment, describes these challenges as social problems in distressed neighborhoods, difficulties with land acquisition and land assembly, financing complexities, regulatory constraints, site contamination, infrastructure problems, community opposition, and historic preservation requirements. It's best to work with a builder who has experience with infills because purchasing them in some locations can be very complicated and expensive.

If you build on an infill, there are several design challenges you must keep in mind. First, you should strive to ensure that your home maintains the architectural look and feel of the current neighborhood. This is very important, especially if the present homes have a common, even historic, design. Not following the styles of the existing homes can make your home look out of place and cause possible friction between you and your neighbors.

Tips & Tools

Visit the homeowners' associations in the neighborhoods in which you are considering building an infill. Give consideration to the style of existing homes when designing your home.

Second, consider the shape and size of the land. Infills generally occupy less acreage than new homes built in new developments. However, it's just as easy to incorporate many green features—including geothermal heating, solar panels, rainwater collection systems, and so on—on a smaller property snuggled between two other properties as it is on a bigger, more remote, site.

The Urban Land Institute also says that urban infill housing sparks neighborhood revitalization. Once new residents build in the area, they pay property taxes and spend money, which then spurs retail stores, office development, restaurants, and more. In larger cities, building an infill home means that residents also have access to local public transportation, as well as the ability to walk and bike to local amenities. Again, this reduces the carbon footprint of the residents.

Adaptive Reuse

An empty building that was once a school, a factory, or an office building sits unused. Thinking out-of-the-box, green builders can convert these empty buildings into multilevel, single-family homes. It's a terrific way of preserving and recycling buildings. One such example of an adaptive reuse is Pioneer Valley in West Springfield, Massachusetts, with the redevelopment of the old Stanley Home Products factory to a mixed-use redevelopment community that contains 75 businesses and 32 homes. And adaptive reuse can lead to much-needed tax dollars coming into the area.

Brownfields Are Green Again

If you have the financial resources, a brownfield can be a potential location for your new home. According to the EPA a brownfield is a property where the expansion, redevelopment, or reuse might be complicated by the presence or potential presence of a hazardous substance, pollutant, or contaminant. It is estimated that up to 1 million brownfields exist in the United States. Why would you want a location like that? It's simple: Clean it up, get it approved, and it already comes equipped with that much-needed infrastructure.

For example, in Pittsburgh, the Summerset at Frick Park residential development was once used as a *slag* dumping ground. A developer purchased the property, rehabbed it, and created the $243 million development.

Although builders are sometimes hesitant to work with brownfields because of the unknowns—the cost and obstacles of cleaning up the property might be prohibitive—other developers started snatching up the properties back in the

def•i•ni•tion

Slag is leftover material and residue from making steel.

1980s when they were inexpensive and nobody wanted to deal with them. These developers would then clean up the hazards, restore the land, have it approved for resale, and then sell it, often at a hefty profit.

In the 1990s, organizations stepped in to help the cleanup process along. The EPA created a voluntary cleanup program by which it provides seed money to local governments. The program launched hundreds of two-year brownfield "pilot" projects. Policies such as the Brownfields Law expanded the assistance by providing new tools to the public and private sectors to promote sustainable cleanup and reuse of brownfields.

Studies from the EPA and other organizations have shown that cleaning up and reinvesting in brownfields …

♦ Increases local tax bases.

♦ Facilitates job growth.

♦ Utilizes existing infrastructure.

♦ Takes development pressures off of undeveloped, open land.

♦ Improves and protects the environment.

These before-and-after pictures are examples of a brownfield project from the California Environmental Protection Agency. The East Bay Asian Land Development Company (EBALDC) purchased seven acres of former industrial property in San Pablo in 2004, and replaced 6,800 tons of soil that was contaminated with petroleum hydrocarbons, lead, chromium, perchloroethylene (PCE), and arsenic with clean soil. Other hazards were removed as well, and the property was sold for the construction of 74 market rate homes.

Greyfields

A greyfield, according to the NAHB, is an obsolete commercial site—an old strip mall or shopping center, for example—in an older suburban area. These greyfields can be revitalized and become potential locations for new development, but unlike brownfields, they typically do not require any environmental cleanup.

Hard Hat Area

Avoid sites with steep slopes because this will cause runoff from that site. One of your green building goals is to contain all runoff water. This can be accomplished with drainage catch basins and drywells, but if possible, it should be avoided.

Sites to Avoid

Although contaminated brownfield land has great potential to be cleaned up, approved, and reused, other environmentally sensitive areas should be avoided because of the impact that building your home will have on the environment. These sensitive areas include wetlands, floodplains, and farmland.

Wetlands

The National Wetlands Research Center, which is a clearinghouse of information on wetlands and aquatic habitats, describes wetlands as transitional areas sandwiched between permanently flooded deepwater environments and well-drained uplands. Wetlands provide shelter for fish, shellfish, and migrating birds, and act as a water filtration system, recycling nutrients and purifying the water. Some studies show that the United States is losing wetlands at an alarming rate. One study shows that Louisiana, which has 40 percent of the nation's wetlands, is losing 25 to 35 square miles per year because of erosion and *subsidence;* however, other studies indicate that more wetlands have been enhanced or preserved. It's vital not to build on wetlands property.

def•i•ni•tion

Subsidence is the motion of a surface as it shifts downward.

Hard Hat Area

According to the Natural Resources Defense Council (NRDC), which works to protect wildlife and wild places, the use of household pesticides and chemicals can damage wetlands. Eliminate the use of these products on your lawn and garden and in your home. Dispose of leftover paint thinners and varnish removers properly—never down the sink or in the street. Use natural cleaning products, such as vinegar and baking soda, instead.

Floodplains

A floodplain is flat land near a stream or river that has a history of flooding. Building a home near a floodplain leaves your home susceptible to frequent flooding. The NRDC says that global warming can lead to extreme weather events such as floods and large storms. These floods and storms can increase in size and frequency, straining the limits of flood control systems, exposing some floodplains and low-lying coastal regions to damage reminiscent of Hurricane Katrina.

Crystal City, Missouri, May 17, 2002—Water stands in a former residential area that state and local officials included in a floodplain buy-out program after the 1993 floods. This is the western edge of this buyout area.

(Anita Westervelt/FEMA News Photo)

Farmland

Over the years, as farmers have struggled to keep their businesses afloat, they have been selling off their land for development at an alarming rate. From 1992 to 1997, more than 6 million acres of agricultural land was converted to developed uses.

def•i•ni•tion

A **conservation easement** is the transfer of usage rights that creates a legally enforceable agreement between a landowner and a municipality or a qualified land protection organization.

Preserving and supporting the remaining farmland has become extremely important, especially after the falling economy in 2008 brought critical awareness to the importance of our own local farms. More people are once again turning to their local farms to shop for meat and produce instead of shopping at the big supermarket franchises.

If you insist on building on farmland, one option is to build your home on one part of the land and obtain a *conservation easement* for the remaining land, thereby ensuring it will remain undeveloped.

Build Some, Save Some

In his day (or night) job, Chuck Leavell is one of the most respected and sought-after piano players and keyboardists in modern music history, as well as a dedicated and revered conservationist. As both a solo artist and as a musician, he has worked with The Rolling Stones, Eric Clapton, George Harrison, The Allman Brothers Band, The Black Crowes, Gov't Mule, Train, and many others and is an inductee in both the Georgia Music Hall of Fame and the Alabama Music Hall of Fame.

In his book, *Forever Green; The History and Hope of the American Forest* (Evergreen Arts, 2001), Chuck tells the story of how he and his wife, Rose Lane White, turned Rose's family plantation near Macon, Georgia, into what has become a textbook tree farm. Their work on Charlane Plantation has been recognized by several conservation organizations, and Leavell, as comfortable on a tractor as a piano bench, is the only two-time recipient of the Georgia Tree Farmer of the Year award.

In 1999, the American Tree Farm System selected Chuck and Rose Lane as the National Outstanding Tree Farmers of the Year. Leavell has also been cited by the National Arbor Day Foundation, the Georgia Conservancy, the Future Farmers of America (FFA), and many other conservation organizations; he's even been recognized by the University of Georgia where the Leavells sponsor a scholarship. He sits on several boards and committees of conservation organizations and is active in forestry and conservation issues.

In 2007, Georgia Governor Sonny Perdue announced that Leavell had donated a conservation easement of almost 300 acres of the Charlane Plantation, an award-winning pine forest plantation and hunting preserve, to the state of Georgia.

It Can Be Done: An Infill and a Brownfield

In 2002, Milwaukeeans Mike and Juli Kaufmann wanted to build a green home. After extensive research, they chose a contaminated city lot in a historic Milwaukee neighborhood. The lot had been vacant for nearly three decades, and it took two years to acquire the land and complete the cleanup in compliance with the brownfield remediation requirements.

The couple built a comfortable 1,600-square-foot home that includes a geothermal heating system (Chapter 11), PEX plumbing (Chapter 12), spray-foam insulation (Chapter 7), reclaimed maple flooring from a nearby warehouse redevelopment, cork flooring, a green roof (Chapter 9), a rain water collection system (Chapter 15), and a xeriscape landscape (Chapter 20).

The installation of a home geothermal heating system.

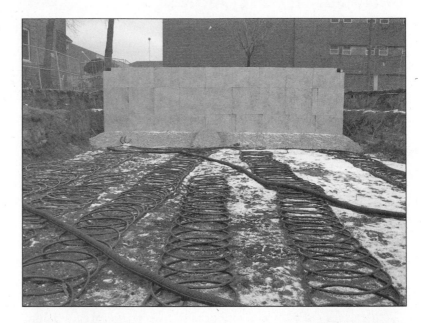

The Kaufmann's new, green home.

The Least You Need to Know

- ◆ Consider a property's history and ecological impact when deciding where to build.

- ◆ Consider building on an empty lot in an already developed area as a way to save resources and make use of existing infrastructure.

- ◆ Farmlands and wetlands should be preserved; brownfields and infills should be used.

- ◆ If farmland is still your dream, put a conservation easement in place to protect land from future development.

Part 2

Your Home's Structure

Green homes no longer need to look like a life-size version of a kids' Playdoh house, nor do they need to be hidden underground. As a matter of fact, today's green homes are often impossible to distinguish from any other house on the block. The difference is in the materials you choose to build with.

Chapters in this part break down each major component of your home's structure—its foundation and roof; windows and doors; and floors, insulation, and exterior—and show you how to choose materials that are sustainable and eco-friendly. When you know your options, your choice will depend on your budget, climate, and taste.

Chapter 7

Homebuilding Techniques

In This Chapter

- Nuts and bolts of framing your home
- The ABCs of SIPs and AFTs
- Make your home an earthship or yurt
- Lessons on heat and moisture
- The inside scoop on insulation

This chapter takes you through the nuts and bolts of building the shell of your home, otherwise known as the *envelope*. We'll review proper green building and insulating techniques for the outside framework of your home—the foundation, framing, insulation, walls, and roof—which are vital to successfully creating a truly energy-efficient home.

Foundations

The foundation of your home is the base, or bottom; it is what holds it up and keeps it from shifting and settling. A strong, well-insulated foundation sets the tone for what comes next—a well-insulated framework, ceilings, floors, crawlspaces, roof, and so on.

Solid wood foundations were once a staple in home building construction. Usually built with a faster-growth southern yellow pine wood, the wood was pressure-treated with chemicals to preserve it and prevent rotting. Because treated wood can emit VOCs, it is not the most ideal choice for green builders. The most common chemical utilized in pressure-treated wood was once chromated copper arsenate (CCA). A few decades ago, this chemical was found to contain arsenic, which can be toxic to the environment and to the user when burned. It has since been banned and replaced with safer alternatives.

Today more builders—even green builders—use concrete for foundations. The concrete is either mixed on site and poured or in premade blocks.

Green Facts

Although relatively uncommon now, green building was once associated with a rammed earth construction. Rammed earth construction is an earth mix that's packed between forms. With the addition of water and sometimes cement, it is an environmentally safe, strong building material. Rammed earth is an ancient earth building technique—the Great Wall of China is made partly of rammed earth—that is slowly being revived, although its use has been limited in the United States.

Concrete is the green material of choice because it minimizes waste—you only buy or mix what you need. In addition, any extra can be returned. It's also becoming a greener material because it's being made with recycled materials such as fly ash, a residue generated in the combustion of coal and used in concrete because of its durability. Concrete is an energy-efficient material and is durable, stands up to high winds, and resists moisture. Compared to some treated lumber, it also has low emissions of volatile organic compounds, or VOCs, that can contribute to a variety of health issues.

New on the market are insulated concrete forms (ICF) and precast concrete walls. These are hollow blocks or panels made up of rigid recycled polystyrene foam insulation and fly ash. The blocks are stacked and reinforced and then filled with concrete, making it very durable, although not impenetrable. It's one of the strongest residential foundation and framing systems around and actually improves with age. It can even withstand hurricane-force winds. Although concrete-built homes are slightly more expensive than traditionally built homes, the benefits long outweigh the extra cost.

Framing

When it comes to the walls, or the framing, of the home, homebuilders have numerous options. In addition to the traditional framing methods, such as timber framing—a greener choice than conventional wood framing since it uses less lumber—other options include structural insulated panels (SIP), concrete form framing, steel, and advanced framing techniques.

Structural Insulated Panels (SIP)

Fast becoming a popular method of framing because of their tremendous energy-efficient features, SIPs are precut and arrive at the job site ready to install. Made of molded expanded polystyrene, they can be used as walls, floors, or roofs. One example of structural insulated panels is strawboard, which is made of compressed wheat or rice straw and covered with recycled paper liners. The panels are fireproof and soundproof and can be treated so they are resistant to insects as well. These panels are a bit pricier than traditional framing options, but your energy savings will offset this cost.

Steel

Steel framing is also becoming a popular alternative framing method for homes. Steel is durable, recyclable, noncombustible, stable, and consistent. According to the Steel Framing Alliance, it's also fire-safe; resistant to pests (especially termites), fungi, and mold; and makes for a strong foundation, which is particularly desirable in areas where hurricanes and earthquakes are a possibility.

> **Green Facts**
>
> It takes about 18 acres of wheat straw, which is replaceable every year, to build a 1,760-square-foot home. It takes the equivalent of 1 acre of clear-cut forest, which takes 30 years to replace, to build the same home.

Steel framing is being used for faster installation into concrete exteriors, floors, and ceilings.

(Integrated Building and Construction Solutions)

Advanced Framing Techniques

The building industry is working hard to reduce the amount of lumber that goes into framing each home. Doing so not only saves valuable resources and energy, but also allows room for extra insulation to be installed, making the home more energy efficient.

One method that reduces the amount of lumber used is called advanced framing technique, also called optimum value engineering (OVE). Using engineered wood, which is stronger than traditional lumber, allows builders to leave wider spaces between studs. This means that there is room for more insulation to be added in the roof, ceiling, attic, and so on. The finished product is a much tighter, more energy-efficient home that has taken fewer resources and less energy to heat.

> **Green Facts**
>
> According to *Green from the Ground Up,* a 2004 Pulte Homes study showed that advanced framing techniques reduced 738 studs from one home, amounting to more than 2,100 board feet of lumber saved. Energy costs in the home (both heating and cooling) were a mere $710 a year, compared to $1,003 per year for a conventional home.

Novel Framing Techniques: Earthships and Yurts

If you prefer more unconventional home styles, you might want to try to build an earthship or a yurt. Although earthships sound like something out of a Stephen Spielberg movie, they are catching on for those seeking a more unique and highly energy-efficient home that is built using traditional earth-friendly materials.

Earthships are typically circular or u-shaped dwellings. The walls are made from recycled tires (exterior) and used aluminum soda cans (interior), which are then covered with plaster or adobe. The owners usually incorporate a means to recycle rainwater, and the homes are equipped with modern-day plumbing. Most earthships are topped off with a green, or living, roof.

Earthships were created by Michael Reynolds, who owns Earthship Biotecture near Taos, New Mexico, where he builds full communities of earthships. Today there are earthships all over the world. They are well-insulated and can generate their own utilities using solar panels and windmills.

The cost of building an earthship is said to be $175 a square foot on average, but can be more as well. However, the cost savings once the house is built can be huge.

According to Pacific Yurts, a manufacturer of yurts, these homes are a modern adaptation of the ancient shelter used by Central Asian nomads for centuries. The shape is compact and energy efficient, yet it is lightweight, low-cost, and extremely weather tight.

Modern-day construction codes do not cover yurts and earthships, and insurance and mortgage companies may not provide any financial coverage for these homes. They can also be extremely difficult to undertake, so it's important to check with your local building department to make sure that the type of home you want to build is permitted in your area. Both of these styles of homes come with their own sets of challenges, so if you are interested in building them, you should consult with an expert in that area. For the sake of this book, we are focusing more on building and remodeling mainstream homes, but we recognize the positive features that these green homes offer.

> **Green Facts**
>
> The Greater World subdivision is located about 13 miles northwest of Taos, New Mexico, and is a unique subdivision in that all the homes are earthships and all utilities are generated from solar and wind power. The community's "Users Code" specifically prohibits outside utility hookups (i.e., there are no water lines, power lines, sewer lines, gas lines, etc.) and prohibits drilling water wells.

Straw Bale Homes

Straw bale homes are inexpensive, well-insulated, very quiet, and can bear heavy loads. Straw bale homes are made by stacking bales of straw on top of one another within a wooden frame and covering the straw with plaster and stucco to keep the straw in place. Typically, the homes cost from 10 percent to 20 percent less than a traditional wood frame home, but the final cost depends on the size and location of your home.

Builders are constructing straw bales that are indistinguishable from traditional homes, making this option more appealing to consumers.

Hard Hat Area _____

Keep drywall out of landfills! When gypsum drywall is disposed in landfills and gets wet, it can actually cause environmental problems. An alternative would be to grind up the drywall and use it as a soil neutralizer.

Heat and Moisture 101

To help grasp the underlying fundamentals of green building, one of the first things you need to know is how heat and moisture affect your home. Let's tackle heat first.

Heat is transferred into your home by three means: conduction, convection, and radiation.

Conduction

Conduction is the transfer of heat from one object to another by contact. For example, during the winter, conduction occurs when the heat is transferred from the studs in the wall to the exterior of the home. You can actually see this happening after an early morning frost: look out on your roof after the frost, and you'll probably see the lines of the roof rafters where they are melting the frost. Your home can experience significant heat loss and heat gain through conduction.

Convection

Convection is the transfer of heat through air or fluid. You can feel convection in your home during the winter if you sit by a closed window. What you're feeling is the cold air coming from the heat loss near the window, dropping, and being replaced by air that is moving across the room. This moving air creates a feeling of coolness. Convective currents can also accelerate heat loss and gain if not kept under control.

Radiation

Radiation is the transfer of heat through space from one object to another. For example, you can see radiation during the summer when the heat shimmers on the road or when you feel a sun-warmed concrete floor in a solar home. In your home, it's important to reduce the harmful effects of radiation and instead enhance its beneficial warming effects.

Once you understand how the heat loss occurs in your home, you can take steps to prevent it from occurring. This can be accomplished through such techniques as increased insulation, insulated windows, and passive solar heating and cooling.

Moisture Movement

Understanding how moisture moves throughout your home will help you to select wall, ceiling, and floor systems that mitigate mildew and mold and prevent structural damage.

Moisture can move through any material by a process called *diffusion*. Moisture moves from areas of high humidity to areas of low humidity, and from areas of warm temperature to areas of colder temperatures. Moisture affects homes in different ways depending on the season and climate.

For example, in the winter, when you seal up your home and heat it to keep warm, the humidity inside your home is typically high. Outside, however, the temperature is colder and the humidity is usually lower. As a result, moisture in the air moves through the walls and ceilings from the inside of your home (the warm area) to the outside of your home (the colder area).

def•i•ni•tion

Diffusion is the movement of moisture through solid materials. Some materials allow more moisture migration than others. The rate of diffusion is referred to as the "perm rate." The lower the perm rate, the less moisture can move through it.

In the summer when you're cooling your home, the movement of the moisture is usually reversed. The outside of your home is warmer and more humid, and the interior is cooler and drier. So when you're cooling your home down in the heat of summer, moisture moves from the outside of your home (the warmer area) to the interior (the cooler area).

Two types of moisture can enter your home—bulk moisture and vapor moisture:

◆ **Bulk moisture** comes from leaks around windows, doors, and roofs, as well as from condensation—when cold air comes in contact with warm pipes—resulting from uninsulated pipes and heating, ventilating, and air conditioner (HVAC) ducts.

◆ **Vapor moisture** is the result of cooking, showering, laundry, general occupancy, and changes to indoor humidity. Showers, cooking, washing, and even breathing can add 5 to 10 pounds of moisture a day into your home. Washing and drying clothes indoors can add another 30 pounds. All that moisture needs to go somewhere. If it doesn't, it accumulates on the ceilings and walls.

Your goal should be to control the amount of moisture in your home and make certain it doesn't get trapped in this process. This is of critical concern because moisture accumulation can lead to structural problems, such as rot, which then leads to structure failure. It can also cause mold and mildew, which can lead to a host of medical problems.

Get It Under Control

To control moisture, the envelope of your home—the foundation, framing, and roof—must be designed to actually enable moisture movement to occur in *both* directions. If it's done correctly, the wall and ceiling cavity will remain dry. Bulk moisture is controlled by utilizing *flashing* techniques around windows and doors, where the roof and walls meet, and on exterior decks and patios to prevent leaks. It is also controlled by limiting the contact of cold surfaces, such as water pipes, and HVAC ducts with warm, moist air by insulating the pipes or placing them in conditioned spaces.

def•i•ni•tion

Flashing is waterproof membranes or sheet metal that is installed around windows and doors to prevent water from entering a structure.

Vapor moisture is harder to control. It moves through solid materials—such as drywall and plywood—and is everywhere. Extra care needs to be taken to make sure the walls and other solid materials cannot allow moisture through that can lead to mildew and mold.

Air flow—and pressure from outside wind pressure and from inside pressure such as exhaust fans and furnaces—accentuates the flow of heat and moisture. This means that any holes in the walls around electrical receptacles and wall penetrations can significantly add to your heat loss and detrimental moisture movement.

What it all comes down to is this: you need to build a home that prevents moisture from entering (vapor barrier) and prevents unwanted air from entering (air barrier) while also having controlled ventilation systems in place to let the home breathe properly.

Air barriers are anything that prevents air flow, such as properly installed drywall and caulking around windows, doors, and other openings.

Vapor retarders help to control moisture in basements, ceilings, crawl spaces, floors, foundations, and walls. They can be made of specially treated paper, thin plastic sheeting, or a low-perm paint. The retarder must have a vapor permeance rate of not more than 1.0 perm. How it is used will depend on where you live. Some climates require that the vapor retarders be placed in the interior of the home while some require it on the home's exterior. In some areas, such as the South, vapor retarders are not recommended.

> **Green Facts**
>
> Aerogel, one of the world's lightest solids, is being dubbed "frozen smoke" and a "miracle material" for the twenty-first century. It can withstand a blast of dynamite and protect against extreme heat. Down the road it might be considered as a green building material because it absorbs pollutants in water, too.

Insulation

In addition to what we've already discussed, insulation also plays a critical role in controlling moisture in your walls, ceiling, crawl spaces, and attic. Insulation creates a heat barrier between the inside and outside of your home, thereby cutting heating and cooling costs.

The Center for Disease Control and Prevention reports that using insulation with an *R-value* of 19 in Hawaii could reduce the indoor air temperature by 4°F and possibly lower the ceiling temperature by more than 15°F. The type of insulation for your home may differ depending on your local climate and your individual home.

Ultimately your goal for using insulation to create a heat barrier is to reduce (or even eliminate) the need for an air conditioner to cool your home. A well-insulated home will need a smaller, and less costly, heating and cooling system than a home that isn't as well insulated.

def•i•ni•tion

> The **R-value** is an indication of how much heat the insulation allows to pass through. The higher the R-value, the more the insulation resists heat transfer.

Properly controlled ventilation goes hand-in-hand with proper insulation. Tightening up your home to prevent air from leaking in and out is vital to energy efficiency, but your home must breathe—good air in, bad air out. You want air to enter, but at the same time you need to eliminate dust, irritants, and moisture from entering your home. It's a fine balance, but you'll read more about proper ventilation techniques in Chapter 17.

If you're not sure whether your home needs additional insulation, check with an energy auditor. Refitting homes with a higher R-value insulation can be expensive unless you already plan on opening the walls for other construction.

A less expensive option is to install extra insulation in your attic or crawl spaces or to create small openings through which to add blown-in insulation (see the following section) in closed walls.

A properly insulated home will reduce your energy use and your heating and cooling costs and is well worth the investment.

Hard Hat Area

Years ago, formaldehyde was a popular ingredient in urea-formaldehyde foam insulation. The popular insulation, which was developed in Europe in the 1950s, was made from a mixture of urea-formaldehyde resin, a foaming agent, and compressed air. It was then injected into the wall as a foam and, when it dried, it hardened and became a very effective insulating material.

Later, homes with this type of insulation were found to have very high levels of formaldehyde, and homeowners began to complain of health problems including watery eyes, burning sensations in the eyes and throat, nausea, asthma attacks, difficulty breathing, and even cancer.

Eventually the building industry banned the use of formaldehyde in insulation. However, research has suggested that residents in homes already insulated with urea-formaldehyde foam insulation are at little risk for health problems because most of the formaldehyde is released into the air when the product is installed and dissipates over time. However, if you are upgrading your home, newer, formaldehyde-free insulation is now available.

Which Insulation Is Right for You?

The type of insulation you choose and how much you should install depends on a number of factors, including ...

♦ Where you live and the R-value specified by local building codes. For example, if you live in Maine, you're going to have different R-value minimum requirements than someone living in Arizona. Ask your builder what your local requirements are. Maine residents should be using an R-19 insulation in the walls and floors and insulation from the high R-30s to the high R-40s for the ceilings. However, mild climates might only be using an R-10 or R-11 in the walls and floors and an R-19 in the ceilings.

♦ Whether you currently have ductwork in the attic (which can require additional insulation in the attic ceiling).

♦ Your home's framing style.

Installing higher R-value insulations helps to keep your home cooler in the summer and warmer in the winter. In Chapter 9, you'll learn how structural insulated roof panels also provide high R-values and, combined with proper attic insulation, can significantly reduce your heating and cooling costs.

It is recommended that builders choose an R-value that's approximately 50 percent above the minimum recommended R-value for your area to maximize energy efficiency. However, don't make the common mistake of buying very high R-value insulation and jamming it into a space where it's not meant to be used. Follow the manufacturer's guidelines.

The two basic types of insulation are those that allow moisture movement and those that do not. The insulation that does not allow for moisture movement is called closed-cell foam. The types of insulation that allow moisture movement are the following:

♦ Loose fill

♦ Batt

♦ Open-cell foam

And then, of course, there's insulation made from your old blue jeans.

Loose-Fill Insulation

Loose-fill insulation is made up of loose particles of fiber, foam, fiberglass, mineral wool, rock wool, slag wool, or cellulose. It is blown into a structure's walls, ceilings, or attic using special pneumatic equipment.

♦ **Fiberglass** contains 20 percent to 30 percent recycled glass and other natural ingredients such as sand.

♦ **Mineral wool** is produced from 75 percent post-industrial recycled content.

♦ **Rock wool,** developed way back in the mid-1800s, comes from aluminosilicate rock (usually basalt), blast furnace slag, and limestone or dolomite.

♦ **Slag wool** is a byproduct of steel production that would otherwise wind up in landfills. Both rock and slag wool insulations are made in part from waste materials. Manufacturers say they use less energy during the production of these types of insulation. Rock and slag wool insulation are also sound absorbent, mold and bacteria resistant, and noncombustible and have a high fire-retardant rating.

♦ **Cellulose** insulation is a "green" insulation made from natural wood and recycled newspaper. Because it is blown in rather than laid in sheets, it fits into odd, tight spaces (such as around pipes) that can be difficult fits for traditional insulation. It also has a very high R-value—even higher than fiberglass and mineral wool insulation, although the R-value for blown-in insulation is determined after the insulation has settled and can be measured. Cellulose has also been given a class-1 fire rating because it has fire-retardant chemical additives.

> **Green Facts**
>
> Between 1992 and 2005, slag wool insulation manufacturers used more than 13 billion pounds of waste blast furnace slag in the production of insulation.

Cellulose insulation must meet the requirements of Consumer Products Safety Commission Safety standards, and a number of qualified independent product testing laboratories have cellulose insulation certification programs to assure contractors and consumers that the materials they buy and install meet or exceed government and industry standards. The National Association of Home Builders National Research Center certifies the quality and performance of cellulose insulation.

If your framing is already up and closed, you can still benefit from this insulation by drilling holes between the wall studs, blowing the insulation into the holes, and then sealing the holes. Consult a qualified professional or discuss this option with your builder.

Keep in mind that over time, cellulose insulation can settle and cause the R-value to change, so it's important to add more cellulose to compensate for this settling.

These walls were insulated with sprayed-on cellulose. Although the insulation value of cellulose is only a little better than fiberglass, it completely fills the wall cavity and, unlike fiberglass batt, fills around pipes and wires and provides a higher-quality installation and better overall wall performance. Cellulose has the added benefit of being a recycled product.

(Davis Energy Group— Springer, David)

Batt Insulation

Traditional fiberglass insulation comes in long, precut rolls that are placed between the studs in your walls, placed in the floor, or rolled out in the ceiling. If not installed correctly, it can lose its effectiveness. According to the California Energy Commission, even a gap as small as a half-inch can reduce the efficiency of the fiberglass insulation by as much as 50 percent! Many types of fiberglass batt insulation are available; discuss the best options with your builder.

Tips & Tools

Direct contact with fiberglass and fiberglass dust can irritate skin, eyes, nose, and throat, so do-it-yourselfers should wear goggles, a mask, and gloves during installation of this and other insulations. Also, do not rub your eyes while working with fiberglass.

Open-Cell Foam

Open-cell foam insulation is a type of soft insulation that comes in sheets that can be cut to fit or can be sprayed into the space, after which it hardens in just minutes. The thickness of the sheets determines its R-value. It's often installed in basements and underneath vinyl siding.

Denim, Cotton, and Soy

Are your old blue jeans worn out or too small? Had enough of your old cotton t-shirts? You'll never look at them the same way when you find out that they can actually help to make your home comfy cozy, save money on your heating and cooling costs, and reduce your energy use. Recycled denim jeans and cotton insulation are rapidly becoming more popular as a way to insulate homes.

Cotton insulation made from recycled jeans is asbestos- and formaldehyde-free; does not irritate the skin, nose, and throat; holds heat well; and absorbs more sound because it is heavier than fiberglass. Denim insulation comes in rolls or batts or can be blown in. This insulation is a bit pricier than traditional fiberglass insulation, but it definitely has its advantages and is well worth the extra cost.

Soy-based spray foam insulation is relatively new and quite pricey, but is slowly catching on. It is manufactured from renewable American-grown soy beans and can expand to 100 times its volume to completely fill every space. It is not affected by moisture, mold, insects, or rodents.

The Least You Need to Know

- ◆ You can't properly insulate your home without properly ventilating it, too.

- ◆ Understanding how heat and moisture move in your home will help you to know how to make your home more energy efficient.

- ◆ To make your home energy efficient, it should contain a vapor barrier, an air barrier, a proper ventilation system, and adequate insulation.

- ◆ Newer technologies, such as soy, cost more but the investment will be offset by your energy savings.

Chapter 8

Windows and Doors

In This Chapter

- ◆ The architectural and functional aspects of windows
- ◆ The biggest energy losers
- ◆ U-factors and low-E grades
- ◆ Window placement and size
- ◆ Energy-efficient and earth-friendly doors

Windows and doors have several functions in your home. They determine what your home will look like architecturally, how much light will come in, and how much energy you will gain from the sun. Windows and doors are part of your home's envelope that includes the roof, floors, framing, foundation, and walls. Installing energy-efficient windows and doors is one of the most important steps you can take to seal your home's envelope properly.

The Importance of Efficient Windows

Are your windows drafty? Do your curtains blow when it's breezy outside, or do you tuck rolled-up towels at the base of your windows and doors to minimize the draft from coming in? Are they poorly insulated, installed improperly, or do they have gaps or cracks? Are the windows just really old and inefficient? These are all signs that your windows are already causing serious problems. These faulty features can account for up to 30 percent of the heat loss in your home. In turn, this can make your heating and cooling systems work harder and lead to higher bills. Either way, you're literally throwing your hard-earned money right out those leaky windows and doors.

Tips & Tools

A professional technician can conduct a blower door test. This test depressurizes the house and measures how long it takes for old air to be replaced by new air to determine how leaky your house is.

def•i•ni•tion

Replacement windows are windows that are removed and changed without actually changing the trim or old window frame.

Today's building technology has significantly improved the energy efficiency of new and *replacement windows* and doors. No longer are windows constructed with just one pane of clear glass. Today, a wide variety of window selections consist of additional energy-saving layers of insulated glass sandwiching argon or krypton, which are colorless, odorless gases that minimize the amount of heat penetrating the window.

Energy-efficient windows are also subjected to intense certification processes to ensure their efficiency. Several associations and organizations conduct these window-testing programs, including The American Architectural Manufacturers Association (AAMA), The Window & Door Manufacturers Association (WDMA), and The National Fenestration Rating Council (NFRC).

According to the AAMA, its certification label means that a window product sample has been tested and conforms to performance standards for air and water infiltration at the specified pressures, structural integrity, and resistance to forced entry.

The WDMA sponsors the Hallmark Certification Program, which identifies products that have been manufactured in accordance to the WDMA's standards.

The NFRC is a nonprofit organization that administers a uniform, independent rating and labeling system for the energy performance of windows, doors, skylights, and attachment products.

NFRC National Fenestration Rating Council® CERTIFIED	World's Best Window Co.

World's Best Window Co.

Millennium 2000+
Vinyl-Clad Wood Frame
Double Glazing • Dynamic Glazing • Argon Fill • Low E
Product Type: **Vertical Slider**

ENERGY PERFORMANCE RATINGS

U-Factor (U.S./I-P)	Solar Heat Gain Coefficient
0.30 Variable ↔ **0.40**	**0.10** Variable ↔ **0.50**
Off/Closed On/Open	Off/Closed On/Open

ADDITIONAL PERFORMANCE RATINGS

Visible Transmittance	Air Leakage (U.S./I-P)
0.03 Variable ↔ **0.65**	**0.2**
Off/Closed On/Open	

Manufacturer stipulates that these ratings conform to applicable NFRC procedures for determining whole product performance. NFRC ratings are determined for a fixed set of environmental conditions and a specific product size. NFRC does not recommend any product and does not warrant the suitability of any product for any specific use. Consult manufacturer's literature for other product performance information.
www.nfrc.org

The National Fenestration Rating Council is an organization that has a rating and labeling system for the energy performance of windows, doors, skylights, and attachment products. Look for this label.

Window Design

To understand how a window can help you save energy in your home, you need to understand how an energy-efficient window actually works. The concept is really quite simple: an energy-efficient window slows down the rate of heat loss between the inside and outside of your home. Because energy moves from warm to cold areas, your window becomes a magnet. In the winter, the warm air inside the house tries to move outside to the colder air; in the summer, the warmer air outside tries to move inside. The air goes to the windows because they are less efficient than most other parts of the house, including the walls, floors, and roof. The air will successfully get out through window cracks, openings in the frame, or right through older single-pane or poorly insulated double-pane windows. Even in well-sealed windows there is still some energy (heat) transfer through the glass since the glass conducts heat via *conduction*.

def•i•ni•tion

Heat **conduction** is the spontaneous transfer of thermal energy through matter, from a region of higher temperature to a region of lower temperature. It acts to equalize the differences in temperature.

Condensation is when water changes from a gaseous state to a liquid state.

Energy-efficient windows include modern technologies to reduce air flow and heat loss. These technologies include glazing, low-E coatings, low-U values, and gases such as krypton or argon between panes (more on all of these in a moment). These efficient windows protect you from the chill in the winter and keep you cool in the summer. In addition, they will also reduce that dreaded *condensation* inside your windows.

How well an energy-saving window performs depends on the construction of the window frame and the spacer material that separates the individual frames of glass inside the pane and the glass itself. And, if your goal is to achieve LEED certification on your home, choosing the correct windows will improve your score. LEED points are given according to the window's U-factor, solar heating gain, size, and other factors. These terms will be explained shortly.

What to look for when shopping for energy-efficient windows.

(ENERGY STAR)

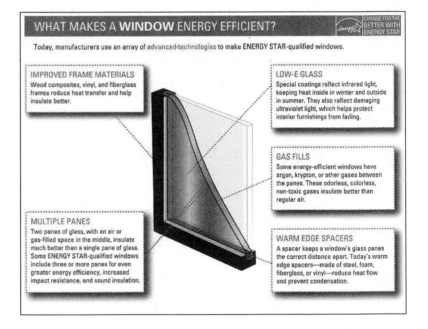

WHAT MAKES A **WINDOW** ENERGY EFFICIENT?

CHANGE FOR THE BETTER WITH ENERGY STAR

Today, manufacturers use an array of advanced technologies to make ENERGY STAR-qualified windows.

IMPROVED FRAME MATERIALS
Wood composites, vinyl, and fiberglass frames reduce heat transfer and help insulate better.

LOW-E GLASS
Special coatings reflect infrared light, keeping heat inside in winter and outside in summer. They also reflect damaging ultraviolet light, which helps protect interior furnishings from fading.

GAS FILLS
Some energy-efficient windows have argon, krypton, or other gases between the panes. These odorless, colorless, non-toxic gases insulate better than regular air.

MULTIPLE PANES
Two panes of glass, with an air or gas-filled space in the middle, insulate much better than a single pane of glass. Some ENERGY STAR-qualified windows include three or more panes for even greater energy efficiency, increased impact resistance, and sound insulation.

WARM EDGE SPACERS
A spacer keeps a window's glass panes the correct distance apart. Today's warm edge spacers—made of steel, foam, fiberglass, or vinyl—reduce heat flow and prevent condensation.

Glazing

Glazing is the term used to describe the glass in a window. A double-glazed window has two panes of glass; triple-glazed has three. An "energy-glazed" window has a coating on the glass or a gas between the panes of glass. The more glazing, the more *solar gain* is reduced.

def•i•ni•tion

Solar gain is the energy that is gained through the window from the sun. In southern climates you want to minimize solar gain, while in northern climates, or heating climates, solar gain is somewhat desirable during the heating seasons.

The three types of solar gain are direct gain, indirect gain, and isolated gain. In direct gain, the sun heats the room directly. In indirect gain, the sun heats one room directly and that heat is distributed to other rooms. Those other rooms are heated by indirect gain. In isolated gain, the sun heats an isolated space—say, a greenhouse or sunspace—and the heat is then circulated to other areas.

Too much solar gain and it will cause floors, carpet, and furniture to fade and add to your cooling costs; however, some solar gain is desirable to help reduce the winter cold. A double-glazed window reduces the solar gain by 10 percent; triple-glazing cuts solar gain by 20 percent. Older homes that haven't been upgraded have single-pane or single-glazed windows. Upgrading to double- or triple-glazed windows can have a big impact on the energy efficiency of your home.

Low-E

Energy-efficient windows have a *low-emissivity* (*low-E*) coating that helps control the amount of heat that comes through the window. This coating is virtually invisible and is applied directly to the window pane, on either the inside surfaces of the panes of glass (surfaces facing each other) or the outside. Low-E coatings allow light to penetrate but reduce the amount of heat transferred through the glass that can escape through the window. In addition, low-E squared and low-E cubed versions of low-E coatings are available. This simply means that the window has two or three coatings of low-E.

def•i•ni•tion

Low-emissivity (low-E) coatings control the amount of heat transfer coming in from the windows.

Low-E coatings are applied in soft or hard coats. Soft-coat low-E isn't as strong as hard low-E and can deteriorate when exposed to air and moisture. On the other hand, although hard low-E coatings are more durable, they aren't as energy efficient as soft coatings.

According to the U.S. Department of Energy, windows manufactured with either type of low-E coating typically cost about 10 percent to 15 percent more than regular windows, but they reduce energy loss by as much as 30 percent to 50 percent. Low-E windows, once available only by special order, are now becoming standard on windows.

> **Tips & Tools**
>
> See Chapter 19 for information on how shading your windows with awnings or deciduous and evergreen plants and trees can further reduce your windows' solar gain.

U-Value

You learned in Chapter 7 that the R-value describes the efficiency of wall and ceiling insulation; the higher the R-value, the greater the insulation. Although windows insulate, they differ from wall insulation in that they react to several factors, including sunlight; outside and inside air temperatures; and wind, rain, and other weather. It only makes sense, then, that window insulation is measured differently.

The industry measures the energy efficiency of windows with a U-value, also called a U-factor. The U-value measures the rate of heat transfer through the window, or heat loss. (You might still see R-values listed on new windows, but you should ignore them because they focus on the center of the window, not the entire window.) When it comes to windows, the lower the U-value, the better. In cold climates, the recommended U-value is .35 or lower.

Windows with double- or triple-glazing and that contain argon or krypton between the pieces of glass also slow the heat from penetrating and contribute to lower U-values.

The Solar Heat Gain Coefficient (SHGC)

The SHGC indicates how well the product blocks solar radiation from the sun. The lower the SHGC, the less solar heat it transmits. The ENERGY STAR program has established specific criteria for windows and doors for three climate zones in the United States. It is recommended that you contact the manufacturer to ensure that the product is ENERGY STAR–certified and that you check the U-value and SHGC numbers. To be eligible for ENERGY STAR certification, products must be rated,

certified, and labeled for both U-value *and* SHGC in accordance with the procedures of the National Fenestration Rating Council (NFRC) at levels that meet the
ENERGY STAR qualification criteria in one or more climate zones.

Frames and Sashes

Energy efficiency is not just about the window panes. Windows are comprised of
frames, too—typically wood frames—that are also exposed to sunlight and harsh
weather. This exposure can lead to decay and, eventually, air loss.

Windows and their sashes can be made from aluminum, wood, a combination of wood
and vinyl or aluminum, or solid vinyl. Wood is the oldest type of frame, has moderate
insulating qualities, and needs the most maintenance of the three types of windows.
It's usually found in the more expensive windows and needs to be maintained by painting to prevent damage from moisture and insect infestation.

Aluminum windows are durable and the least expensive, but they need a "thermal
break" to prevent the transfer of heat through the frame. Pre-finished aluminum
clad wood windows are similar to wood windows—and have the recycling aspect of
aluminum—but don't need as much maintenance as wood.

The American Chemistry Council states that vinyl window frames require three times
less energy to manufacture than aluminum frames, and using vinyl window frames will
save the United States nearly 2 trillion BTUs of energy per year. However, vinyl is
made with PVC, which is not a good green building feature.

Fiberglass windows are less expensive than
wood windows and have better insulating
qualities and less maintenance. Another
frame and sash option is composite recycled
wood fiber and vinyl composition frame and
sash material.

No matter what frame type you choose,
it's vital that they be installed correctly and
weather-stripped properly to avoid leaks.

 **Hard Hat Area**

If you are using a wood
frame and plan on painting
it, be sure you use an environmentally safe low- or no-VOC
paint.

Window Placement and Size

Where you place your windows is just as important—if not more important—as the
type of windows you purchase. Proper window placement encourages good ventilation,

which lessens your dependence on mechanical cooling (i.e., air conditioners). It can also minimize heating costs by providing adequate solar gain. When it comes to choosing windows, it is definitely not a one-size-fits-all situation. Each section of your home might actually require a different type of window. For example:

◆ **South**—To calculate how many windows should be installed, south-facing windows' square footage should be 7 percent of the finished floor area (cumulative). If you are incorporating passive solar, the ratio can increase to 12 percent but other solar features, such as a thermal mass, need to be included in this calculation. Too much glazing on the south will add to your cooling costs. These windows help to heat up your home in the cold, frosty winter, but prevent it from entering in the summer (combined, of course, with proper shading techniques, which you can find in Chapter 19).

◆ **East and west**—Use low solar heat gain, or low-E, coatings for all-around energy efficiency. East-facing windows should have a 4 percent ratio of finished floor area to glazing area; west-facing windows should have 2 percent.

◆ **North**—Windows on the north side of your house should also have a 4 percent ratio of finished floor area to glazing area. In addition, make sure there is adequate insulation in the framework on this side of the home.

Skylights

Skylights—windows that are built in to the roof—can make an attractive addition to your home. Skylights allow more natural lighting into the home during the day, thereby reducing the need for electric lights.

The three types of skylights are ventilating, fixed, and tubular:

◆ Ventilating skylights open and are primarily used in kitchens and bathrooms to keep the moisture out and let air pass through, but can be found in other rooms as well. These open either manually or electronically.

◆ Fixed skylights don't open and are used strictly for allowing light into the home.

◆ Tubular skylights are smaller, fixed skylights and are used in hallways and smaller areas.

Skylights come in different shapes and sizes including flat, round, pyramid, polygon, and dome (or "bubble"). Special shapes and sizes—other than flat—can cost significantly more.

When purchasing skylights, consider the same factors as you do when buying windows—energy efficiency, insulation, and UV protection. ENERGY STAR does have specifications for skylight energy efficiency, depending on your climate zone, so check the ENERGY STAR website before making your purchase.

Low-Budget Upgrades

If your windows need upgrading but you can't afford a complete transformation just yet, there are other energy-efficient and lower-cost options available.

Storm Windows

Storm windows are installed over your current windows. They provide extra insulation and protection and are a more affordable option to replacing all your windows. They can help reduce heat loss through the windows by 25 percent to 50 percent and should have low-E and low-U ratings.

You can choose between interior and exterior storm windows, although interior storm windows are easier to install and require less maintenance than outdoor storm windows.

Similar to traditional windows, storm windows can be made of wood, aluminum, and vinyl. Wood storm windows have a tendency to expand and contract during the seasons and require regular maintenance. Aluminum windows conduct heat—something you're trying to avoid. Because they require little maintenance, vinyl remains the best option for storm window framing material.

Window Film

Solar protection film can be applied to the inside of the windows and can screen out more than 50 percent of the sun's heat load while also screening out almost all the sun's *ultraviolet rays* (*UV*). Keep in mind that some manufacturers require that their film be professionally installed.

def•i•ni•tion

Ultraviolet rays (UV) from the sun can be useful to humans (it induces the body's vitamin D production) or potentially harmful (sunburn, skin cancer). Many windows have UV protection, but because skylights usually get more direct sunlight, it's more common to see UV protection for skylights.

Installing the 3M Prestige Series of Window Films, a clear nonmetallic window film that blocks heat and UV rays.

Some films are metallic based and have been known to corrode in humid or coastal areas. They also sometimes interfere with wireless or cellular signals. Fortunately, new clear non-metal-based films are available that block up to 66 percent of heat penetrating the window, resulting in less stress on air-conditioning systems and lower overall energy costs. Because these films allow more natural light to enter a home or building than traditional window films, they can also help homeowners reduce their use of artificial lights.

Caulking and Weatherstripping

Although upgrading your windows should be a top priority with larger budgets, homeowners with smaller budgets can still reduce air loss through the windows. Spend a weekend caulking and weatherstripping your windows and doors. (Be sure to purchase caulk that is specifically meant for windows.) Stopping air infiltration will actually have a quicker payback than upgrading the glazing. A good caulk installed with care will accomplish a lot at a fraction of the cost.

Also refer to Chapter 19 for a discussion of how to use landscaping, canopies, shutters, and awnings to help further cool and heat your home in an affordable and environmentally safe manner.

Smart Windows

One of the latest innovations in window design is called "smart windows." Smart windows technology alters window settings based on what is occurring in the environment. This can be done automatically (called *photochromic* and *thermochromic* smart windows) or by a switch (*electrochromic*). To understand how photochromic windows work, think of sunglasses that darken when you go outside. These windows respond to a change in light just like those sunglasses. Thermochromic windows automatically change from clear to white in response to heat.

Doors

Doors welcome your friends and family into your home. And like windows, they also protect you from the outside elements. Choosing the right door is no different from selecting any other building material for your home. You need to consider, among other things, their insulating properties and·what they are made of. Several key factors in purchasing energy-efficient doors are as follows:

- ◆ **Building material**—As beautiful as traditional exterior wood front doors are, they are not as energy efficient as some other options. A better option is to purchase a wood-clad steel or fiberglass door that is filled with polyurethane foam. If you absolutely insist on having a wood door, choose one that has been made of sustainably harvested materials (for example, recycled wood fibers) or one that has been certified by the Forest Stewardship Council (FSC), which promotes environmentally appropriate, socially beneficial, and economically viable management of the world's forests.

- ◆ **Certification**—Just like windows, doors are also certified by the NFRC, so be sure to look for labels and compare.

- ◆ **U-value**—Doors, like windows, are also given a U-value rating. The lower the U-value, the better the efficiency of the door. A recommended U-value for a steel door with a foam-core interior is .35. If the door has windows, follow the same recommendations for buying a window—look for double- and triple-glazing, argon or krypton gas between panes, and low-E coating.

Tips & Tools

When designing your new home, you should also consider installing mud rooms or foyers at your entrance doors to serve as air buffers between the outside and inside of your home.

Garage Doors

Currently no ENERGY STAR guidelines exist for selecting energy-efficient garage doors. However, garage doors are available with energy-efficient double-paned windows, and you can purchase doors with polyurethane foam insulation inside.

Sliding Glass Doors

Think of sliding glass doors as big windows. Follow the same guidelines for choosing a window and make sure that there is adequate weatherstripping near the sliders because that is the area most prone to letting in air.

Interior Doors

When choosing interior doors, energy efficiency isn't as important unless the door opens to a garage, sunroom, or other such room. More important, when it comes to interior doors, is the kind of wood they are made of. The commonly used hollow interior doors aren't very environmentally friendly. Both hollow and medium-density fiberboard doors are made with urea formaldehyde adhesives, which can contribute to indoor air quality problems. Instead, choose solid wood doors, which are a little pricier but are a healthier choice. Make sure they are FSC-certified. MDF, or fibercore doors, are also available with low urea-formaldehyde material.

The Least You Need to Know

- Invest in windows with low-E and low-U factor ratings.
- Check with the NFRC before purchasing to ensure that your windows are suitable for your climate.
- If you can't afford to upgrade your windows, take less-expensive steps, such as adding storm windows, caulking, weatherstripping, and window film to make them more energy efficient.
- Avoid hollow wood interior doors and select those that have been made with sustainable resources.

Chapter 9

Roofing and Siding

In This Chapter

- ◆ Roof responsibilities
- ◆ Climate control
- ◆ White roofs
- ◆ Straw bale roofs

Your home's roof and siding carry a lot of responsibility. Think of the roof and siding as the hat and coat for your house. They protect it, help moderate its temperature, and shelter it from the elements while insulating it from the heat and cold. Your roof and siding are also principally responsible for maintaining and controlling the air and moisture in your home. Aesthetically speaking, they are also a large part of your home's *curb appeal* (landscaping being the other large part).

There are more green alternatives to roofing and siding materials than ever before. There are roofing materials that cool your home better than traditional material and others that reflect heat very well. There are ENERGY STAR–rated roofing products and a wider variety of recyclable, sustainable

def•i•ni•tion

Curb appeal is a real estate term that means the first impression that a potential buyer has when they drive up to your property. If your home has curbside appeal, the buyer likes what they see.

products to choose from. These new products contribute to a reduction in your home's energy usage and costs.

Roofing and siding materials last a long time, often for decades, so it's important to weigh all your options carefully before making the investment. Making the right choice will bring you peace of mind for years to come.

Roofing Styles

Although from a decorative point of view, you have many styles of roofs to choose from, for the sake of green building, we're going to limit the discussion to three types of roofs:

- **Steep-sloped roofs**—These are good for cold climates that get a lot of snow, allowing the melting snow to run off and away from the home. These roofs have slopes that are from 2 inches to 12 inches.

- **Low-sloped roofs**—These have a nearly, but not completely, level slope.

- **Flat roofs**—These are just that, flat. Unless you have a water drainage system installed, flat roofs can be more prone to water accumulation and leaking than sloped roofs. Although it's best to choose a low- or steep-sloped roof to prevent the accumulation of snow, ice, or rain on top, if you already have a flat roof, you can either convert to a sloped roof or create a living roof (also called a green roof) equipped with a drainage system to keep the home cool and dry (more on these in Chapter 19).

Whether you choose a steep-sloped, low-sloped, or flat roof will depend on …

- What architectural look you desire.

- Whether you are replacing a current roof or building a new home. If you are replacing a roof, you may have some limitations based on your current roof and home structure. Your home was built to support your current roof, and your home's foundation and framing may not be sturdy enough for a heavier roof. When building a new home, discuss the roofing choice with your architect and builder so they can make any necessary design adjustments. For example, heavy concrete tile roofing may require additional framing support and would need to be designed by your architect.

◆ The climate you live in. Colder climates need a roof that can withstand heavy snow loads while warmer climates that are prone to fire require a roof made from a nonflammable material (although this is a wise choice for all areas).

Tips & Tools

If you are planning to install solar panels on your roof at some point, consider designing and installing them when you have your roof installed. You might pay a bit more at the beginning of your project, but it will cost you more to add them on later. You'll begin to recoup your investment immediately by utilizing the sun's rays to lower your home's energy usage and heating and cooling costs.

Climate Control

Your home's roof gets hot, very hot—as high as 200°F or more in some climates. Two factors determine exactly how hot the roof gets: how much sun the roof can reflect away, known as *solar reflectance;* and how the roof releases the heat it absorbs, known as *thermal emittance.* If the roof fails to release the heat, it seeps into the home, increasing your energy use and cooling costs. Installing an ENERGY STAR–rated roof that reflects the sun's rays and keeps it cool ultimately lowers your home's temperature.

ENERGY STAR roofs can reduce the heat in your home and your dependency on air conditioning by 10 percent to 15 percent.

Remember, although choosing the right roofing and siding helps to reduce your heating and cooling costs, combine it with the right amount and type of insulation, the proper ventilation systems, and energy-efficient windows to maximize your energy savings and efficiency.

Green Facts

Americans spend about $40 billion annually to air-condition homes and buildings. The amount of energy devoted to air conditioning constitutes one-sixth of all electricity generated in this country.

Types of Roofing

You have decided on the shape of your roof, but what roofing material do you install on top of the roof? There are many alternatives, all of which come with their own pros and cons, including weight and cost.

Shingles and Shakes

Asphalt shingles are the most common roofing material today due to their durability and affordability. How long the shingles last depends on their thickness. Standard asphalt shingles will last for 10 to 20 years. However, thicker shingles will last for up to 50 years, making them a much greener choice. A 50-year shingle typically costs about three to four times as much as a 20-year single, although the cost varies depending on region.

An example of asphalt shingles.

Cedar shake shingles are preferred by many homeowners for their aesthetic appeal and because they are a long-lasting and maintenance-free shingle, but they are prohibited in some areas due to potential fire hazards, so check your local building codes. Green builders should purchase shingles that have been certified by the Forest Stewardship Council (FSC), an organization that ensures that the wood is sustainable.

Shakes made to resemble cedar can also be made with recyclable materials including hemp fiber, soda bottles, and tires. Their cost is comparable to premium roofing and premium cedar, and they're fairly easy to install. Cedar roofs are about two to three times the cost of 50-year asphalt roofs.

Tile

Tiles, which are effective at reflecting the sun's rays, come in a variety of styles, including clay and concrete. Clay tiles come in interlocking and overlapping styles and are preferred by many builders because of their fireproof qualities, durability, and lack of thermal conductivity (they don't get too hot) that makes them good for warm climates. Clay tiles aren't as common today as they used to be because they are more expensive compared to other newer alternatives. They are also heavier than other roofing materials. Tile is also prone to breaking due to frost and, because air is able to flow underneath the tiles, water from melting frost can also seep in and cause water damage.

Clay tiles on the roof of a home in the southwestern United States.

Concrete

Concrete roofing tiles are becoming more popular in all climates. The concrete can be manufactured to look like slate, wood, or clay, so if you're looking to build a Tudor-style home, you can do so with concrete tiles. These tiles are more expensive than shingles, but they last longer and are better at reducing heat buildup. Concrete tiles allow for more controlled ventilation in the home, providing up to a 22 percent savings on energy costs. Concrete is eco-friendly and durable; it lasts for years.

Concrete tiles are durable and can be molded in various shapes and designs. These are MonierLifetile Concrete Slate Shingles in Hickory.

(MonierLifetile)

Slate

Slate is a natural stone that has been mined from the earth for more than 500 years. According to the American Slate Company, slate is chiefly comprised of quartz and illite, with mica, calcite, and minor quantities of other various minerals. Slates vary in color, but are most commonly seen in black, gray, red, purple, and green. It is very durable, is a low water absorber, and resists acids and chemicals. It comes in various thicknesses and different textures, with different combinations being used to provide different roofing looks. It's just as heavy as concrete.

Slate is a pricey material, but with a life span of more than 100 years, it can save you money in the long run. However, the life span depends on the type of slate and the climate. A slate roof can cost as much as 10 to 12 times the cost of a 20-year asphalt shingle roof.

Metal Roofs

Metal roofing actually reflects heat very well and fits into the green building philosophy nicely because of its low maintenance, durability, and high resistance to fire. In addition, metal roofing can contain up to 50 percent recycled material, and aluminum roofing contains 100 percent recycled material.

Several EPA ENERGY STAR–labeled metal roof products are available for residential use.

Adobe

Adobe is a completely natural building material made from sand, clay, sticks, water, straw, and other natural materials. It's shaped into bricks and dried in the sun. Buildings made of adobe are more common in the hotter southwestern parts of North America as well as in other countries, including North Africa and Spain, because of their durability and ability to keep a home much cooler than traditional building materials. However, adobe is difficult to insulate. To insulate an adobe home, a double wall can be created on the interior of the home with insulation placed in between.

Hard Hat Area

If you are considering an adobe roof, it's important to consider the weight of this material, which often requires additional framing support and can cause cracking.

Green Roofs

A green roof is a contained space filled with plants and vegetation built on top of a roof. By absorbing sunlight, shielding the roof from the elements, and acting as a natural insulator, the plants on a green roof can lead to substantial savings by reducing air-conditioning costs and extending the life of the roof. A green roof can actually reduce the temperature of a home or building by more than 100 degrees! In turn, this reduces your cooling costs significantly.

This goes a long way toward explaining why you might want to consider encouraging vegetation to take up residence on top of your home. How much you actually save depends on the size of your home, the climate, and the type of green roof that you have planted. Countries such as Germany, France, Austria, and Switzerland have embraced the green roofing concept.

Green roofs also play an increasingly important role in storm water management, absorbing much of the water that would otherwise run off in a storm and filtering pollution from rainwater.

In urban areas where homes are close together, a green roof can have a substantial impact on the urban heat island effect. A green roof can counteract that effect by providing shade and evapotranspiration, which is the release of water from plants to the surrounding air.

> **Green Facts**
>
> When celebrated architectural firm Cesar Pelli & Associates designed The Solaire, a 293-unit residential building in Manhattan's Battery Park City, they incorporated two green roofs: an intensively planted 5,000-square-foot terrace green roof on the 19th floor and a 4,800-square-foot extensive green roof on the 28th floor.

A study by the Los Angeles–based Heat Island Group has found that rooftop-cooling efforts on buildings and homes could lead to annual energy savings of $16 million. A climate model developed through the United States Department of Energy revealed that increased reflective roof surfaces and urban re-vegetation could result in temperature reductions in New York City alone of 3.6°F.

However, some structures are not suitable for a green roof, including homes with steeply sloped roofs, some historic homes (depending on the requirements of the neighborhood), and roofs that have an insufficient load capacity (which means they may not be strong enough to hold the greenery). In addition, before deciding to install a green roof, you need to consider what plants or vegetation to plant and how much sun exposure your roof gets.

Consult with a structural engineer and landscape design firm to determine whether your roof is suitable for "greening" before your architectural plans are drawn. The engineer can determine where to place the water supply and water drainage systems and what waterproofing techniques will be used.

Pricing for such a project is hard to estimate. It depends on the complexity of your roof design as well as the design and size of the green roof. Extensive green roofs can cost more than traditional roofs because they require more material and labor for installation.

Cool Roofs

When you want to stay cool in the summertime, you wear light-colored clothes because they don't absorb the sun's rays as much as dark-colored clothes do. The light-dark concept holds true for your roof, too. The lighter the roof's color, the more it will reflect the sun's rays away from your home. Light-colored roofing can also help to reduce the urban heat island effect, an effect that occurs in denser communities when numerous hot roofs can actually heat up the surrounding area by a few degrees.

To reflect the sun's rays and cool a low-sloped roof, a coating, otherwise known as a *white roof*, can be applied. This coating is similar to thick white paint and is applied with a sprayer or roller. It can last up to 20 years. The cost of applying a cool roof application depends on the size of the job and the current condition of an existing roof.

Installing a cool roof may also qualify you for rebates through your local utility company, so be sure to check on that.

Siding

Your home's siding is also exposed to the elements all year round and needs to be made from a long-lasting, durable material. Siding is also expensive to replace, so it's important to do it right the first time.

Wood

Wood siding was once a popular siding material. Cedar shakes are a traditional siding in some parts of the country. They are durable and resistant to rot, but they are pricey and time-consuming to install. Other types of wood siding include western red, redwood, northern white, and Alaskan yellow. As with any other wood product you are considering using for your home, be sure to confirm that the wood you are choosing for your siding is certified by the FSC. Most importantly, however, when it comes to siding, you also should ensure that it is fireproof, which really means that wood is not the best option.

Cement and Brick

Two strong siding candidates for green building are fiber cement and brick. Both are environmentally friendly and fireproof. Fiber cement siding is a mixture of sand, cement, and cellulose fibers. It is formed into boards that are installed so they overlap (similar to shingles) on the side of the home. Installation can be tricky, so a builder should have experience installing a fiber cement siding.

Brick is one of those green building materials that takes a lot of energy to make but lasts for a long time. To balance the energy the brick-making process expends, the product should come from a local kiln. The farther it is transported, the less green it is.

Vinyl

Vinyl siding is affordable and durable and rarely requires maintenance. However, the biggest issue with traditional vinyl siding is the fact that it's made from polyvinyl chloride (PVC), which makes it one of the least green choices for building and remodeling. The EPA explains that acute (short-term) exposure to high levels of PVC in the air has resulted in central nervous system problems, such as dizziness, drowsiness, and headaches, in humans. Chronic (long-term) exposure to PVC through inhalation and oral exposure in humans has resulted in liver damage. The EPA classified vinyl chloride as a Group A human carcinogen.

It should be noted that the vinyl industry is making strides to develop safer vinyl siding, and there are certification programs in place to monitor the product. In the meantime, ENERGY STAR has certified a no-maintenance vinyl siding with a solid foam core and an R-value of 4.0 (higher energy efficiency) compared to other vinyl sidings with an R-value of less than 1.0. Insulated vinyl siding is also an option.

According to the NAHB, insulated vinyl siding typically costs 20 percent to 30 percent more than traditional vinyl siding, but homeowners can earn the investment back by reducing their heating and cooling costs.

Aluminum Siding

Aluminum is a very affordable siding that is very durable. It makes a great green siding option since it is made of recycled materials. It requires basic cleaning maintenance with a biodegradable detergent and power washer. If the color fades over time, aluminum siding can be painted.

Exterior Paint Job

Choosing exterior paint is different from choosing interior paint. Because the outside of your home is exposed to harsh weather and the elements all year round, the exterior paint needs to have a chemical protectant mixed into the paint to protect it from the elements. As a result, exterior paints do emit some VOCs, but the air dissipates those toxins pretty quickly (more on interior paints in Chapter 10). Although the industry has responded with low- and no-VOC interior paints, these less-toxic options are not as durable as an exterior paint.

A green alternative to traditional exterior paint is a lime wash. Lime wash has been used for thousands of years; it has traditionally been used on historic buildings and homes and in hospitals. Lime is durable, odor-free, low-cost (a few hundred dollars' worth should cover the exterior of a standard-size home), nontoxic, and soaks into the pores of the material it is covering. It can also be colored and acts as a mild fungicide due to its high pH factor.

It Can Be Done: Alys Beach, Florida

Alys Beach is a beautiful new resort town located along Florida's Scenic Highway 30A. All Alys Beach homes are required to be built to the Green Home Designation Standard of the Florida Green Building Coalition.

Alys Beach, Florida. An environmentally friendly development.

Alys Beach is also a Traditional Neighborhood Development (TND), making it one of the most environmentally friendly forms of land development. It utilizes the white cool roofing application that was discussed earlier in the chapter. Beautiful white exterior walls and rooftops reflect the sunlight, keeping the homes and neighborhoods significantly cooler than they otherwise would be.

Alys Beach's careful design encourages walking and bicycling, allowing for more parks and conservation areas. A 20-acre preserve along the northern end of the town features wetlands and a longleaf pine forest, providing a vibrant habitat for native birds, small mammals, and other wildlife. The development even comes with a full-time Environmental Program Manager who oversees all environmental aspects of the growing town, including the use of green building materials.

All homes and streets in Alys Beach are carefully oriented to allow passive heating and cooling from the sun, as well as from the steady Gulf breezes (every major street is an open thoroughfare straight to the Gulf). Beautiful white exterior walls and rooftops reflect the sunlight, keeping the homes and neighborhoods significantly cooler. Storm water runoff is minimized through the use of streets and parking courts made from pavers hand-set in gravel, allowing 35 percent of all rainfall to filter directly into the ground.

The landscaping is also carefully managed to be drought-tolerant and pest-resistant, including extensive use of native plants. All exterior lighting is carefully planned and regulated to illuminate only where needed and to avoid glare, thus reducing energy use, preserving the view of the night sky, and minimizing intrusive light on the beaches (which can disturb the neighbors, including nesting sea turtles and their hatchlings!).

The Least You Need to Know

♦ Choose a sustainable and durable roofing material.

♦ The lighter the roof's color the better. White roofs reflect the sun's rays.

♦ Keeping roofs cool is about more than just the material you've chosen. It's about proper insulation, ventilation, and landscaping.

♦ Vinyl siding is *not* recommended for green building due to the toxic nature of the material. However, research is being done on more environmentally friendly alternatives.

♦ Choose a siding product that is both durable and environmentally friendly.

Chapter 10

Floors and Walls

In This Chapter

- Green flooring options
- The wonders of wood
- Eco-friendly carpet options
- Nontoxic wall coverings

Now that the walls and floors are up, it's time to cover them. Popular flooring choices have always been hardwood, linoleum, carpeting, and tile; while paint, wallpaper, or perhaps a little paneling are commonplace on the walls. Not much has changed in these areas. Those materials are still available, but manufacturers have given them a makeover, making them more environmentally friendly than in the past.

In addition, the selection of natural materials has grown to include such nontraditional materials as cork, bamboo, leather, and linoleum.

The Facts on Flooring

When it comes to choosing sustainable flooring, you want something that's going to make your feet feel good while being natural, durable, safe, and (hopefully) recyclable. Flooring is an element of your home that you'll keep in place for a long time, so it's important to make the right choice now so you're not dealing with the expense of replacing it later. So what, exactly, are you looking for?

- **Durability**—Flooring takes a beating from active children, drops, spills, pets, and more, so it needs to withstand the pressure of constant abuse. Not every type of flooring is meant for every type of family, nor is every type of flooring meant for every room. Wood flooring is great for the kitchen, living room, hallways, and other living areas, but it is not recommended for bathrooms or other areas frequently exposed to moisture. The moisture can cause buckling, warping, and staining in certain types of hardwood.

- **Comfort**—You'll be walking on the floor for years, so you want it to be easy on your feet. For example, if your home is in a cold climate, you might want an oak or maple hardwood floor versus a cooler concrete floor, especially if you do not have or have chosen not to install *radiant floor heating*.

- **Safety**—Keep in mind that flooring, carpeting, and wood floor finishes contain volatile organic compounds (VOCs), which have been proven to cause a multitude of health problems. Select flooring that does not contain these toxins.

def•i•ni•tion

Radiant floor heating is a heating system that is installed in—and radiates through—the floor. The system works best with a concrete floor, so the piping (hot water) can conduct heat and distribute it to the room. Hardwood flooring will work, although it's not as effective. Chapter 11 goes into more detail on this type of heating system.

- **Natural**—Carpets should have little or no chemical treatments.

- **Non-petroleum-based**—Some carpet padding can contain unsustainable resources including petroleum-made plastics, so either choose a carpet that needs no padding or purchase padding made from recycled materials.

- **Adhesive-free**—Choose sustainable flooring that doesn't need adhesives such as chemical-based glues. Today, you can install a carpet with water-based low-VOC glues or no glues at all.

- **Recyclable**—Choose flooring that you can recycle when you do finally replace it.

The Wonders of Wood

Fortunately for homeowners who love the look, feel, and durability of hardwood floors, becoming eco-friendly doesn't mean those fabulous features need to be sacrificed. Today, homeowners have sustainable hardwood flooring choices that are just as durable as traditional woods. You can choose from such popular styles as cherry, maple, red birch, rosewood, and *cumaru*. Although sustainable hardwood might be slightly more costly than conventional flooring—maybe as little as $1 more per square foot than standard, but it can also be considerably less—these renewable materials offer you style, comparable or even superior durability, and peace of mind.

Unfortunately, the sustainable wood industry has been plagued with its share of shady businesses that conduct illegal logging practices, so it's important to exercise caution when choosing flooring. For example, as consumers become more aware of the benefits of bamboo, some growers are entering the industry and either using hazardous pesticides on the plant or cutting them before their prime just to meet demand. Choose your flooring from businesses that participate in legal logging, by purchasing wood that earned a label from either the Forest Stewardship Council (FSC) or the Sustainable Forestry Initiative (SFI). The SFI is a program based on the premise that responsible environmental behavior and sound business decisions can coexist to the benefit of landowners, manufacturers, shareholders, customers, the environment, and future generations. The SFI program integrates the perpetual growing and harvesting of trees with the protection of wildlife, plants, soil, water, and air quality.

def•i•ni•tion

Cumaru is a wood that comes from Central and South America and is also known as Brazilian Teak. It has a warm brown color with some reddish tones.

The FSC promotes environmentally appropriate, socially beneficial, and economically viable management of the world's forests. This label will let you know that the business has obtained its products legally.

Reclaimed Wood

Reclaimed wood is wood that has been taken from another structure—perhaps from a home or building that has been condemned or is about to be destroyed—and has been refinished for use as a flooring material.

One company, Elmwood Reclaimed Timber in Kansas City, Missouri, uses reclaimed timber from places such as old redwood bridge beams in the Sierra Nevada and old cherry barn beams in West Virginia. Some companies specialize in reclaiming lost logs from the bottom of rivers and lakes. These reclaimed logs are well preserved, even after having been underwater for decades.

Reclaimed wood can come in many styles and patterns, including walnut, rustic oak, maple, and ash, and can add great character to your rooms.

Laminated Wood

Laminated wood flooring looks like hardwood and is versatile and durable. It is made like plywood in that it has *laminations*. The base laminations can be made of fast-growth wood such as aspen; only the top veneer is made from slow-growth hardwood. This is an efficient use of material, but care should also be taken to ensure that the product you buy uses only low-urea formaldehyde glues and low-VOC finishes. Due to the laminations this flooring does not "move" as much as solid wood flooring.

def•i•ni•tion

Lamination means sandwiching two or more layers of material together and sealing them to form a solid product.

Plantation-Grown Wood

New on the market, plantation-grown wood is hardwood flooring that has been grown on plantations, thereby preserving natural habitat ecosystems. The wood is a hybrid of two eucalyptus trees and has no knots, holes, or gum pockets.

Bamboo

Bamboo is a massive, fast-growing grass that is strong and stable, making it a good flooring option, especially if you have kids, pets, or lots of foot traffic. Strand bamboo is a recycled bamboo material that is pressed together, making it stronger than both traditional hardwood flooring and regular bamboo flooring. Bamboo stalks are harvested when the plant reaches maturity. It is then sliced into strips, boiled (to remove the starch), dried, and laminated into boards.

As long as the roots are not killed when the plant is harvested, bamboo can continue to be harvested indefinitely. Bamboo flooring can be made in both light and dark shades and can be created to look and feel like traditional hardwood.

Stone

A stone floor—whether it's sandstone, marble, granite, limestone, or slate—is beautiful and natural, but it's one material you need to look at from both sides of the environmental equation before deciding whether it's best for you.

First, as striking and as durable as a stone floor is, stone is not a truly renewable resource, and the actual process of obtaining the stone from the earth is not environmentally friendly. Stone is often located deep in the earth and hard to excavate. In addition, transporting it from its original location to your home requires more energy than it does for other styles of flooring and, therefore, contributes more to global warming problems. On the flip side, stone is biodegradable and its durability also means that it has less of a chance of needing to be repaired or replaced.

Most importantly, from a health perspective, stone is a boon for allergy sufferers for the following reasons:

- It doesn't emit any chemicals.

- It doesn't need chemicals during installation because it uses cement or mortar to seal it.

- It is moisture and bacteria resistant.

Several styles of stone are available, each with its own unique features:

Marble: Mined in India, Italy, and Egypt, marble is a much softer stone and is very costly. It stains easily and so it must be sealed. However, some marbles develop a desirable patina from staining.

Limestone: A softer stone than marble, limestone needs a sealant to prevent any moisture from seeping through. It is not good for high traffic areas, such as kitchens, or areas where spills are possible.

Sandstone: Similar to limestone and marble, it's a durable stone that needs a sealant but can last a lifetime.

Slate: Less expensive than marble and granite, slate doesn't need sealant, but one is recommended to prevent staining.

Terrazzo: This mosaic stone is all natural and made from combining stone pieces, such as marble, with a sand or cement mix. This makes it a recyclable stone, but it does need to be sealed.

Price wise, stone is significantly more expensive than plastic laminate, ranging in price from below $75 a square foot to well over $100 a square foot. The most important thing to keep in mind regarding stone from a green perspective is how it's mined and shipped. The environmental impact might outweigh its benefits and beauty.

Ceramic Tile

Like stone, ceramic tile is also very durable and comes in a wide range of patterns, colors, and textures. However, it can also require just as much energy to manufacture as stone does to excavate. Today, some companies offer recycled ceramic and glass tiles. These are made with recycled content such as bottles, lightbulbs, and more.

Ceramic tile does not require much in the way of maintenance. Handmade tiles will need to be sealed and maintained similar to stone. The grout between the tiles will require sealing. Ceramic tile costs less than stone on average.

Cork

Who would've imagined that cork—the same material used to plug wine bottles—would make great flooring? Cork is a renewable, albeit limited, resource that is harvested from the dead outer bark of the cork oak tree about every 9 to 15 years. It is native only to Spain and Portugal. Cork makes for a warm, natural floor. It is available in a variety of colors, textures, and patterns, and can even be made to look like hardwood, parquet, or tile floors. At one time, cork was used underneath wood or tile floors because it is a great sound insulator. Today, those same properties make it a good stand-alone flooring choice.

Because cork can resist moisture and does not absorb dust, it's also a great option for allergy sufferers. However, cork should be avoided in bathrooms because excessive moisture can eventually damage it. Cork is springy, making it a perfect choice for your kitchen or other areas where you stand for long periods of time.

Cork is sold as either tiles or planks of various sizes and thicknesses, and is available with interlocking edges that glue together. This allows you to remove a damaged tile and replace it with a new one, reducing the cost of any replacements.

Linoleum

Let's set the record straight: linoleum isn't vinyl and vinyl isn't linoleum.

Vinyl flooring is not an environmentally friendly material. It is made from polyvinyl chloride (PVC), a known carcinogen. Linoleum, on the other hand, is made from renewable raw materials, including cork, linseed oil, wood flour, resins, mineral pigments, and *jute*. Also called marmoleum, linoleum has antistatic and bacteria-resistant qualities that help to eliminate dust and pesky microorganisms, and it's easy to take care of and repair because scratches and burns can be easily buffed out. It can last for up to 40 years, and it's biodegradable. However, this versatile flooring choice should not be used in the bathroom because it might suffer from excess moisture.

def•i•ni•tion

Jute is a cheap, natural fiber made from two Asian plants. It's used to make rice and grain stacks and is strong and durable.

Concrete

Once banished for use only in garage or basement floors, today concrete is being introduced to the main part of the home—as flooring as well as for countertops and fireplaces. It is preferred flooring for radiant heat and passive solar applications due to its ability to store heat.

Thanks to a process called *acid staining*, in which acids are used to color or stamp new or old concrete, a variety of colors and patterns are available. No two slabs are ever the same. The concrete is cleaned, diamond-grinded smooth, and sealed to achieve this exquisite result. Not all acid stains are environmentally friendly, though, so if you hire a company to perform such a task, ask them which products they use.

Be sure to ask for "green-manufactured cement." In regular cement, the raw ingredients are mined, heated, and cooled in a not so eco-friendly way, so if you don't specify green-manufactured concrete, you might not get it. The only negative thing about installing cement floors is that they can be a little hard on your feet and knees; they also tend to be chilly unless you install radiant heat flooring.

This concrete surface has been acid stained.

(http://specialeffexonline.com, Craig Adamson)

Leather, Coconut, and Other Exotics

Coconut palms produce nuts for up to 80 years, after which they can be harvested and milled for flooring. It is one of several exotic flooring options available.

Coconut palms sand well and are resistant to splitting when they are nailed. The palms are naturally free of knots and repellent to insects, especially termites. The coloring is similar to other rainforest hardwoods, ranging from golden to ebony. However, some environmentalists are concerned that the cultivation of these palms threatens the rainforest because the palm is often planted and grown in land cleared for that purpose.

Leather, or recycled leather, flooring might not appeal to all homeowners, but it is durable and actually improves with age. Leather is also completely renewable within five years and is sold in hides or tiles that can be removed and reinstalled if one is damaged. The installation adhesive stays on the subfloors, and the material can be chiseled up with little damage, although the process is best left to the professionals.

If you are considering an exotic flooring, keep in mind that they might have limited applications, so consider the practicalities of them when deciding whether they are the right style of flooring for you.

Carpeting

Although carpeting covers nearly 70 percent of all floors in the United States, it can actually contribute to poor indoor air quality. Carpets are known to emit VOCs, as do the adhesives and padding that come with them. Carpet traps dust and chemicals from the outdoors and brings in more than 100 of its own chemicals when installed. As a result, exposure to newly laid carpeting might result in eye, nose, throat and skin irritation; headaches; shortness of breath; fatigue; and other symptoms.

The good news is that the carpet and rug industry is working hard to reduce the number of emissions. In 1992, the Carpet & Rug Institute (CRI) launched its Green Label program that tests carpets, cushions, and adhesives to help identify products that carry low VOCs.

CRI also launched Green Label Plus, a voluntary industry testing program for carpet and adhesive products that establishes the highest standard for indoor air quality (IAQ) ever set by the carpet industry. Green Label Plus identifies carpets and adhesives that are tested by an independent, certified laboratory and meet stringent criteria for low chemical emissions.

Some carpet manufacturers are making new carpet by recycling old carpet with recycled plastic soda bottles. The recycled carpet is about the same price as a regular carpet, but it produces fewer emissions, which helps to reduce indoor air pollution. When purchasing recycled carpet, be sure to ask about its content and the process used to create the carpet.

Hard Hat Area

To reduce exposure to emissions from any carpet, unroll the new rug at least two days before it is installed and air it out in a clean, well-ventilated area. Avoid being in the home during and a few days after installation, if possible, and open windows to ventilate the air.

Paints

Paint is the most versatile, affordable option to put on your walls. It's usually available in a seemingly endless variety of colors. If, for some reason, the manufacturer doesn't have a color you want in stock, they can usually create it while you wait. Although paint is affordable and versatile, it also has its downsides.

The ABCs of VOCs

Paint comes in two standard varieties: oil and latex. Although it's durable and popular, latex paint is a water-based paint that contains resins, solvents, pigments, and additives. It can be highly toxic to the environment, harming fish and wildlife and polluting groundwater when dumped. Often, homeowners hazardously stockpile empty or practically empty latex paint cans in their home. Today, to combat this problem, recycled latex paint—which is made from leftover latex paint—is now available. It is sold at a lower cost than standard paint and is available in more colors than ever before.

Another downside of paint is its smell or, more importantly, what that odor is made of. Those fumes are caused by VOCs, which can trigger serious health reactions in those who inhale them. Over the last few years, the paint industry has responded to this by introducing low- and no-VOC paints. Although they are a bit pricier, preventing the potential hazards and damage to your indoor air quality are well worth the cost. Many paint companies—including Benjamin Moore, Dutch Boy, and Cloverdale—rely on the certification of their low-emitting VOC paints through GreenGuard and Green Seal (see Chapter 2) to test their products. Look for these certifications on your paint can.

Some oil paint has been modified to qualify as a low-VOC paint as well.

Get the Lead Out!

If you are repainting or otherwise remodeling a home that was built before 1960, there is a chance that the paint already on the walls contains lead. In 1991, lead was named the number-one environmental threat to the health of children in the United States. The danger comes from when lead is removed—either by scraping, sanding, or burning—and high concentrations are released into the air and inhaled or when a child ingests a piece by biting on a surface, such as a window sill, covered in lead-based paint.

Exposure to lead can cause a host of health problems in both children and adults, including adversely affecting the brain, central nervous system, blood cells, and kidneys. It has also caused birth defects and delays in mental and physical development in children.

> **Hard Hat Area**
>
> When remodeling your home, The Department of Housing and Urban Development recommends keeping the living section of your home protected from the remodeling section by using a poly sheeting barrier over doors, windows, and return registers for heating and cooling systems. Make sure to adequately ventilate your home, too.

On March 31, 2008, the EPA issued a rule requiring the use of lead-safe practices and other actions aimed at preventing lead poisoning. Under the rule, beginning in April 2010, contractors performing renovation, repair, and painting projects that disturb lead-based paint in homes, child care facilities, and schools built before 1978 must be certified and must follow specific work practices to prevent lead contamination.

Tips & Tools

For more information on lead, visit the National Lead Information Center website (www.epa.gov/lead/pubs/nlic. htm) or call 1-800-424-LEAD [5323].

Wallpaper

Wallpaper is experiencing a renaissance as a popular wall covering option. Unfortunately, many traditional wallpapers are coated with vinyl and can trap moisture between the walls and the wallpaper. This can lead to the buildup of mildew and mold. The best practice is to have a "breathable" wallpaper that allows a wall to dry out. You can also look for recycled wall coverings that, like recycled hardwood, are made from sustainable resources.

The Least You Need to Know

- Not all flooring is good for every room. Be sure you consider the rooms before you make your choice.

- Recycle your current carpet before installing a new one. Contact Carpet America Recovery Effort and find out how to keep it out of the landfills.

- Paint is the easiest and most economical way to change a room in your home. Be sure to use low- or no-VOC paint.

- If you're painting an older home, hire a professional to remove any lead-based paint before beginning your project.

- If you choose to use wallpaper, select breathable styles that do not have a vinyl coating.

Part 3

Energy

Energy efficiency is an important component of any green home. When you use more energy-efficient systems, you are not only using fewer nonrenewable resources and thereby decreasing your impact on the environment, but are also saving money. It's a win-win situation!

And don't worry, being green doesn't mean reading and eating by candlelight. Thanks to today's special energy-efficient lightbulbs and unique lighting tricks, you can save energy and still have a bright, well-lit home.

Chapter 11

Heating and Cooling

In This Chapter

- ◆ Heating more efficiently
- ◆ Warmth from the hearth
- ◆ Heat from the sun
- ◆ Geothermal heat
- ◆ Air conditioners and fans

It's a wonderful feeling to know that your home keeps you comfortable in any weather. When the heat beats down and your home heats up, the air conditioning kicks on, cooling off you, your family, and your pets. In the wintertime, when old man winter is beating down your door, the furnace makes your home warm and cozy.

Green building and remodeling doesn't take away your comforts of home. But there are some environmental and financial side effects to heating and cooling systems that need to be seriously reconsidered. First, both of them are fueled by gas, oil, propane, or electricity. As a result, they use a substantial amount of energy and increase greenhouse gas emissions, which contribute to global warming.

Second, the rising costs of gasoline, oil, propane, and electricity are pushing the costs of running these systems higher and higher every year. The Alliance to Save Energy says that the average household spent almost $2,100 on home energy costs in 2007, with heating and cooling accounting for about one-half of the typical residential utility bill. It's time to take a look at heating and cooling your home in a way that's safer for the environment and easier on your budget.

However, before we talk about greening heating and cooling systems, it's important to first talk about the basics of these important systems.

Warming Trends

The common types of heating systems are: forced hot water (also used in radiant heating) and steam heat (also called hydronic systems), forced hot air, electric, floor heating, heat pumps, and of course fireplaces and wood stoves. Most of these systems use gas, oil, propane, or electricity. Reducing the dependency on these fossil fuels will help to reduce your heating and cooling costs and reduce the effect your systems have on the environment.

Forced Hot Water

Forced hot water is the most prevalent heating system because it rapidly delivers hot water to radiators and continues emitting heat even after your home has reached the desired temperature and the boiler shuts off (which means your home might become 1° to 3° warmer than the temperature setting you program into the system).

The hot water is delivered through the pipes to room radiators or baseboard units. In one-pipe heating, the water is at its hottest in the beginning of the heat circuit. Hot water is then transferred to the first radiator, reenters the same pipe, and heads to the next radiator, and so on. In such a system, the last radiator in line ultimately gets cooler water than the first one. In the more common two-pipes systems, heat is more evenly distributed throughout your home. One pipe carries the hot water throughout the home, while the other pipe returns the cool water to the boiler.

Forced hot water is also used in radiant floor systems, but the system delivers hot water to tubing in your floor, not to your radiators (more on that later).

Forced Air

A forced air system uses fans or blowers to circulate air through registers or diffusers in the ceiling, floor, or walls. The system is relatively quiet and allows temperatures within your home to fluctuate: when the desired temperature is reached, the system shuts off and then restarts when the temperature begins to fall.

There are a few downsides to this system: first, the heat fluctuates more with hot air than with hot water. Hot water, especially radiant heat, is much more consistent. Second, the air in your room can get very dry. Many homeowners have installed humidifiers to combat this in the past, but as you will see in Chapter 17 there is a better and healthier option. Another downside of forced air is that it can circulate dust and other airborne particles. These stirred-up particles can cause an increased incidence of allergies and other health problems in those who are sensitive. Newer, greener, and healthier options to this age-old concern are addressed in Chapter 17.

Floor Heating

Also called radiant heat, floor heating is actually forced hot water that is run through plastic tubing laid out in the floor.

A boiler heats the water, which is circulated through the pipes. When the piping is in a thermal mass, such as concrete, for radiant floor heating, the heat is transferred to the thermal mass and it provides a very consistent heat. It is considered green because once the thermal mass is "up to heat" (it takes a bit more energy to get it there) it consumes less energy because it needs only to maintain the heat. It has the added benefit of being one of the most comfortable kinds of heat available.

If there is no thermal mass, then the piping can be run through metal fins that radiate the heat. This type of system can be installed below hardwood floors. There are systems available today that have the grooves already in plywood sheets with aluminum backer so the heat is radiated.

Green Facts
Using body heat to warm a building? That's what developers are trying at Kungsbrohuset, a new environmentally friendly building in Stockholm, Sweden. The claim: the building will be partly heated using body heat generated by the 250,000 people who pass through nearby Stockholm Central Station daily. Using standard heat exchangers in the ventilation system, the excess heat will be converted to hot water, which will be pumped to the nearby office and used to heat the building.

Tubing is laid out for radiant floor heating.

(Plastic Pipe and Fittings Association)

Heat Pump

A heat pump extracts heat from the outside air and delivers it inside your home, but it delivers cooler temperatures than with a typical furnace, which might make you feel slightly uncomfortable depending on the outside temperature. Heat pumps are really practical only for warmer climates.

Warmth from the Hearth

In the past, Americans burned wood to heat their homes. Today, thanks to the known dangerous effects of fossil fuels, many homeowners are returning to wood-burning stoves. Although it might sound cozy to throw a log on the fire to stay warm, determine whether fireplaces, pellet stoves, and wood stoves are adequate forms of heating your home and good for the environment.

Pellet Stoves

Pellet stoves are relatively new. The technology is also being used in clean-burning heating appliances and barbeque grills. Pellet stoves are minimal polluters and need minimal electricity to work, but they do not yet require certification by the EPA.

Wood Stoves

Wood stoves produce almost no smoke, produce minimal ash, and require less firewood, and although they were once used to heat only the rooms they were in, they can now be used to heat an entire home. Unfortunately, wood-burning stoves and fireplaces can still emit air pollutants such as nitrogen oxides, carbon monoxide, organic gases, and other pollutants that can have serious consequences on your health. It's best to purchase the most energy-efficient appliance that has been certified by the EPA or another testing and certification body for safety. EPA-certified wood stoves should produce only 2 to 5 grams of smoke per hour.

According to the Department of Energy, the rule of thumb to properly measure a wood-burning stove is that a stove rated at 60,000 British thermal units (BTU) can heat a 2,000-square-foot home, while a stove at 32,000 BTUs can heat a 1,300-square-foot space.

Tips & Tools

The Hearth, Patio, and Barbecue Association (www. hpba.org) developed a cost-effectiveness calculator to compare the cost savings of stoves and fireplace inserts. One study showed that replacing all outdated wood-burning stoves in Libby, Montana, with more efficient ones dropped the outdoor air particulate levels by 28 percent.

Bigger Is Not Necessarily Better

It's important to keep in mind that when it comes to green building, heating and cooling your home isn't about installing the biggest air conditioner or furnace. It's quite the opposite: your goal is to install a system that is correctly sized for your home. But first you must take steps to conserve energy while maximizing your home's design to work with nature and its natural warmth and cooling abilities.

In the past—and maybe even recently if the builder hasn't adopted environmentally friendly building principles—a builder or contractor would determine the size of your heating or cooling system by relying on a rule of thumb, such as "1 ton of air conditioning per 500 square feet of room." He gave little consideration to anything else but the size of the room.

Today, before a contractor even considers installing or upgrading your heating/cooling units, you must first make other energy conservation changes in your home. These changes include sealing all the air leaks in the envelope; upgrading the insulation; installing a *programmable thermostat*; upgrading to higher insulated windows; and using trees, awnings, etc., to provide window shade from the outside. After these measures have been taken, the green-building contractor can then take into consideration the following elements to determine what size heating/cooling system is right for your home:

◆ How much and the type of insulation that was installed

◆ The position of your home to the sun

◆ The size of the home

◆ The number of windows in your home

def•i•ni•tion

A **programmable thermostat** programs your heating and cooling system to raise or lower the temperature of your home. They are easy to install and will shave off approximately 10 percent of your heating and cooling bills, according to the Alliance to Save Energy.

How do you know if you should replace your old system? If you have a furnace that's more than 20 years old, consider replacing it, but only if you have already installed additional insulation, sealed up air leaks, and improved your windows. The American Council for an Energy Efficient Economy also suggests that you upgrade your system if you have an old coal burner that was previously switched over to oil or gas or you have an old gas furnace without electronic ignition. Also, if your system has a standing (or constantly burning) pilot light, it was probably installed prior to 1992 and has an efficiency of about 65 percent (compared to the least efficient systems today, which are 80 percent or greater).

Building a new home provides a bit more flexibility in picking out heating and cooling systems compared to remodeling since you are not forced to stay with an existing delivery system and you can design around other energy conservation measures, such as duct location within the envelope, better insulation and windows, and so on.

Green Heat

Newer technologies on the market today rely on the warmth of the earth and the sun and not on the burning of fossil fuels in order to heat and cool your home. As a result, they are healthier for you, your family, and the environment. However, they carry much higher up-front installation costs than traditional systems, but you will begin to recoup your money almost immediately with the savings on your heating and cooling bills. Be sure to check with your local utilities company for additional money-saving discounts and other incentives for using these new technologies.

Solar Heating

Capturing the sun's heat and using it to warm your home will cut your energy costs tremendously (the sun's rays are free, although you're paying for the technology to harvest the heat). Capturing the sun's heat can also provide energy to your solar hot water heater, space heater, and pool heater. It is a viable, renewable, and clean way of heating your home.

There are two types of solar heating: passive and active.

- **Passive solar** heating takes advantage of the warmth from the sun transferred through your windows (especially those on the south side of your home). The word *passive* means "lacking will," which means you don't have to do much to take advantage of the sun's heat.

- **Active solar** means that the sun's energy is collected and then distributed through your house by mechanical means, such as with a fan, water or glycol, or a mix of both.

The costs associated with passive solar heating are usually absorbed into the cost of construction, such as the size and location of the windows, the materials used to absorb the heat, and the shading provided for the cooling season. These are all items that are accomplished at the design stage and therefore much less expensive than adding them at a later time.

Installing solar panel systems in a remodel can be costly and, again, should be done when all other energy conservation methods have been implemented. There used to be tax credits for consumers who installed solar heating systems, but the credit criteria and the credits are constantly changing. For updated information, check the U.S. Department of Energy or EPA websites.

Active solar comes in a number of varieties—the most common collects heat in roof panels and then distributes it to the house via a liquid. Another solar panel system uses fans to blow heated air that is collected in dark-colored boxes. Commercial applications use much more sophisticated systems that include mirrors to increase the sun's energy and tracking systems that follow the sun across the sky during the day. Some utility companies are experimenting with solar "farms" that utilize large arrays of these systems to create energy.

Geothermal Energy

The word *geothermal* comes from the Greek words *geo*, which means Earth, and *therme*, which means heat. Geothermal systems utilize the earth's constant temperature (around 55°F) to heat and cool your home. It involves a well or a horizontal loop that circulates a liquid to exchange heat with the earth. The liquid is circulated through a heat pump to provide the heating and cooling for the home. Instead of using the outdoor air—with temperatures that can fluctuate wildly creating an increased energy need—geothermal heat uses a more constant 55°F temperature inside the earth. Geothermal energy is a renewable energy source because the water is replenished by rainfall and the heat is continuously produced inside the earth.

There are two types of geothermal systems—closed and open.

- In a **closed-loop system,** the most common system, the piping is buried underneath your property and filled with water and an antifreeze solution, and the warm water is piped throughout your home or to a heat pump for conversion to forced air. These closed-loop systems are broken down even further to horizontal (the most economical choice), vertical, slinky coil, and pond loops. Which closed-loop system you use depends on a variety of factors, including the type of soil in your area, the amount of land available, the climate, and the accessibility to a pond or stream.

- An **open-loop system** extracts water from one well, or source, cycles it through the heat pump, and then discharges that same water into a second well or source. Open-loop systems require a good source of water, such as a well or a pond, and for that reason the closed-loop system is preferable in many areas. In addition, there are restrictions on the use of an open-loop geothermal system, so check with your local jurisdiction before investing in this type of system. The open-loop system may also need more maintenance depending on the quality of the water. Hard water will cause scaling on the heat exchanger, which can decrease the efficiency of the system and shorten its life span.

As noted previously, geothermal systems are very expensive to install (they can run tens of thousands of dollars). On the upside, the financial payback starts almost immediately. But because of the high costs, you should consider it only after implementing all other energy-conservation measures first.

Fuel Efficiency Standards for Your Home

When upgrading or choosing a new heating system, you want a system with a high annual fuel utilization efficiency (AFUE) rating. You can find this information in the product literature. If a salesperson tells you the rating, be sure to verify it by reading the label.

The AFUE is the measure of the amount of heat delivered from your furnace through your house. For example, a furnace with an efficiency rating of 70 percent means that the furnace converts 70 percent of the fuel you supply to heat. What happens to the other 30 percent? It's lost. The higher the AFUE percentage, the better the efficiency. Good efficiency units today are 85-plus for furnaces and 90-plus for boilers.

Cooling Down: Air Conditioners and Fans

Typical home cooling systems include ceiling fans, window-unit air conditioners, and central air conditioners. Air conditioning units and central air conditioners use electricity to run, emitting greenhouse gas emissions. By reducing your dependency on these systems, you can also reduce your greenhouse gas emissions and reduce your monthly cooling costs.

Just like upgrading your heating system, you must implement other energy-saving cooling techniques before you install or update a new cooling system. These techniques include shading the outside of your home with awnings and trees, adding insulation so the cool air can't escape through cracks and openings, and properly ventilating your home. After you complete these energy-conservation measures, you might find that you can get by with a smaller air conditioner or central air unit or you might even be one of the lucky ones who doesn't need a system at all and can cool your home with just a few fans.

If you still need a cooling system, however, keep in mind that biggest isn't always best. The air conditioner you buy is going to depend on which room you are cooling, its size, and how many people typically use that room. Energy efficiency is an important part of selecting the right air conditioner for a room.

Room Air Conditioners

Room air conditioners are typically installed in windows and are sized according to their cooling capacities. The higher the BTU, the more powerful the air conditioner. To determine how much BTU your room needs, measure the room that you want to cool. The larger the area, the higher the BTU air conditioner capacity required. As a rule of thumb, an 8,000 BTU air conditioner can cool two small rooms (10×12 feet) or one large room (15×20). Add additional BTUs for any sunny rooms in your home, for rooms typically occupied by more than two people, and in kitchens. Smaller units start at $100, with higher-end units costing upward of thousands of dollars.

A home that is poorly protected against the heat can require double the air-conditioning capacity of a well-weatherized house; that's why weatherization is the first step to cooling your home.

Tips & Tools

Always shade the outside of your air-conditioning unit to prevent the sun's rays from hitting the unit and causing it to use more energy.

Manufacturers are required by the federal government to list the energy rating, or the Seasonal Energy Efficiency Ratio (SEER), on each unit. The SEER system was defined by the Air Conditioning and Refrigeration Institute, a trade association that represents manufacturers of air conditioning, heating, and commercial refrigeration equipment. In 2006, the minimum SEER rating for central air conditioners was 13. Today the SEER ratings start with 11 and go up to 19. ENERGY STAR recommends a SEER of at least 13. The ENERGY STAR rating follows the SEER number.

There are ENERGY STAR–qualified air conditioners on the market that use at least 10 percent less energy than conventional models and offer timers for temperature control. According to ENERGY STAR, if every room air conditioner sold in the United States were ENERGY STAR–qualified, it would prevent 1.3 billion pounds of greenhouse gas emissions—the equivalent emissions from 115,000 cars!

The most efficient room air conditioners have higher-efficiency compressors, fan motors, and heat-transfer surfaces than previous models. A high-efficiency unit reduces energy consumption by 20 to 50 percent.

Central Air Conditioning

It's a more costly system to purchase and install, but central air conditioning cools off an entire home and uses the same duct work that heats your home during the winter.

ENERGY STAR recommends replacing any central air-conditioning system that is more than a decade old with an ENERGY STAR model; this can reduce your energy consumption for cooling by 20 percent.

Whether or not you choose a room unit or a central air unit depends on how it is being used. If a window unit is used only to provide the cooling for one room or on a select few days, then it is a pretty good option. Trying to cool an entire home with a window unit is definitely *not* a green thing to do.

Facts About Fans

Ceiling and window fans are a less-expensive method of cooling your home and less harmful to the environment. Whole house fans are large fans that can cool effectively in temperatures up to 85°F. This type of fan draws hot air out of a home into the attic; that air is then replaced with cooler outside air from open doors and windows. A whole house fan is not the same as an attic fan, which only removes the hot air from the attic. Whole house fans don't use as much electricity as an air conditioner and can reduce the interior temperature of a home by 10 to 15 degrees.

Passive Cooling

Passive cooling techniques involve using the home's structure to help move convective currents out of the home. The architecture of the South has a perfect example of passive cooling. The wide porches commonly seen in the South were very effective in providing shade for the home. Another common feature of large southern homes is cupolas on the center of the roofs. On hot days, the windows of the cupola are opened and the hot air that rises through the home and out the cupola creates an airflow that pulls the shaded and cooler air from the porch, through the windows, and up through the house. Nowadays, the same can be accomplished with centrally located skylights, attic fans, or by designing an old-fashioned cupola.

Tips & Tools

Before you implement any suggestions in this chapter, refer to Chapter 19 to learn more about how landscaping techniques can help to cool your home. These should be designed in conjunction with these heating/cooling systems for maximum efficiency.

The Least You Need to Know

- Heating and cooling your home properly starts with energy-conservation measures.

- Consider solar and geothermal heating and cooling only after smaller measures have been implemented.

- When you apply all conservation measures, you might find out you don't need an air conditioner or central air.

- With the proper heating/cooling measures taken in your home, a fan might be all you need.

Chapter 12

Water Heating

In This Chapter

- ◆ Water on demand
- ◆ Solar water
- ◆ PEX not PVC
- ◆ Water-saving measures

Here's a typical scenario: you turn on the water—whether it's for washing the dishes, shaving, or taking a shower—and let the cold water rush down the drain as you wait for the warm water to come (insert *Jeopardy* theme song here). Not only does this method of heating water waste water, it also wastes energy. Your hot water heater must work to keep the water hot for you at all times, whether it's needed or not. When you stop to really think about it, it doesn't make a lot of sense, does it? Fortunately, today there are better, and greener, methods of heating water.

Water Heaters

Traditionally, water is stored in a tank and heated by electricity, gas, or oil (again, a greenhouse emissions hazard) with conventional water heaters that lose energy due to what's called *standby heat loss*. This is heat that has been lost in the transfer of water through the pipes from the tank to the final destination (say, your bathroom sink). In addition, when this stored hot water is not being used, it cools down as it sits in the pipe. As a result, when you need hot water, gallons of perfectly good unused cool water go running down the drain.

On-Demand Hot Water Heaters

On-demand hot water heaters, also known as *tankless heaters*, solve the problem of all that wasted water. In an on-demand system, water is supplied to a small suit case–size unit that heats the water when you turn on the tap labeled "hot." When you turn the faucet, the pressure in the water pipe drops, and this change in pressure starts the water heater. A heater with a high British thermal unit (BTU) rating warms the water as it flows through the system.

The closer the unit is to the point of use (i.e., the bathroom or kitchen), the less water and energy is wasted. Most manufacturers recommend a unit being no more than 20 feet away from its source.

A tankless hot water heater can handle multiple bathrooms and fixtures, but your builder or plumber needs to properly calculate the flow required for multiple fixtures on the same heater to purchase the correctly sized heater. Larger homes can benefit from multiple on-demand heaters. In some areas, tankless heaters require maintenance to keep them clean of calcification. A tankless heater will cost a little more money than a standard water heater—from $1,500 to $3,500 or more depending on the size, BTU, and flow rate.

Green Facts

New ENERGY STAR criteria for water heaters were established on April 1, 2008. These are applied to solar water heaters, advanced drop-in integrated heat pump water heaters, and three gas-fired designs (high-performance storage tank, condensing, and whole-home tankless water heaters). The first set of standards are due to save more than 4 million tons of carbon-dioxide emissions and will be released January 1, 2009. Even stronger standards will take effect on September 1, 2010.

Indirect Heaters

Indirect water heaters work with your boiler to heat water using gas, oil, propane, electric, or solar energy. That hot water is then sent through a heat exchanger that is in the storage tank, and the tank stores the warm water until it is needed, thereby reducing your need to turn your heater on and off too often. If you install a high-efficiency boiler with a well-insulated storage tank, you can significantly reduce your energy use and cost savings. These systems can work with hydro-air systems and hydronic or radiant floor heating systems as well. These units are very efficient when you are using a high-efficiency boiler to heat the water.

Solar Water Heaters

Yes, you can use the sun to heat your water, too.

On your roof you can install solar panels holding piped loops of water. This water is heated by the sun and then piped back to the hot water heater to heat the domestic water. It's a very efficient system because the only energy expended is the electricity used by the pump. The system requires a backup system for cloudy days and other inclement weather.

Solar panels range widely in price: they can be homemade and relatively inexpensive or can cost thousands of dollars for the panels, piping, and storage tanks.

If solar panels aren't financially feasible, simpler solar hot water systems are available. One such product is made by Velux (the skylight people) and costs about $7,500. However, it is not for a do-it-yourselfer and takes a certified Velux installer. Homeowners who purchase and install a solar hot water system might be eligible for federal solar energy tax credits through 2008, but confirm this with your tax specialist.

Tips & Tools

According to solarenergy.com, when a solar hot water heating system is included in the financing for a new home, the typical cost of the system ranges from $13 to $20 a month. And because the system is included in the home's mortgage, the homeowner can take advantage of a federal tax deduction.

Drain Water Recovery Systems

Drain water recovery systems recover the energy from the warm water that goes down the drain. This water has already been heated, so these systems recapture that heat and send it back to the hot water to "pre-heat" the water. A coil is wrapped around the drain pipe and fresh water is circulated through the loop to preheat the water. It is then sent to the hot water heater, thus making the hot water heater more efficient.

Hard Hat Area

Check with the local plumbing codes since drain water recovery systems are not allowed in some areas.

Recirculation loops are loops that circulate the hot water so it is available "on demand." Hot water that is delivered more quickly results in less energy and less water being wasted. However, it takes energy to keep the circulating water heated. There are a number of innovative techniques to add to the recirculation loop that will save on energy. For instance, some builders and consumers have put a pump on the loop and had the pump controlled by a motion detector. When a person enters the bathroom, or needs hot water, the motion detector turns on the pump and hot water is circulated. Or you can simply put the pump on a switch and turn on the hot water loop just like turning on a light.

Piping

People don't usually give much thought to the pipes that carry their water to and from their sinks, showers, and other fixtures. The pipes are installed in the walls, the walls are closed up, and the pipes are all but a distant memory—that is, unless one breaks. Unfortunately, some types of piping—especially PVC piping—contain toxins that can end up in your drinking water.

Good-Bye PVC

Over the years, the most commonly used piping has been made with either copper or polyvinyl chloride (PVC), which is still widely used in traditional construction work because it's cheap, durable, flexible, and easy to assemble. PVC is also found in packaging, home furnishings, children's toys, automobile parts, building materials, and hospital supplies. However, it is far from a healthy material and shouldn't be used when you are building or remodeling a green home.

With any building material, you should look at the life of the product from beginning to end. You want materials that have the least environmental and health impacts.

Greenpeace USA calls PVC one of the most dangerous plastics around today. Greenpeace describes PVC as "one of the most toxic substances saturating our planet and its inhabitants." PVC contaminates humans and the environment throughout its lifecycle: during its production, use, and disposal. Few consumers realize that PVC is the single most environmentally damaging of all plastics. Since safer alternatives are available for virtually all uses of PVC, it is possible to protect human health and the environment by replacing and eventually phasing out this poison plastic.

Hard Hat Area

With PVC, special additives such as phthalate and organotins can be used to make the PVC even more flexible. PVC is also made with the carcinogen vinyl chloride and produces such toxic chemicals as dioxin and ethylene dichloride when it is burned. Dioxin is known to cause cancer and reproductive disorders. Because of this and other additives, PVC is very unhealthy for the environment.

Hello PEX

There are good alternatives to PVC, including a new product called cross-linked polyethylene (PEX) piping. PEX tubing was developed in the 1960s and was used in European countries before it was introduced to the United States in the 1980s. It is becoming more popular as consumers discover that it does not have the same health concerns as PVC. This piping also helps to conserve water since the inside diameter is smaller than traditional piping. This means that less water can travel through the pipe, but it's delivered with the same force and rate as traditional piping. A homeowner can't see any difference in their water pressure at all.

A PEX system is also quieter than rigid piping, and its smooth interior will not corrode. PEX systems have fewer joints and are easier to install. From a cost perspective, this lowers the cost of installation compared to using traditional plumbing materials. Additionally, the chemical structure of a PEX pipe allows for substantial expansion, so if there is a freeze, the pipe will expand quite a bit before it bursts (unlike copper).

PEX piping is generally easier to install and, including labor and materials, generally costs about the same as copper piping. Of course, with the volatility of copper pricing, this is constantly changing.

Insulation

Remember in our example at the beginning of this chapter, when we described running the cold water out of the pipes before the hot water could get through? Typically, hot water is stored in pipes that are located in chilly, uninsulated areas of the home—such as in the garage or crawl spaces—and can lose its heat by the time it reaches the inside of the house. To help prevent loss, water pipes should be insulated.

Insulation is often associated with walls, attics, and crawl spaces, but pipes located in un-insulated areas take more energy to warm up, thereby contributing to energy loss and water waste. Furthermore, pipes located in uninsulated areas run the risk of freezing.

Water is typically stored at temperatures greater than 100 degrees; when that water is exposed to temperatures below 100 degrees, it will lose heat. To reduce exposure to colder temperature, all you need to do is cut fiberglass insulation to fit the pipes and tape it around the pipes. You can use specially made pipe sleeves that look like foam wrapping to insulate pipes as well.

Insulating hot water pipes can reduce heat loss and raise water temperature by 2 to 4 degrees. This enables you to lower the temperature on the water heater but still get the same temperature water from the faucet! As a result, you'll save money on your water bill and energy costs. In addition, you'll be conserving water.

Tips & Tools

In addition to wrapping the piping, your water heater should be wrapped as well. Older water heaters can cause significant heat loss (up to 45 percent), unless they have a high insulation value.

Warmer pipes mean warmer available water, which reduces the amount of time the boiler or hot water heater is on and the water is running. It's an easy, affordable method to conserve energy and cut costs.

Cold water pipes should also be insulated to minimize the formation of condensation, which can lead to moisture problems inside your home.

Insulated hot water pipes.

Water Temperature

The flipside to our previous problem is this: how many times has the hot water arrived in your faucet or showerhead for you to find that it's *too* hot? Then you spend a good minute adjusting the water while it continues to run down the drain.

Sound familiar?

Well, many water heaters are automatically programmed at 140°F for certain appliances, including dishwashers and washing machines, but this can lead to wasted water and serious burns, and is particularly dangerous if you have young children or babies in the home. A quick and easy way to avoid more water waste and the risk of burns is to turn down the thermostat on your hot water heater. Not only is reducing the temperature a smart safety issue, but it's a water-saving technique and helps to reduce mineral build-up and erosion in the pipes.

When you go on vacation, turn down the thermostat even further—just be careful that this doesn't lead to frozen pipes in the middle of winter.

In Chapter 17 you will learn how to further reduce your water usage by installing low-flow shower heads and toilets.

The Least You Need to Know

- ◆ Water down the drain is water and energy wasted. Upgrade to on-demand water heaters.

- ◆ Tankless heaters can be energy efficient and water usage efficient.

- ◆ Recirculation loops can provide a very efficient method of hot water delivery when used with a high-efficiency boiler.

- ◆ PVC piping is toxic and should not be used anywhere in your home.

Appliances and Countertops

In This Chapter

- When to replace old appliances
- ENERGY STAR standards for appliances
- How to make your laundry greener
- Environmentally friendly interior cabinets

The average homeowner spends about $2,100 on home energy costs per year, and typically a home's appliances (refrigerator, oven/stove, dishwasher, and washer/dryer) and home electronics (computers, televisions, and stereo equipment) count for 20 percent of that bill. Replacing inefficient appliances is one of the easiest ways you can conserve energy, lower your bills, and save some hard-earned cash. But what is an energy-efficient appliance, and how can you determine what size appliance meets your needs? Honestly, the options can seem overwhelming.

When to Upgrade Your Old Appliances

If you are remodeling, you are probably eager to upgrade your current appliances to more energy-efficient models, but don't go ordering your new unit just yet. First, consider the age of the present appliance. If you bought it within the last few years, reconsider replacing it for now. If it was manufactured before 2001, or if it is not functioning efficiently anymore and cannot be repaired, you should consider replacing it.

When you're choosing new appliances, look for the ENERGY STAR certification and the EnergyGuide label.

Tips & Tools _____

Before purchasing an appliance, check with your local utility company to see whether they offer rewards or incentives for upgrading older appliances, including rebates or coupons toward ENERGY STAR replacements.

Look for the ENERGY STAR label on all new appliances you buy.

DESIGNED TO EARN THE ENERGY STAR

The estimated energy performance for this design meets US EPA criteria. The building will be eligible for ENERGY STAR after maintaining superior performance for one year.

The ENERGY STAR certification means that the appliance has met standards that make it an energy-efficient unit. ENERGY STAR models use from 10 to 50 percent less energy and water than federal standards require. Today's models are 75 percent more efficient than those produced 30 years ago. This efficiency translates into less air pollution and better water conservation.

An ENERGY STAR–qualified appliance must carry an EnergyGuide label. This label estimates how much energy the appliance uses, compares energy use of similar products, and lists approximate annual operating costs. For example, the label on new refrigerators tells how much electricity—in *kilowatt hours*—a particular model uses in one year. The smaller the number, the less energy the refrigerator uses and the less it costs you to operate it. Your exact costs will depend on your local utility rates and the type and source of your energy.

Typically, you can expect to pay more for an ENERGY STAR appliance, but since the life span of these better-performing units can be up to 20 years, you can expect to save much more money through lower utility and water bills.

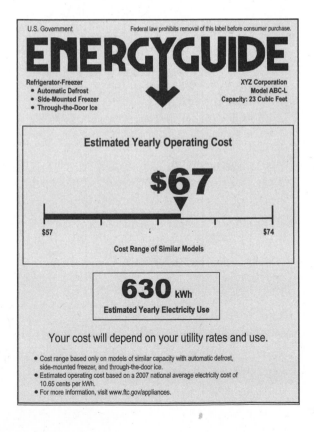

Look for this ENERGYGUIDE label on appliances. It indicates the estimated energy consumption compared to similar models and the estimated yearly operating cost based on the national average cost of electricity.

Other factors to keep in mind when shopping for new appliances include the following:

- **Size**—Make sure the appliance you are buying suits your needs. Unless you entertain often or have a large brood, oversized refrigerators and multiple appliances of the same kind are a waste of energy and money.

- **Gas versus electricity**—Appliances that run on natural gas are more energy efficient than those that run on electricity, so whenever possible, choose natural gas appliances. (Unless, of course, you have access to alternative energy methods such as photovoltaics or wind power.)

Stoves and Ovens

For most households, the kitchen stove is not a big energy guzzler. So the kind of oven or stove you purchase should be based on your individual cooking preferences.

> **Green Facts**
>
> ENERGY STAR provides a list of energy-efficient ventilating fans. ENERGY STAR–qualified ventilation fans that include lighting use 70 percent less energy on average than standard models, saving $120 in electricity costs over the life of the fan. These fans are also more than 50 percent quieter than standard models.

> **Hard Hat Area**
>
> The flames on your stove should always be blue. If your stove is giving off a yellow flame, it might not be getting enough air and burning inefficiently. This must be repaired immediately. And always contact your local utility company if you smell gas.

Some people prefer to cook on a gas stove versus an electric stove because of the temperature control that gas provides. Even if you prefer cooking with gas, you should consider purchasing a stove with an electric ignition switch rather than a continuously burning pilot light. You'll also need to ensure that your kitchen is adequately vented for a gas stove.

A relatively new stove option is an induction cooktop, which heats up by transferring electromagnetic energy to the pan. The cooktop cooks faster and more evenly and saves a bunch of energy—up to 90 percent. Remove the pan and the heat is gone. Keep in mind if you invest in an induction cooktop that you may have to purchase new pots and pans. This type of system only works with cast iron, stainless steel, or enameled iron.

A convection oven is an oven that has a constant flow of air, keeping temperatures even throughout and cooking food more evenly. A convection oven is, on average, 20 percent more energy efficient than a conventional oven.

One final feature, a self-cleaning oven, is also worth considering. Self-cleaning ovens are made with more insulation and are therefore more energy efficient than standard ovens.

Refrigerators and Freezers

ENERGY STAR–qualified refrigerators made after April 28, 2008, must be 20 percent more efficient than the previous federal standards. According to *Consumer Reports* magazine, the difference in energy consumption between refrigerators sold in 2006 and those made after April 28, 2008, "might amount to only a few dollars a year per household. Yet, if the almost 3.5 million ENERGY STAR–qualified refrigerators sold in 2006 had met the new criterion, we'd have used 90 million fewer kilowatt hours of electricity per year, equivalent to the greenhouse gas emissions of 12,500 cars."

Studies also show that the average energy efficiency of new refrigerators nearly tripled from 1972 to 1999—the average electricity use of new refrigerators declined from 1725 kWh/yr in 1972 to 685 kWh/yr by 1999.

Tips & Tools

To see how much your model of refrigerator is costing you each year and how much you can save by replacing it with a more efficient model, visit www.energystar.gov/index.cfm?fuseaction=refrig.calculator.

Keep in mind, however, that newer refrigerator models are larger and have more features, including side-by-side doors, icemakers, and more. Some of these added features can use more energy than standard-size refrigerators with fewer bells and whistles. For example, although side-by-side refrigerator/freezers look sleeker and are quite popular, they actually use more energy than models with top freezers. Units with icemakers also use more energy than those without. There really isn't much of a difference efficiency-wise when comparing refrigerators with either top or bottom freezers, but studies show that both types perform better than the side-by-side units.

After you've bought your new refrigerator, you need to maintain it to keep it running as efficiently as possible. To do so, follow these guidelines:

◆ Make sure the refrigerator temperature is between 36°F and 38°F and the freezer temperature is between 0°F and 5°F.

◆ Check the refrigerator and freezer door seals and gaskets on your refrigerator to make sure that no air is leaking out.

◆ Defrost regularly. Letting ice build up makes your unit work harder.

Tips & Tools _____

Conduct the dollar bill test: close the refrigerator door with a dollar bill half in and half out of the refrigerator. If the dollar bill slips out easily, air might be escaping from the unit and you might need to replace the door seal.

Washing Machines and Dryers

More than 1,100 loads of laundry are started every second in the United States, which comes to a staggering 35 billion loads per year. Washers and dryers use 2.6 percent of the total residential energy use. The majority of the energy consumed is used for heating the water in the washer and drying the clothes in the dryer. Washing machines are also one of the biggest water wasters in your home.

Tips & Tools _____

Go one step further in your green efforts and be sure to use environmentally safe detergents for your appliances.

When you are shopping for a new washer, you of course want one that's up to the challenge of your kids' grimy sports outfits and your baby's juice-stained bibs. But buying a bigger machine that uses more water doesn't necessarily mean that your clothes are going to get a better wash. Front-load washers—which are more energy and water efficient—wash clothes very effectively by using an agitator instead of filling up an entire drum. Today's top-loading washers are now being manufactured to use less water as well.

Replacing a pre-1994 washer with an ENERGY STAR model will have several benefits. First, it can shave up to $110 a year from your utility bills. Also, ENERGY STAR washers save 7,000 gallons of water a year. Over the 11-year life of a typical washer, that's enough water to fill up three backyard swimming pools, or provide a lifetime of drinking water for six people. According to ENERGY STAR, look for a machine with a high _modified energy factor_ (_MEF_) and a low _water factor_ (_WF_).

Another benefit of a new machine is that they use less than 25 gallons of water per cycle, compared to 40 gallons of water for older models. Other new machines, such as the Whirlpool Duet Steam, a washer and dryer combo, incorporate steam to clean clothes more quickly while using less energy and water.

And finally, upgrading your washing machine is better for the environment. Statistics show that if most U.S. households change over to high-efficiency washing machines by 2010, U.S. carbon emissions will be reduced by 28 million metric tons of carbon per year.

def•i•ni•tion

A **modified energy factor (MEF)** is a measure of energy efficiency that considers the energy used by the washer, the energy used to heat the water, and the energy used to run the dryer. The higher the MEF number is, the more efficient the washer. **Water factor (WF)** measures the water efficiency of the unit as gallons of water consumed per cubic foot of capacity. The lower the WF number, the more efficient the clothes washer.

A clothes dryer costs about $85 to operate annually and about $1,100 to operate over its lifetime. At the present time, there are no energy requirements for dryers, since ENERGY STAR states there is little difference in the energy use between models. It has been recommended that dryers that still function well shouldn't be replaced until the end of their functioning life. However, using a washing machine that has a faster spin cycle speed will help to eliminate excess water more efficiently and, in the long run, will cut down on the amount of time needed to dry your clothes.

One benefit of newer dryers is that they spin clothes much more quickly than older models, thereby reducing the amount of time your clothes are in the machine. Some new models even come with an automatic moisture sensor that senses when your clothes are dry and shuts off, cutting down on energy usage.

Tips & Tools

Want a completely free, no-energy way to dry your clothes? Install an indoor or outdoor clothesline in your backyard or garage and let your clothes air-dry. Some municipalities in the United States, Canada, and Europe have actually banned clotheslines for aesthetic reasons, but new awareness on energy savings have lawmakers considering striking down these laws.

Dishwashers

According to the American Council for an Energy-Efficient Economy (ACEEE), 70 to 90 percent of the energy used by a dishwasher just goes toward heating the water, so washers that use less hot water also use less energy.

Another big energy waster is the electric heating element that runs during the drying cycle. New dishwashers offer a no-heat drying option that uses room-temperature air circulated by fans.

When buying a new dishwasher, the ACEEE recommends units with an energy factor (EF) of at least 0.65, or an estimated energy use of less than 340 kWh/year. This is about 40 percent better than the federal standard. The EF measures the number of cycles that can be run with 1 kWh of electricity. Some dishwashers use much less water and have different wash cycles so they can be tailored to your specific dishwashing needs.

Disposing of Old Appliances

What do you do with your old appliances after you've replaced them? Whatever you do, don't leave them on the curb hoping someone will come and pick them up—it's not only dangerous to leave them out where young children can climb inside and get trapped, but there are greener ways of disposing of them. First, check with your utility company to see whether it offers an appliance recycling program. Some utilities even transport the appliance to a recycling center; others have drop-off spots.

If your utility company does not take appliances, consider giving them away to a family member or friend or selling them or giving it away on websites such as Freecycle and Craigslist (refer to Chapter 5 for more information on these websites).

Countertops

Kitchen and bathroom countertops need to withstand the abuse of everyday living—chopping and pounding in the kitchen, water in the kitchen and bathroom—and take the heat—think hot pots and curling irons—without suffering scratches, stains, and cracks. Countertops also need to be aesthetically pleasing and made of durable, and nontoxic, materials.

The most popular styles of kitchen countertops used to be Corian, Formica, tile, marble, and granite, but by now you've learned that just because something is popular does not mean it is an environmentally sound choice, and countertop materials are no exception.

Countertops to Reconsider

Corian, made by DuPont, is a man-made solid surface material composed of acrylic polymer and alumina trihydrate. Avonite is a manufactured composite made from acrylic or polyester resins and mineral filler. Plastic laminates are man-made countertop materials that were invented almost a century ago and are heat-resistant.

Stones such as granite, limestone, and marble make gorgeous countertops and are very durable, but stone has several environmental downsides. First, it is not a renewable resource. In addition, these countertop materials require a lot of energy during production and shipping and cause a great deal of environmental wear and tear, depending on how they were mined. If you are set on a stone countertop, try to find a nearby quarry to purchase the stone from.

Countertop manufacturers are developing new versions of existing products that include recycled content as well as introducing some altogether new and exciting materials that are environmentally friendly and aesthetically pleasing.

Paper Composite

Paper composite surfaces are made of paper and other fibers that have been saturated with resin, which is a natural secretion of many plants and used as an adhesive. The resin itself does not come from recycled sources, but it constitutes only a small amount of the material.

PaperStone is one example of a countertop made from recycled paper products. It is certified by the Forest Stewardship Council (FSC), Smartwood, and the Rainforest Alliance. Most PaperStone products are made from post-consumer paper waste, recycled paper, and petroleum-free resins. According to PaperStone, the use of this product can contribute up to five LEED points to a home striving for certification and is best recommended for kitchen counters, window sills, and door thresholds. According to GreenHomeGuide.com, the average price of a paper composite countertop is $50+ per square foot.

Recycled Glass

Recycled glass countertops are some of the newest green products on the market and are absolutely beautiful while being sustainable and potentially recyclable. A countertop made of recycled glass and concrete contains almost 95 percent post-consumer recycled content.

IceStone is a product made from recycled glass combined with concrete. Another recycled glass countertop is Vetrazzo, which takes discarded glass from windshields, used bottles, and plate glass windows, and transforms it into countertops. According to Vetrazzo, using its recycled glass products can help your home qualify for LEED certification. This product is not currently available nationwide but is catching on quickly, and the company is expanding. This type of countertop doesn't require much maintenance. All you need is a nontoxic cleaner.

Concrete

Concrete, known more for its use as sidewalks and driveways, has made a comeback inside the home as flooring and countertops.

Concrete countertops are highly durable but must be sealed periodically to protect against staining. The type of seal depends on the contractor. Whether a concrete countertop is 100 percent green depends on the type of cement used, but by using concrete that contains recycled materials, you are lessening your environmental impact.

Concrete countertops are either premade in a shop or built onsite. You can mold concrete into custom shapes and integrate such features as the sink. Concrete can be dyed almost any color imaginable (you can purchase custom or standard color samples from your concrete contractor). You can also add materials, such as bits of glass or broken tile, for a unique look.

Green Facts

Fu-Tung Cheng, designer and founder of the Concrete Exchange, is considered a pioneer in the concrete design industry, making countertops, fireplaces, and indoor water features from this sustainable material. Cheng enjoys the ability to color, texture, and sculpt concrete into any design he or his customers choose. Each piece is then a one-of-a-kind original that offers the same smoothness of marble and granite.

Concrete is known to form hairline cracks that are the result of curing and drying; these cracks can create a unique and desirable look; however, if the cracks are bothersome, they can be patched.

The price of concrete countertops is similar to other natural stone. Special features, including unique shapes and custom edging, can increase the cost of your one-of-a-kind countertop. According to GreenHomeGuide.com, the average price of a standard concrete countertop is from $60 to $75 per square foot, with custom-made details driving the price higher.

Recycled Ceramic Tiles

Ceramic tiles are a popular style for countertops, but recycled ceramic tiles are more environmentally friendly than their nonrecycled counterparts. Recycled tiles contain up to 70 percent recycled glass and are moisture and stain resistant, making them useful as both kitchen and bathroom countertops. There are a number of recycled ceramic tile manufacturers, including Terra Green, which makes their tiles with 58 percent recycled aviation glass. Because they can stain, you'll need to use a low-VOC sealant. According to GreenHomeGuide.com, the average price of a ceramic tile countertop is from $10 to $20 per square foot and from $5 to $12 per square foot for porcelain.

Glass Tiles

For a different tile look, you may want to try glass tiles. Glass tiles are beautiful and environmentally friendly because they contain 100 percent recycled materials. However, they are not recommended for use as the primary countertop surface because they can scratch easily. Instead, glass tiles are perfect for use as a backsplash or accent tile. Use a safer water-based grout that seals tiles without harsh solvents. According to GreenHomeGuide.com, the average price of a glass tile is from $15 to $40 per square foot.

Tips & Tools _____

If you like the look of glass tiles, visit local artisan shops to find hand-made glass tiles sintered by local artists. Sintering is the production process for recycling glass into tiles.

Recycled Plastic

Recycled plastic countertop material is durable and moisture resistant and can be obtained in a wide variety of colors, patterns, and textures. Some plastic countertop manufacturers provide a product that looks similar to Terrazzo. Be careful, however, because recycled plastic countertops can burn and scratch more easily than other materials. According to GreenHomeGuide.com, the average price of a recycled plastic countertop is from $50 to $100 per square foot.

Terrazzo

According to the National Terrazzo & Mosaic Association (NTMA) terrazzo flooring has a long history that dates back more than 1,500 years. Terrazzo was created by Venetian workers utilizing the waste chips from slab marble processing. Today, terrazzo contains glass, porcelain, and other recycled materials.

Overall, terrazzo is a better choice than many other countertop materials because it is a low-maintenance, durable material that will typically last for years. It also includes a great deal of recycled content and can be recycled at the end of its life. Companies such as EnviroGlas and IceStone offer countertops with higher levels of recycled content.

The biggest concern about this countertop material is its adhesive. Some contractors use an epoxy version, which can't be recycled and can be toxic.

According to GreenHomeGuide.com, the average price of a terrazzo countertop ranges from $20 to $50 per square foot.

Other Countertop Options

Just about any wood can be used as a countertop material. The downsides are that wood can burn and stain and, depending on the type of wood, might require a great deal of maintenance—including regular applications of mineral oil. The upsides are that it can be fastened without adhesives and can be recycled at the end of its shelf life. If you are in the market for wood countertops, look for a certified FSC label on the product and be sure to use a nontoxic finish. According to GreenHomeGuide.com, the average price of a wood countertop ranges from $50 to $75 per linear foot.

Stainless steel is another countertop option that is commonly used in restaurant and other commercial kitchens, and it is gaining popularity for use in residential kitchens. It is a durable material, but it scratches easily. According to GreenHomeGuide.com, the average price of a stainless steel countertop is from $45 to $65 per square foot.

Although bamboo is more popular right now for flooring and outdoor fencing it is slowly catching on as a countertop material. For more information on bamboo, refer to Chapter 10.

Kitchen and Bathroom Cabinets

For years, kitchen and bathroom cabinets have been made with particleboard that contains formaldehyde. As we've discussed in previous chapters, the offgassing from formaldehyde is a huge health and indoor air quality problem, but you can reduce your exposure to formaldehyde emissions by choosing formaldehyde-free medium-density fiberboard or plywood cabinets. As you should do when shopping for any wood products for your home, look for cabinets made with FSC-certified wood.

The Kitchen Cabinet Manufacturers Association developed the Environmental Stewardship Program (ESP) to encourage practices that benefit the environment and society. The voluntary program gives cabinet manufacturers a way to demonstrate their commitment to sustainability and helps you identify products that are better for your home, your family, and the environment. Some of their requirements for cabinets are as follows:

- 75 percent of particleboard, medium-density fiberboard, and plywood used in the cabinets must be third-party certified to meet low formaldehyde emission standards.

- 75 percent of cabinets must be finished domestically. Finishes must emit no greater hazardous air pollutants than allowed by local plant operating permits.

- 75 percent of particleboard and medium-density fiberboard used in cabinets must contain 100 percent recycled or recovered fiber content.

According to the Healthy House Institute, the clear finishes that are used on the cabinets are worse for the environment and your health than the cabinet material itself. These finishes include a urea-formaldehyde clear finish that takes from four to six months to outgas.

A better alternative is recycled wood products such as resawn old timbers, plantation-grown materials, bamboo, and so on.

Holding Them Up

The surface on which you lay your countertops should be just as green as the countertops themselves. Be sure to choose FSC-certified plywood, wheatboard, or formaldehyde-free medium-density fiberboard rather than particleboard or medium-density fiberboard (MDF), which contain formaldehyde.

The Least You Need to Know

- Sometimes the greener option is to keep your existing appliances rather than replace them with newer, more efficient models.

- Upgrading your appliances to more energy-efficient units is an easy way to reduce your energy usage and help the environment.

- When choosing new countertops, consider the material and how durable it is.

- Formaldehyde is a common—and dangerous—ingredient in cabinet construction.

Chapter 14

Light and Power

In This Chapter

- ◆ What you need to know about lightbulbs
- ◆ Daylighting
- ◆ Accent lighting
- ◆ Power sources

Energy costs have skyrocketed in the past few years, and it has been estimated that they will continue to rise even more for quite some time. At the same time, the demand for energy is increasing. Americans own more electric appliances than ever before—just count up how many computers, telephones, televisions, air conditioners, stereo and video game devices, and kitchen appliances you own. Keeping these items running uses a tremendous amount of energy. In addition, the emissions from the fossil fuels used to generate the energy contribute to the rise in greenhouse gases and, ultimately, global warming.

In August 2003, New York City's high demand for energy to power the air-conditioning systems during a sweltering summer led to a major blackout.

Even though New York's energy systems are some of the most modern in the United States, the state's reserve of energy is actually 40 percent lower than regulators say it should be. That is one reason power companies are proposing the construction of more power plants. But is building more power plants really the best solution to our energy crisis?

The bottom line is that the nation needs to implement serious conservation measures in order to reduce costs and provide enough electricity to a growing population—in other words, use less power. Reduce the demand. Generate more power using newer, greener methods. While New York and other states are doing their part, your part starts at home. Find ways to reduce your electricity usage. By doing so, you'll save energy, reduce your greenhouse emissions, and save money—a triple play!

Education on Electricity

At a traditional electric power plant, electricity is generated by a spinning generator. What spins that generation might be a water wheel in a hydroelectric dam, a large diesel-powered engine, or a gas-powered turbine. The power is collected and delivered to your home through a power grid of aboveground and underground cables.

Lighting

One of the easiest ways you can cut back on how much electricity you use is by changing how you light your home. When Thomas Edison improved on the idea of the incandescent lightbulb, he succeeded at bringing luminosity into the home. Edison wasn't too concerned with how much energy his invention used, but today we know better. Incandescent bulbs are huge energy wasters.

> **Green Facts**
>
> Have your lights ever gone out momentarily with no explanation as to why? It might have been a brownout. A brownout is deliberately enacted by your utility company to reduce power consumption when the demand gets too high for the supply.

Inefficient lighting can consume up to 15 percent of your home's energy needs. Energy-efficient lighting can reduce consumption by 50 percent or more. One of the most effective ways to reduce your energy use is to switch to more energy-efficient lightbulbs, such as compact fluorescents (CFLs) and light-emitting diodes (LEDs). Other ways include daylighting and lighting controls.

Tips & Tools _____

To reduce your electrical usage, don't just turn off the appliances that aren't being used. Unplug them. An appliance that is turned off but plugged in continues to use electricity. This can add up to hundreds of dollars in electricity costs every year.

Compact Florescent Lights

According to ENERGY STAR, if every American home replaced just one traditional incandescent lightbulb with an ENERGY STAR–qualified bulb (such as a CFL), enough energy would be saved to light more than 3 million homes for a year; cut more than $600 million in annual energy costs; and prevent greenhouse gases equivalent to the emissions of more than 800,000 cars. An amazing impact for one little lightbulb.

CFLs emit as much light as regular incandescent bulbs but can last from 8 to 10 times longer and use anywhere from 50 to 75 percent less electricity. Matching the right CFL to the right fixture helps ensure that it will perform properly and last. ENERGY STAR offers these tips:

- CFLs perform best in open fixtures that allow airflow, such as table and floor lamps, wall sconces, pendants, and outdoor fixtures.

- For recessed fixtures, it's better to use a reflector CFL than a spiral CFL because the design of the reflector evenly distributes the light down to your area.

- If a light fixture is connected to a dimmer or three-way socket fixture, you'll need to use a special ENERGY STAR–qualified CFL designed to work in these applications.

- Choose a qualified CFL that offers a shade of white light that works best for you. For example, while most CFLs provide warm or soft white light for your home, you might want to choose a cooler color for task lighting. Task lighting is intended to provide light for a specific job and is a brighter, whiter light.

- To choose the CFL with the right amount of light, the CFL should be labeled as equivalent to the incandescent bulb you are replacing. Lightbulb manufacturers include this information on the product packaging to make it easy for consumers to choose the equivalent bulb.

*A low-mercury compact fluo-
rescent bulb. Although these
lights cost more, they are
more efficient and last about
10 times as long.*

(Greenlite Lighting Corporation)

GREENLITE

If you haven't made the switch yet, in a few years you're not going to have a choice. The 2007 Energy Bill phased out incandescent bulbs starting in 2012, forcing all consumers to purchase energy-efficient CFLs, halogens, or LEDs. Under this new bill, all lightbulbs must also be 25 to 30 percent more energy efficient by 2014. By 2020, the bulbs must be 70 percent more efficient. This major change should cut electricity use from lightbulbs by up to 60 percent, for a savings of $18 billion annually.

Hard Hat Area

CFL bulbs contain small amounts of mercury, although it's less than the mercury generated by an electrical plant for an equivalent incandescent bulb. Mercury can cause health problems if there is contact with it, but some studies have shown that the amount of mercury in a CFL bulb is extremely small.

Halogens

Halogen lighting creates light through heat and is only slightly more efficient than incandescent. However, the light is much hotter and brighter and therefore emits more lumens (measurement of light emitted) over their incandescent counterparts.

Light-Emitting Diode (LED)

Light-emitting diode (also known as LED) lightbulbs are another green lighting option. Known mostly for their use in traffic lights and as those little red power-on lights on our electronics, LED bulbs can provide up to 50,000 hours of light and are more efficient than CFL lighting. And unlike CFLs, LEDs do not contain mercury, making them a more environmentally friendly lightbulb. Once used just for accent lighting, the lights are now available for ambient and task lighting.

Like any new green building product, these lights are still a little pricier than incandescent and CFL bulbs, but as customers begin to demand more of them, the price will come down. In the meantime, it's still a good investment that will begin to pay off immediately.

Design for Your Lighting Needs

When you are designing your new home or remodeling project, keep in mind that not every part of your home requires the same kind of lighting. For example, a bathroom isn't going to require the same amount of light as a reading room or a hallway. However, we have the tendency to just pop in the same wattage for the entire home. This is overkill and a huge waste of energy. Instead, design for your needs, whether it's ambient, task, or accent lighting:

- **Ambient lighting**—Lights up a whole room. It produces general illumination.

- **Task lighting**—Provides illumination for a specific job. For example, task lighting for sitting at your desk would come from the desk lamp and not the ceiling light that illuminates your entire room.

- **Accent lighting**—Focuses the lighting on a particular area or item, such as a piece of artwork in your home.

The proper design plan should include ambient lighting that works in conjunction with task and accent lighting. This reduces the need for ambient lighting and will save on costs.

Tips & Tools _____

Use a "cooler" or brighter light for task lighting and use warmer light for living areas.

For example, in the bathroom, you might want to use a warm, or more yellow, ambient light to accentuate your flesh tones. The same is true in your dining room. In your den or library, where you spend a lot of time reading, you should install a whiter light for task lighting that provides a stronger contrast.

Artificial vs. Daylight

In addition to installing new energy-efficient bulbs, you can cut back on your energy usage by relying on the sun's natural light.

During the day, natural light from the sun pours into your home through your windows. One green building and remodeling goal is to capture as much natural daylight as possible and limit your reliance on artificial (or electric) lighting.

Hard Hat Area _____

In Chapter 9, we talked about keeping the sun's rays out through insulated windows, shading, window film, and so on, which seems to contradict what we are discussing in this chapter. However, you can successfully allow indirect daylight into your home while shielding out the sun's heat and radiation. The use of shading through roof overhangs and plantings will still let the natural light enter your home while stopping the harmful direct rays that heat up your home.

Don't fall into the trap of thinking that daylighting simply involves installing more windows or skylights to let the sun shine in. Too many windows can actually work against you, causing an abundance of heat and glare. Proper daylighting design for your home depends on several factors, including the position and location of your home, the position of the sun, and how many floors your home has. Once these are factored in, your builder can determine where to place your windows for maximum daylighting and determine what additional lighting you will need in what room.

Discuss your individual needs with your architect, contractor, or builder when planning your project. They may need to discuss your project with a lighting specialist (who could be at your local lighting retail store) or a lighting designer (who is a certified lighting professional).

Lighting Controls

Lighting controls, such as dimmer switches, three- or four-way switches, and motion detectors can create certain moods in your home while also saving energy.

Dimmer switches enable you to reduce the intensity of light at any given time. You can lower the lights for an intimate dinner and then raise them to read the evening paper. Three- or four-way switches allow you to turn on lights from multiple locations. This facilitates people turning off lights when leaving the room.

Although mostly used outside the home for security reasons, motion detectors can also be installed inside. The lights go on only when motion is detected in the room and turn off a few minutes after motion stops. Some motion detectors are now equipped with energy-saving LED lights and batteries. Lights that shut off automatically when not in use save energy and save on your electric bill.

Hard Hat Area

If you attempt any electrical work inside your home, make sure the electricity is turned off to prevent any injuries.

Power!

Why depend entirely on the public utility for your electrical power? How great would it be to have the utility company pay you for the power you have saved them? That's what living off-the-grid is. Living off-the-grid means you're not dependent on public utilities for electricity. You have created your own power, which is not only a money- and energy-saving bonus, it's also a liberating feeling. Consumers might be a little timid relying on their own system for power, but generating electricity from alternative energy sources is becoming more and more popular as the search for money-saving and energy-saving alternatives continue.

Tips & Tools

Visit www.treehugger.com, a terrific site with blogs on green topics. One blog follows the trials and tribulations of consumers who experimented and went off-the-grid.

> **Green Facts**
>
> Actress Daryl Hannah lives in·the Rocky Mountains in an old stagecoach shop that she restored. She generates electricity using solar power, and she also has a backup generator that runs on bio-diesel fuel such as soybean, canola, and other waste vegetable oils. Her water comes from a spring located next to the home.

Solar Power!

Let the sun run the power in your home. The sun's energy is captured by solar panels that are installed on (not in) the roof of your home—similar to skylights—and that use photovoltaic (PV), or solar, cells, to change the sun's rays into electricity.

To use solar power, you need to have a roof area or yard exposed to sunlight throughout the day. Because the panels create electricity in the form of direct current, you also need an inverter to change the direct current to alternating current (AC) power.

> **Green Facts**
>
> The popularity of solar power systems made a huge leap forward when utilities started giving net metering credits. Net metering is, in essence, letting the meter run backward. In other words, on sunny days a home may produce more electricity than it consumes and the meter would run backward, meaning that you are selling power back to the utility. This eliminates the·need for expensive battery storage and backup systems. When you need additional power—on cloudy days, for example—you simply use your credits with the local power company.

The only drawback to this type of electrical system is that the amount of sunlight on a given day isn't a consistent thing—it depends on clouds, rain, snow, and other weather conditions; the location of your home; and the time of year.

The system can be relatively expensive to install, with a payback of around 10 years. Technologies are improving, so hopefully costs will be coming down.

Other energy-saving measures should be implemented before investing in a solar power system.

Wind Power!

Wind power is the conversion of wind energy into more useful forms—usually electricity—using wind turbines. It's one of the fastest-growing forms of alternative energy in the United States, especially in regions that are prone to a lot of wind. Statistics show that growing from almost nothing in 1980, wind-powered turbines generated 11,605 megawatts of electricity in the United States in 2006. Although it's still less than 1 percent of the national power supply, it's a good start.

A wind turbine captures wind, an alternative source of energy.

(Skystream)

Utility companies are even beginning to create wind farms on hilltops and coastal regions. For homeowners, smaller wind power units are available and, as the technology improves, are becoming more efficient. Wind power might not be allowed in local zoning laws, so be sure to check with your municipality. Depending on your area, there might also be a height restriction for the wind turbines that are installed on your property. Typically, the units need to be over 40 feet tall to clear the "turbulent region" above trees.

The major objection to wind mills on residential property is visual. Some people do not want to see towers or hear the noise it emits, which is a loud oscillating hum. Different designs are coming on the market that reduce noise and that can capture wind energy in the turbulent zone.

The Least You Need to Know

◆ Add CFLs and LEDs to your shopping list. They are a little more expensive than incandescent but are worth the extra cost and energy savings.

◆ Design your home to take advantage of free sunlight; supplement the design with an energy-efficient lighting plan.

◆ All lighting isn't equal—there are different options available for each part of your home and each task at hand.

◆ Let your utility company pay you for powering your own home. Alternative forms of energy require a large up-front investment but can be well worth the financial and environmental rewards!

Part 4

Water and Air

We often take clean air and water for granted, assuming they will always be there. The truth is that the water supplies in many parts of the country are in serious jeopardy, and many homes have very poor indoor air quality.

In this part, you'll learn how to capture and use rainwater and even reuse your home's greywater—the water that goes down the drain—for irrigation. In addition, you will learn how low-flow fixtures and piping can save a tremendous amount of water. Finally, you'll find out how to clean up the air in your home by improving your ventilation system and choosing products that don't emit toxic pollutants.

Water Preservation and Conservation

In This Chapter

- ◆ The growing water crisis
- ◆ Keep your water pure
- ◆ How to harvest rainwater
- ◆ Greywater reuse systems

Everybody is talking about saving water. We're told to take shorter showers; turn the faucet off while brushing our teeth; and install low-flow restrictor valves on our toilets, faucets, and shower heads (see Chapter 17). But why bother? If you go into any grocery store, there certainly seems to be an ample supply of the stuff, with bottles lining the shelves in a seemingly endless variety of flavors. So is it really necessary to conserve water?

Absolutely.

Unfortunately, too many people take the availability of clean, safe drinking water for granted. Want some to drink? Grab a bottle out of the fridge. Want to wash some dishes? Turn on the tap. Want a long, hot shower? Go for it. Although we act as though there's an endless supply, there isn't. As a matter of fact, the demand for water far outweighs the supply!

The U.S. population has doubled over the last 50 years and has put a serious stress on our water supplies. According to the EPA, Americans use an average of 100 gallons of water each day—enough to fill 1,600 drinking glasses!

In the meantime, more and more states—36 as this book goes to press—are in the midst of a water shortage or anticipating one by 2013. North Carolina and Georgia are suffering from one of the worst droughts in recorded history. Florida's population is growing, but its water supply isn't. Reservoir levels are dropping to record lows. Internationally, the situation doesn't look a whole lot better. Australia is in a severe 30-year dry spell, and some studies show that by 2050 up to 2 billion people world-wide could be facing shortages. That's less than 50 years away!

Building Green Protects and Preserves Our Water

Green building and remodeling emphasizes the conservation and preservation of water by taking measures inside and outside of the home to manage the supply. With some simple steps, both during the building/remodeling process and in your daily habits, you can significantly reduce water consumption and help reduce water pollution.

Green Facts
According to UNICEF, more than 1.1 billion people internationally don't have safe drinking water and another 2.6 billion lack adequate sanitation. Every day, 5,000 people die from water-related illnesses and nearly 2 million die each year, mostly children. For more information, visit UNICEF at www.unicef.org.

Water Quality

In addition to worrying about water conservation, we also need to be concerned about water quality. We often take it for granted that the systems that our country has in place keep our water clean and free of pollutants.

However, many of our lakes, rivers, and groundwater wells contain polluted water. Although natural occurrences such as volcanoes and earthquakes can contribute to the pollution, we must take responsibility for what we have contributed through the toxic products we use and the negative habits that we have. For example, applying lawn and garden pesticides, allowing automobile oil and grease to drip on our driveways, and sending Fido out for a bathroom break in the backyard without picking up after him are just a few examples of how we contribute negatively to water pollution. You see, when it rains, water hits the ground, puddles, and flows to the nearest drain, which channels the water directly toward waterways that ultimately lead to oceans, lakes, and streams. Along the way, the water runoff picks up toxins from the ground, such as Fido's waste, automobile oil and grease, lawn and garden pesticides, and other chemicals.

In the United States, most of our drinking water comes from municipal systems that pull water from these same rivers, lakes, and reservoirs that we pollute. Although treatment makes the water drinkable, the knowledge that the water has been exposed to all these nasty substances can be revolting, especially when a few simple changes in both our personal habits and home building practices can prevent this from occurring.

> **Tips & Tools**
>
> In 2006, Americans drank about 167 bottles of water each, but only recycled an average of 23 percent of those bottles. That leaves 38 billion water bottles in landfills. Instead of buying bottled water, invest in a water filtration system for your faucet, such as Brita, and fill up reusable containers.

Make Changes

For example, it doesn't take much effort to change to safer cleaning products, and it only takes a moment to stop and reconsider pouring cleaning products and other household hazardous waste—such as bleach, cleansers, automobile oil, engine oil, fuel, and even insect and rodent poison—down the drain. Communities now have facilities that can take these substances from you and dispose of them properly.

Better yet, carefully read labels and switch to products that are nontoxic. Take it one step further and make your own cleaners. Vinegar, baking soda, and lemon make a terrific nontoxic cleanser.

In new construction, it has become common practice to pave over natural areas with blacktopped driveways and concrete walkways. This reduces the amount of natural areas available to absorb the rainwater which prevents it from running down the drains. By simply switching to pavers that allow water penetration to the ground below, you've made a huge difference.

The good news is that communities and developers are also starting to do their part by developing stormwater management systems, whereby rainwater is diverted to areas where the ground can absorb it or it is collected and reused. Many builders are automatically including permeable pavers into their designs as well. The even better news is that there are several water conservation techniques that you, the homeowner, can easily implement into the design or remodel of your home.

Use Rain Barrels

Years ago, before large water treatment plants and distribution systems took over the job, people captured rainwater and stored it in cisterns or barrels to be used when they needed to water the garden or grass. Today, rainwater harvesting is enjoying a resurgence among homeowners as an easy, affordable method of conserving water and preventing stormwater runoff.

Tips & Tools

Chapter 21 explains how irrigation systems can be installed—and even used in conjunction with your rain barrel—to deliver the right amount of water to your plants with no waste. You can also select plants for your yard that don't require much water at all.

Hard Hat Area

Rain barrels are not meant for long-term storage. Use up the water every week to avoid attracting mosquitoes, which only need 7 to 10 days to lay and hatch eggs. If you want to store the water longer, mosquito repellants are available.

Why fill your pool or water your garden with water you have to pay for when you can collect hundreds of gallons (or even more) for free? All it takes is a barrel or tank to collect and store it. Rain barrels can also be used to divert stormwater to another area of your property.

You can buy a ready-made rain barrel catchment system or make one yourself if you're handy (there are websites that provide step-by-step directions for do-it-yourselfers). Each rain barrel should be protected from the penetration of the sun's rays (which can change its chemistry) and come with a cover to keep out insects, wildlife, and curious children. Complete rainwater systems are equipped with storage tanks that sit either above or below the ground as well as filtration systems for drinking, although rainwater is more commonly used for watering plants, filling pools, etc.

Depending on how much rainwater you want to capture, you can connect one gutter downspout to a small barrel that holds about 60 gallons or so or install a more elaborate system that collects hundreds of gallons from multiple downspouts and other areas and transports it to one, or several, barrels. As long as there is a way to channel the water to a drain, you can harvest rainwater from any sloped roof.

These rain barrels are from the Terra Eden Landscaping OASIS Rainwater System. The OASIS system uses rain from natural resources, such as gutter downspouts, to hydrate your existing landscape.

(Terra Eden Landscaping)

How much rain you actually collect will depend on the average amount of rainfall in your area. In an example used by the Texas Water Development Board, using a collection rate of 0.62, a system efficiency of 85 percent, and an average annual rainfall of 32 inches for a city in Texas, a resident can expect to collect about 34,000 gallons of rainwater per year ($0.62 \times 0.85 \times 2,000 \times 32 = 33,700$ gallons per year). On the other hand, a resident of El Paso with an average annual rainfall of 8.5 inches can expect to collect only about 9,000 gallons ($0.62 \times 0.85 \times 2,000 \times 8.5 = 8,950$ gallons).

The system doesn't keep all the water it collects. Some might splash out, evaporate, or miss its intended target completely. Therefore, systems are said to have an efficiency of 75 to 85 percent.

Can you drink this rainwater? Yes, but it needs to be treated first because contaminates can find their way into the water and can cause serious illness. Rain barrels can be purchased with a filtration system. Currently, no federal or state standards exist for harvested rainwater quality, but you might have local testing requirements before you can use the water for drinking, so contact your local health department.

The cost of rainwater systems vary. Smaller barrels that hold up to 100 gallons of non-drinkable water might cost only a few hundred dollars, while full systems that include storage tanks and water treatment capability might run a few thousand. If you choose to store your water underground, you'll have to factor in excavation costs as well.

When considering a rain harvesting system, consider combining it with an irrigation system at the same time. The rainwater can be shuttled underground to provide the exact amount of water you need for your plants and trees. (See Chapter 21 for more information on irrigation systems.)

Reuse Greywater

Greywater is the water that goes down the drains in your home—such as after you take a shower, wash the laundry, or do the dishes. It is important to distinguish greywater from blackwater, which is all the water that flows from your toilet.

With the rising costs of water and the limited supply of this precious resource, more homeowners are installing systems that direct that greywater to an irrigation system (more on that next) to water plants, grass, and gardens, or reuse it to flush toilets.

A San Diego homeowner had a greywater system installed by ReWater Systems (San Diego, California) that includes an automatic self-cleaning filter unit and controller that also controls the irrigation system. The system comes with a water meter to determine how much greywater has been used.

(www.ReWater.com, San Diego, California)

Reusing greywater is a very successful water conservation technique, but not all municipalities allow it. State regulations vary, so you need to make sure this system is legal in your area. For example, in Arizona and New Mexico, greywater can be drained directly onto your lawn without a permit, while other states require one. California allows greywater reuse, but only with their approved systems.

A piping system must be installed to separate the greywater from the blackwater and drain it away from the house. If you are building or remodeling and installing piping systems into the home and aren't sure if you want to reuse your greywater quite yet, it's wise to install the appropriate plumbing now for possible future use. Installing it at a later time would be much more costly. If you live in a colder area, remember that piping should be installed lower in the ground to prevent freezing.

Create Rain Gardens

The stormwater that has been pouring off your roof has to go somewhere. If you opt not to harvest it for reuse, you might consider creating a rain garden to use up the water instead. Rain gardens, also called "bioretention systems," soak up rainwater before it flows down the drain. They are located in an area filled with grasses and other plants, such as wildflowers, that soak up the runoff from the roof.

Rain Gardens of Michigan (www.raingardens.org) has a valuable website dedicated to the topic and suggests that before you design your rain garden, you should identify the direction that water runs off of your property and where it ultimately collects. The best spot to locate a rain garden is downhill from your foundation. Rain gardens are built with a depression—up to 6 inches deep to allow for evaporation time—to catch the water. Any deeper and the water may not be soaked up or evaporate swiftly enough, leaving it prone to breeding mosquitoes. Also, avoid creating a rain garden that is flush up against your foundation. This can lead to a leaky basement. Ideally, rain gardens should be located 10 feet away and down a slope from the house.

Hard Hat Area

Mosquitoes cause more than itchy skin. They can also transmit serious diseases, especially West Nile Virus. The best way to avoid mosquitoes is to seal open water areas or outside water containers. Change water in bird baths regularly, keep your gutters clean, and monitor any stored water on your property that might breed mosquitoes, including the pool.

What plants can you put in your rain garden? The choice is yours, but it's best to use plants that are native to your area and are already acclimated to your climate. Rain Gardens of Michigan recommends adding mulch, which plays an important role in removing pollutants from the soil.

Depending on where you live and the type of soil you have, you might need to take additional steps to create your rain garden. Rain Gardens of Michigan offer a step-by-step guide to creating your garden, including preparing the site, designing the borders, improving the soil, and selecting the plants.

The Least You Need to Know

◆ Pause and think before you pour something down the drain that adds to water pollution.

◆ Rainwater is free, so preserve it and use it to water vegetable gardens and flower-beds.

◆ You can drink harvested rainwater, but you *must* first treat it according to local health codes.

◆ Greywater is water that goes down the drain but can be diverted and used in gardens and yards.

◆ Rain gardens help to soak up rainwater and prevent it from going down the drain.

Chapter 16

Faucets and Fixtures

In This Chapter

- ◆ Low-flow toilets
- ◆ Eco-friendly faucets
- ◆ Aerators, sensors, and temperature controls

In Chapter 15, you learned about the urgency of the world's water shortage and how you can take steps to reuse greywater and rainwater. This chapter concentrates on some of the biggest water guzzlers inside your home today—including your toilets, leaky faucets, and that long hot bath you like to take after a hard day.

For example, just one leaky faucet—at the rate of one drip per second—will waste more than 3,000 gallons of water each year. Your relaxing bubble bath can require up to 70 gallons of water each time you soak. Even a five-minute shower will use 35 gallons of water. And a single leaky toilet can waste about 200 gallons of water every day. Bottom line: it's time to stop throwing your money, and water, down the drain.

Upgrading to low-flow toilets or adding new, more efficient showerheads will conserve a tremendous amount of water and reduce your water bill.

Remember, however, that green building and remodeling means integrating your home as a whole to make sure all systems run well together so you can maximize their efficiency and savings. So even though this chapter focuses on toilets, showerheads, and fixtures, it's important to install or upgrade to PEX piping, which uses less water (see Chapter 12), and to properly insulate all hot water piping. With PEX piping and properly insulated pipes, you'll be saving even more water and money.

Toilets

The toilet concept is simple—press a handle and water pressure removes the waste. However, this great invention is one of your home's worst water wasters. Why? A whopping 40 percent of your home's indoor water use will come just from flushing the toilet and any water leaks it may have! The older your toilet is, the more water it wastes. To understand why toilets, especially older models, are huge water wasters and why you should replace them with low-flow models, you first need a quick lesson on toilet mechanics.

Toiletry 101

Plain and simple—you go, you flush. But what you don't see is that when you push down the lever, it pulls up a chain inside the tank that is connected to a flapper (think of it as a sink stopper). The flapper opens to allow the water to go down the drain and more water to come into the bowl. When the water in the toilet reaches a predetermined level, the flapper closes and the water stops flowing. How much water flows into the tank before the flapper closes? That depends on how old your toilet is.

Tips & Tools _____

To determine whether your toilet has a leak, add a few drops of food coloring to the tank water. If the color shows up in the bowl without flushing it, you have a leak.

Toilets made before 1980 use approximately 5 gallons per flush (GPF). Toilets manufactured between the 1980s and 1992 use approximately 3.5 GPF. Today, more efficient toilets—called ultra-low flush toilets (ULFT)—use only 1.6 GPF.

If you're unsure what your toilet's GPF is, you can look for a stamp on the rim of the bowl. If you don't see one there, lift the tank lid; the toilet's make, model, and manufacture date should be stamped on the inside back of the tank. If the toilet is dated earlier than 1980, it's time to upgrade.

Green Facts
Think Thomas Crapper invented the toilet? Don't bet on it. Although Crapper was a plumber who helped to improve the toilet in the 1800s, it was Sir John Harrington who came up with the prototype of a "flushing water closet" and installed it in the palace of Queen Elizabeth I, his godmother.

Low-Flow Toilets

In 1992, the federal Energy Policy Act mandated low-flow toilets and, in 1996, WaterSense, a program sponsored by the U.S. Environmental Protection Agency (EPA), was founded to help consumers identify high-performance, water-efficient toilets and fixtures that can reduce water use in the home. Statistics show that by installing a WaterSense-labeled high-efficiency toilet with efficient faucets and *aerators*, each American home can save more than 100,000 gallons of water every year. These toilets can also save a family of four more than $90 annually on their water bill and $2,000 over the lifetime of the toilet. Look for their logo on water-efficient toilets.

def•i•ni•tion

An **aerator** is a device that is screwed into the end of a faucet that mixes the water with air to help reduce water usage.

WaterSense helps consumers identify water-efficient toilets. Look for this logo.

EPA
WaterSense

Certain brands of high-efficiency toilets (HETs) even go above and beyond the federal minimum (by 20 percent) and use only 1.28 gallons. These toilets qualify for LEED certification. (There has been some concern that the decreased amount of water in HETs doesn't create enough pressure to push the waste through the pipes. According to WaterSense, a limited number of tests were conducted on these toilets and the organization says that the HETs are able to carry the waste the appropriate distances.)

As much as you're trying to save water, toilets do need water pressure to push the waste away. Federal guidelines state your water district should have a minimum pressure per square inch (PSI) of 40, but if you own a well it should have a pump and a minimum of 25 PSI.

These toilets cost slightly more than standard toilets, but you will see a return on your investment through your water bill. Shop around and compare prices and styles that you prefer. They can range from $300 to $600 depending on style:

- **Gravity-assisted**—The most common and most affordable style of toilet. Gravity-assisted toilets use tank water to create a siphon action that pulls the waste through a trap. These toilets work pretty much the same way as older, water-guzzling toilets.

- **Pressure-assisted**—Pressure-assisted toilets use trapped air to force the water into the bowl and push the waste away. Generally, you'll find the much louder pressure-assisted toilets in such commercial places as restaurant and mall bathrooms, but newer, quieter models are finding their way into homes.

- **Vacuum-assisted**—Flushing activates a vacuum chamber, which acts like a siphon to get the water into the bowl. Vacuum-assisted toilets are quieter than pressure-assisted toilets.

- **Dual-flush**—A dual-flush toilet has *two* buttons located on the top of the tank to push the waste away. Press one button to eliminate liquid waste and the other button to get rid of solid waste. The solid waste button uses a little more water than the liquid waste button. Dual-flush toilets have been very popular in other parts of the world and are now catching on in North America. Dual-flush toilets have a siphonic flushing system—the water swirls around the bowl and creates a vacuum in the trap area, and the water pulls the waste out of the bowl. They are the most expensive toilets on the market, starting at $250 and up. Check with your utility company to see whether it offers rebates and/or cash incentives.

Installing low-flow toilets in your home will greatly reduce the amount of water used to flush and, if you have well water, reduce how often you draw on the well.

A dual-flush, water-efficient toilet. One handle flushes away liquid waste, while the other provides more power for solid waste removal.

(TotoUSA; www.totousa.com)

Most low-flow toilets are either a one- or two-piece construction and come in various shapes, sizes, and colors, so you're sure to find one to meet your needs. From a cost perspective, a two-piece toilet is typically less expensive than a sleeker-looking one-piece toilet, but a one-piece toilet has less of a chance of leaking between the bowl and the tank. One-piece models are also costly to repair in comparison to their two-piece counterparts, since you must repair the entire unit.

Tips & Tools

If you are building or remodeling your home for adaptive use, consider installing a taller low-flow toilet bowl that meets the accessibility guidelines of the American Disabilities Act.

It might take some time to get used to the difference in the amount of water and the sound of the flush of a low-flow toilet, but these toilets are much more productive than their older counterparts, and you'll soon realize that you don't miss the difference.

Showerheads

Speaking of water pressure, one of the biggest misconceptions of the green market today is that a low-flow showerhead will not yield the same water pressure compared to older, nonrestricted models. Years ago, plumbers and builders were known to have manipulated low-flow models and removed the restriction device to make their customers happy.

Today, the available low-flow fixtures allow you to have an enjoyable—and penetrating—hot shower and still do your part to conserve energy and water.

Like toilets, showerheads were once water wasters. In 1992, they typically had a flow rate of 5.5 gallons per minute (GPM). Today's federal regulations state that flow rates can't exceed more than 2.5 GPM. To max out your water efficiency, go one step further and select a showerhead with a flow rate of less than 2.5 GPM.

To determine how much water your current showerhead provides, measure 2.5 gallons of water in a bucket so you know where the level is and mark it. Fill the bucket from the shower for one minute. If the amount of water goes over the mark, then your showerhead sprays more than 2.5 GPM and it's time to get a new one.

There are two basic types of low-flow showerheads:

- **Aerating showerheads**—These mix air with water to produce a mist.
- **Laminar-flow showerheads**—These provide individual streams of water.

The showerhead you choose will depend on your personal preference and your location. If you live in a more humid climate, you might want a laminar-flow showerhead because it doesn't give off as much steam and moisture as an aerating head does.

Low-flow showerheads can also come as fixed or handheld showerheads. Fixed showerheads are permanently attached to the shower, while handheld heads are attached to the wall by a tube.

From a pure cost perspective, low-flow showerheads are a terrific low-cost investment that can regularly save you money on your water bills and on your energy bills.

You can find low-flow showerheads for under $100. At the time of this writing, WaterSense does not have an approved showerhead, but they are working on the specifications for developing one.

Faucets

Do you turn off the faucet while you brush your teeth? If you're like many people, you don't, but you might decide to start when you realize that this bad habit wastes as much as 3,000 gallons of water per year!

To help reduce the water lost from faucets, WaterSense helps to identify high-performance, water-efficient bathroom sink faucets and faucet accessories. Like toilets and showers, older faucets had a very high flow rate years ago, as high as 3 to 7 GPM. Today, federal law mandates that new faucets must not exceed 2.2 GPM.

To earn the WaterSense label, faucets must be independently tested and certified by a licensed certifying body to meet the EPA's water-efficiency and performance criteria. To meet the criteria, faucets and accessories, such as aerators, cannot flow at a rate of more than 1.5 GPM or less than 0.8 GPM.

By installing these water-saving faucets and accessories, an average household will be able to save more than 500 gallons each year. Also, these savings reduce the demands on water heaters and help you save energy.

Aerators

If you're not ready to replace your entire faucet, you might want to consider installing flow restrictors or high-efficiency aerators, which can be screwed onto the end of faucets and cost as little as $5. An aerator introduces air—and pressure—into the air stream usually through a series of little holes at the tip of the faucet. A flow restrictor is a device inside the faucet that reduces the amount of water flowing out.

Sensors

Who hasn't forgotten to turn the faucet handle all the way to the off position at least once in their lives? Sensor technology has found its way from public bathrooms into residential bathrooms to help avoid this problem. Sensor faucets turn on when you put your hands under the faucet and turn off when you remove them. The Delta Faucet Company even offers a faucet with touch technology. Sensor faucets can range from $300 to $500, depending on size.

Another hands-free alternative usually reserved for public bathrooms but now finding its way into homes is a spring-loaded faucet, which slowly returns the faucet to the off position after it has been turned on.

Some low-flow faucets even come with foot controls. These products can be a bit pricier, from $200 to $700.

The Least You Need to Know

- In addition to replacing leaky toilets and faucets, think about improving the pipes feeding the fixtures.

- Low-flow faucets and fixtures are more costly than standard fixtures but will help you save money on water bills and, ultimately, will pay for themselves.

- Low-yield showerheads let you reduce water use while still having an enjoyable shower.

- Faucet aerators and sensors and touch technology cut down on wasted water.

Chapter 17

Air Quality

In This Chapter

- How your home can make you sick
- The scary reality of radon
- Moisture, mold, and mildew
- What to know about filtration
- Where to put the garage

If you worked inside a building that you knew was making you sick, would you continue to work there? Probably not. But what if it was your home that was making you sick? It's a scary thought, but the place you turn to for relaxation, solace, and safety might actually be making you, your family, and your pets sick.

According to the American Lung Association (ALA), Americans spend 65 percent of their time in their homes, yet the pollution inside our homes may be up to five times higher than outside. As we mentioned earlier in the book, even the EPA ranks indoor air quality as one of the top-five environmental risks to public health. Add in the exposure to pollutants in your office buildings and schools, and you and your family are likely being exposed to high levels of indoor air pollutants every day.

Concerns about indoor air quality (IAQ) have increased since energy conservation measures were instituted in office buildings during the 1970s. At that time, buildings and homes were sealed tight to conserve energy. Although making homes and buildings airtight helps to conserve energy and prevents outdoor air pollutants from seeping in, sealing up a home or building too well without proper ventilation leaves no place for toxic pollutants—such as mold, tobacco smoke, pest control products, dust, fireplace emissions, formaldehyde from furniture and cabinets, and more—to escape; instead, they build up and linger. Energy conservation might have been a big issue 30-plus years ago, but at the time the side effects from such poor ventilation weren't even considered.

Our homes need to be ventilated—to be able to breathe. In other words, they need to be able take in good, clean air and to expel old, contaminated air. Without ventilation, occupants are exposed to unhealthy toxins, leading to a host of health problems—including asthma, allergies, headaches, infections, and even cancer.

Know Your Home's Air Pollutants

As we mentioned, indoor air quality pollutants come from commonly known sources, such as tobacco smoke, cleaning and pest control products, mold, mildew, dust, poor ventilation, and moisture problems. Even your wood stove, gas stove, and fireplace can contribute toxic pollutants to the air.

And, if you've read the previous chapters, you know that contaminants can come from items you probably never even considered hazardous to your health before, such as your furniture; cabinets; wall coverings; flooring; and the building materials used in your home, such as pressed wood and particle board. Have you ever noticed how many of these products emit an odor when brought into your home? This "new smell" is caused by offgassing, which is the evaporation of chemicals called volatile organic compounds (VOCs).

Tips & Tools

Install a carbon monoxide alarm near bedrooms and on each floor of your home. Carbon monoxide detectors should meet the CSA CAN/CGA 6.19 standard or the Underwriters Laboratories (UL) 2034 standard, have a long-term warranty, and are self-tested and reset to ensure proper operation. You can buy dual-function devices that detect both carbon monoxide and smoke.

VOCs

Amazingly, the offgassing of VOCs can continue for years after you've installed your new rugs, flooring, or kitchen cabinets. Here is just a short list of VOCs that can be found in your home or building materials and the health hazards they can cause:

◆ **Formaldehyde**—As discussed in the chapters on flooring and insulation, formaldehyde is a strong-smelling gas that's used as a preservative. It can be found in your home in particle board, household products, glues, permanent press fabrics, paper product coatings, fiberboard, and plywood. Urea form-aldehyde foam insulation (UFFI), a once-popular type of home insulation, is no longer used because of its form-aldehyde content. Formaldehyde can cause asthma attacks, nausea, difficulty breathing, and has been labeled a car-cinogen.

Tips & Tools

The GREENGUARD Environmental Institute (www.greenguard.org) is a nonprofit organization that establishes acceptable indoor air standards for indoor products, environ-ments, and buildings. It compiles an online guide that features products that have been tested to ensure their emissions meet acceptable IAQ pollutant guide-lines and standards.

◆ **Methylene chloride**—Also known as dichloromethane, this comes from paint strippers, adhesive removers, and aerosol spray paints. Breathing in too much methylene chloride can lead to dizziness, nausea, and tingling in the fingers and toes (similar to carbon-monoxide poisoning). It has also been known to cause cancer in animals and can cause burning and redness of the skin.

◆ **Benzene**—This is both a natural and manmade substance. According to the Centers for Disease Control (CDC), indoor air generally contains levels of ben-zene higher than those in outdoor air. The benzene in indoor air comes from products that contain benzene, such as glues, paints, furniture wax, and deter-gents. It also comes from tobacco smoke. Benzene can cause the production of too many or too little white and red blood cells. People who breathe in high lev-els of benzene may develop dizziness, rapid heartbeat, headaches, confusion, or unconsciousness. If levels are extremely high it can lead to death.

◆ **Carbon monoxide**—A colorless, odorless, tasteless gas, this is one of the most dangerous indoor pollutants. Exposure to significant levels of carbon monoxide (CO) can cause death. Each year, more than 200 Americans die from carbon-monoxide poisoning and thousands more are treated. Carbon monoxide is pro-duced by running cars; motorcycles; and other fuel-burning motor vehicles, appliances, and heating systems.

Radon

Radon is a tasteless, odorless gas that comes from the breakdown of uranium in soil, rock, and water. It can get into your home through cracks in the foundation and by seeping into well water. Breathing in this natural radioactive gas can lead to lung cancer. In fact, radon is a leading cause of lung cancer in the United States, claiming approximately 20,000 lives each year.

Over time, the amount of radon in your home can build up to dangerous levels, but measures can be taken to reduce it and prevent it from seeping into your living areas. Your builder can test the homesite for radon before construction begins and install features during construction—including the piping, stone, and vapor barriers under the slab (or foundation)—to deter the radon away from the inside of your home.

You or your contractor can buy a radon test kit before beginning any remodeling projects to see whether your home has a radon leak. Short-term and long-term test kits are available. A short-term test, which lasts for just a few days, requires closing windows and outside doors and fans or anything else that will bring in outside air. Place the kit in the lowest, regularly lived-in level of the home and leave it there. That's all you do. After two or three days, you just reseal it and send it to the lab, where it is analyzed. The results will be sent to you in a few weeks. During long-term tests, the kit remains in your home for more than 90 days.

Hard Hat Area

Up to 1,800 deaths per year are attributed to radon exposure through household well water. Such tasks as showering, washing dishes, and laundering can release radon gas into the air. If you have tested the air and discovered radon, test the water, too.

The amount of radon in the air is measured in pico-Curies per liter of air (pCi/L). The EPA estimates that 1 in 15 homes has a radon level of 4 pCi/L or more, which is considered high. If yours scores that high, there are ways to fix the problem.

Every state has a radon contact (you can find yours by visiting www.epa.gov/iaq/whereyoulive.html and clicking on your state) and specific requirements associated with providing radon measurements. If you have a radon problem, a venting system can be installed to remove it. Test the area again after the remodeling or construction is complete.

Know Your Moisture

Moisture—both too much and too little—can have a serious impact on your indoor air quality. People tend to feel more comfortable when the relative humidity is between

35 and 50 percent. When the humidity in the room is too high, meaning there's too much moisture in the air, it can cause the room to feel stuffy. According to the ALA, other signs of too much humidity are the following:

- Condensation on windows

- Wet stains on walls and ceilings

- Moldy bathrooms or other areas

- Musty smells

- Allergic reactions or ongoing allergies

During heating season, the natural tendency is for moisture to flow from the interior to the exterior of the home through any leaks in the home's envelope (in a nongreen house). Because the moist, warm air is leaking outside, the interior temperature falls. The furnace comes on and pressures the house even further, driving more warmth and moisture out. It's a vicious cycle! The combination of a leaky house, warm air under pressure from the furnace, and the natural movement of moisture makes the house too dry.

Hard Hat Area

When necessary, humidifiers can be incorporated into a green building—but only in extreme cases—and they need to be monitored closely to make sure they aren't making the house too moist. On the other hand, homeowners should strongly consider using dehumidifiers to keep moisture in check. Although air conditioners dehumidify the air, they are not as efficient as a good dehumidifier.

On the other hand, too much moisture turns the room into a breeding ground for bacteria, leading to serious rotting, mildew, and mold problems on drywall, caulk, grout, wood, and carpet. Mold is typically found in homes affected by water damage. When mold is disturbed, spores are released into the air and produce chemicals called mycotoxins which, when ingested or inhaled, can cause reactions in people who are sensitive to them or who are exposed to them in large amounts or over a long period of time. The most common symptoms of mycotoxin exposure are runny nose, eye irritation, cough, congestion, and aggravation of asthma.

Controlling mold is as simple as controlling moisture. Make sure your home's envelope is air tight and constructed in such a way as to allow the wall cavity to dry on the inside. Building scientists recommend that the wall cavities be designed so they are air tight. This means that holes and gaps need to be sealed (i.e., caulked) to prevent air leaks and that materials need to have a perm rating that allows moisture to move out via diffusion.

Although you can remove small mold growth problems on your own, if the home is already affected by mold that is more than 2 square feet in diameter, or if it has gotten into the carpet or drywall, every inch of affected material must be thoroughly cleaned—or removed and replaced—before permanent repairs are made. This should be done by a health and safety professional with experience performing microbial investigations—particularly if heating, ventilating, air conditioning (HVAC) systems or large occupied spaces are involved. Simply sponging off or covering up a mold problem after it has a foothold in masonry or flooring only exacerbates the problem as the mold continues to grow unabated.

Professional mold remediators are skilled in finding hidden contamination and may use several methods of testing—they will inspect the area to determine the type of mold involved and obtain a small sample with a sterile swab or piece of adhesive tape. The sample is transferred to a culture plate and tested more thoroughly. Mold professionals can also use controlled air tests to determine the amount of spores floating around a given space, moisture meters to identify the extent of water damage inside a wall, and fiber optics to look inside walls and ceilings to find patches of contamination that their physical inspection might have missed.

Tips & Tools

Keep water away from the inside of your home: make sure gutters and downspouts are clear of debris that can block the flow of water from your roof. Your downspouts should be properly graded so that rainwater flows away from the foundation. Splash blocks and downspout extensions can help rainwater to flow in the proper direction.

Today, ventilation systems and contamination controls are a must in your home to control mold and other toxins and improve indoor air quality. Ventilation systems cycle contaminants out of the home and move in the fresh air. In addition, improving indoor air quality also means building and remodeling using products that are free of pollutants. When you make these changes, you, your family, and your pets will be breathing easy.

Ventilation

Ventilation is a simple, yet very significant, green building concept—good air in, bad air out. Ventilation provides a controlled method to maintain the correct indoor relative humidity (and control mold and mildew) along with exhausting the harmful pollutants.

Yes, you want your home to be airtight, but at the same time it needs to be able to eliminate any pollutants that have accumulated inside. Otherwise, poor ventilation can lead to several problems, including soot accumulation, carbon-monoxide poisoning, and *backdrafting*.

def•i•ni•tion

According to the EPA, **backdrafting** occurs when we exhaust too much air from the home and the home becomes depressurized. Instead of allowing combustion products—such as carbon monoxide—to be released up the chimney, depressurization, or the lack of combustion oxygen, pulls them back down the flue and into the home. Because substances such as carbon monoxide can be fatal, backdrafting can create a very dangerous situation.

Proper ventilation will prevent depressurization by balancing the good and bad air in and out of your home (otherwise known as air changes). The American Society of Heating, Refrigeration and Air-Conditioning Engineers (ASHRAE), a national organization that sets standards in the heating, ventilation, air conditioning, and refrigeration industry organization recommends a minimum of 0.35 air changes per hour (ACH), which means the air would be completely changed in approximately three hours. Green builders, however, recommend that you go above the minimum so that there are even more air changes and better ventilation.

Ventilating a house can be done two ways:

◆ Spot ventilation

◆ Whole-house ventilation

The best ventilation strategy is actually a combination of both, otherwise known as a balanced system.

Spot ventilation is the use of a properly sized exhaust fan or ventilation hood in an area such as the bathroom or kitchen. For example, some commercial ranges require a fresh air intake near the back to provide combustion air for all the burners. Exhaust fans can come with timers and humidity sensors.

Whole-house ventilation systems are just like they sound—they are designed to ventilate the entire home. They have intake and exhaust so the house stays in balance.

Heat recovery ventilators (HRV) and energy recovery ventilators (ERV) are specialized whole-house ventilation systems. Heat recovery ventilators, also known as air-to-air heat exchangers, push the stale air out of your home and pull the fresh air in. As it's doing so, it extracts the heat or cold from the air it is expelling.

Broan SmartSense Ventilation System monitors manual usage of the fans and automatically operates them, if necessary, to meet ventilation requirements by digitally communicating over the home's power lines. This provides homeowners with the ongoing fresh air distribution needed to maintain good indoor air quality, all without ever having to think about it.

(Broan-NuTone)

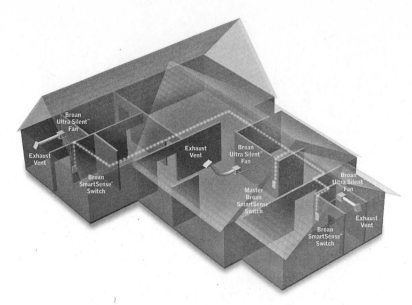

For example, if it's cold outside, the cold air coming in gets heated when it enters your home. When the air is ventilated back outside, the HRV takes the warmth out of the outgoing air and uses it to warm up the cold air coming in. It also removes the pollutants. In the summer, the HRV pulls in hot air from the outside and cools it. When the air is expelled, the HRV takes the cool air and uses it to warm the air that it is coming in.

HRVs save a tremendous amount of energy, up to 80 percent of the temperature that would have been lost. The cost of HRV systems is relatively low, ranging from $800 to $3,000, depending on the size of your home and how many units are installed.

ERVs, which are commonly used in warmer climates, transfer the moisture from the air coming in to the air going out. ERVs tend to cost a bit more than HRVs.

ERVs and HRVs are available as individual room units or, more commonly, as whole-house units. These systems require a bit of upkeep—filters need to be changed or cleaned—and you need a basic understanding of how they work so you can maintain them. The installation of either of these units, which will make your home healthier and more energy efficient, should be done by qualified HVAC contractors.

Air Quality Tests

Although you can purchase indoor quality test kits from hardware and building supply stores, we recommend that these tests be done only by an environmental consultant.

According to the Indoor Air Quality Association, an environmental consultant is a professional who can identify the causes of poor indoor air quality even when problems seem vague or unrelated to visible causes.

Combustion Venting

Homes with older HVAC systems should upgrade to newer models. Here's why: older models might need what's called combustion ventilation, or make-up air. These older furnaces and boilers draw oxygen from the house. When oxygen needs to be replaced, it is drawn through cracks and leaks in the home's envelope. However, with homes getting even tighter, an older unit will now require a duct or pipe that brings in fresh air from the outside to that unit or into that room (spot ventilation). The new, high-efficiency furnaces and boilers have their own pipes that bring in the oxygen needed for combustion and exhaust. It is a sealed system so the air needed for combustion and its exhaust never mingles with the indoor air.

A Few Words About Humidifiers

Many homeowners complain that the air in their home seems too dry. Rather than mask the problem by using a humidifier, you should look into the reason the air in your home is dry. Often, it's because your heating system is too big for your home or your home leaks warm, moist air to the outside during the winter. As a result, your furnace runs longer than necessary, drying out the air in your home.

Installing a properly sized furnace and ventilation system and properly sealing your home is a much more efficient way to achieve adequate levels of humidity and moisture.

Filtration

Ventilation systems help to remove pollutants from the air, but an air filtration system can go even further by trapping and removing more particles, including pollen, dust, and pet dander. According to the ALA, there are several types of filters on the market:

♦ **Panel filters**—These are standard furnace filters that are installed in the ductwork or air conditioning systems, but they do little to remove contaminates from the air.

Green Facts

More than 70 percent of Americans have forced air heating and/or central air in their homes. Yet nearly 50 percent do not change the filters when recommended. Ten percent have never replaced the filter. Replace your filter when recommended for better ventilation and energy efficiency.

Washable/reusable filters are also a poor choice because it's very difficult to clean them thoroughly.

◆ **Pleated filters**—These are slightly better than panel filters but still not the best choice.

◆ **High Efficiency Particulate Air (HEPA) filters**—These are made of fine fibers that slow down the movement of air. They are usually installed in the return air duct near the furnace or air handler. When the air is slowed, the particulates are captured on the fiber. The filter is folded back and forth over corrugated separators that add strength to the core and form air passages between the pleats. These types of filters stand on their own and do not fit most furnaces.

Green Facts

Air particles are measured in microns and range in size from fairly large to microscopic. To better understand the size of a micron, a human hair is about 70 microns in diameter. Your nose, sinuses, and windpipe are designed to filter out particles 3 to 5 microns in size and keep them from becoming lodged in your lungs.

◆ **Electronic filters**—These use an electronic field to trap particles (similar to the static-cling effect). They can be installed in central heating or cooling system ducts and work well at trapping particles.

ASHRAE has developed a standardized rating system for air filters called a Minimum Efficiency Reporting Value (MERV) rating. The higher the MERV rating, the smaller the particles it removes. The ALA's Healthy House guidelines require a MERV rating of 10 or higher.

Tips & Tools

Replace your air filter at the manufacturer's suggested intervals—usually the first day of every season. Replace it more often if you are introducing higher levels of particulates into your home, such as when you are doing renovations. Consider even more frequent changes if you have a family member with asthma, allergies, or another lung disease.

Garage Exhaust

When making green modifications, people tend to give their garage scant attention. Yet your garage plays a huge part in the green building process, especially when it comes to indoor air quality. A typical garage shelters your cars and stores your fertilizers, toxic paints, and solvents. If not properly sealed, these pollutants can seep into your home.

How do you cope with garage toxins? Consider designing your new home with a garage that's separated from the rest of your home. You can either separate the garage completely or attach it to your home via a covered walkway. At the very least, install weatherstripping on doors between your garage and your house to prevent vapors from entering the main part of the home. You could also install a small fan that exhausts the garage only. This would depressurize the garage and any air leaks between the house and garage would leak house air into the garage instead of leaking the garage air into the house.

Treat your garage like you treat your home and make sure to provide adequate ventilation and filtration while sealing cracks, caulking, and insulating walls and pipes.

Duct Cleaning

To maintain the environmental health of your home, it's vital that the HVAC system remain clean.

According to the Environmental Protection Agency, duct cleaning generally refers to the cleaning of various heating and cooling system components of forced air systems, including the supply and return air ducts and registers, grilles and diffusers, heat exchangers, heating and cooling coils, condensate drain pans (drip pans), fan motor and fan housing, and the air handling unit housing.

The EPA says that if these systems are not properly installed, maintained, and operated, their components may become contaminated with particles of dust, pollen, or other debris. Contamination can cut down on the efficiency of your system, making it work harder. On top of that, if moisture is present, the potential for mold to grow is increased and spores from such growth may be released into the home's living areas.

Duct cleaning contractors can start the cleaning process by looking inside your air ducts and chutes. With use of photo and videotape equipment, you can see before and after views of the equipment and make certain that the contractor completely cleaned the system.

The National Air Duct Cleaners Association (NADCA), a nonprofit association of companies engaged in the cleaning of HVAC systems, does not endorse one kind of equipment over another, but explains there are two main types of vacuum collection devices: (1) those mounted on trucks and trailers, and (2) portable units.

Truck/trailer-mounted equipment is generally more powerful than portable equipment. However, portable equipment can often be brought directly into your home, allowing the vacuum source to be located closer to the ductwork. Both types of equipment can clean to NADCA standards. It is important to note that companies offering just vacuuming or brushing will not get an HVAC system clean. Both tools are required to thoroughly clean a system. In addition, the contractor should use vacuum equipment that exhausts particles outside of the home or uses only high-efficiency particle air (HEPA) vacuuming equipment if the vacuum exhausts inside the home.

The EPA says that duct cleaning services typically range in cost from $450 to $1,000 per heating and cooling system, depending on the services offered, the size of the system to be cleaned, system accessibility, climactic region, level of contamination, and type of duct material.

The Least You Need to Know

◆ Just like we need to breathe in and out, so do our homes.

◆ Many building materials emit toxic gasses that can affect the air we breathe. Choose responsibly.

◆ Good indoor air quality is achieved by both properly sealing and ventilating your home.

◆ Toxic offgassing can seep from the garage to the house. Separate the garage from the house or install proper ventilation techniques to prevent toxins from entering the main home.

Part 5

Outdoors

You've taken care of the inside of your home, so now it's time to move outside. Fortunately, having a "green" landscape doesn't mean you have to forgo a lush and lovely outdoor environment.

You'll learn how using natural pest controls prevents toxins from entering the water systems and your home and how to use trees and shrubbery to protect your house from the elements, including the sun, wind, and cold weather. This part also helps you plan a yard that requires less irrigation and that prevents erosion from stormwater runoff.

Many people are relieved to learn that going green doesn't necessarily mean forgoing a swimming pool, hot tub, or grill. You will learn what steps you can take to "green" your pool, decking, and barbecue.

Chapter 18

The Great Outdoors

In This Chapter

- Go native with your lawn
- Eat what you grow
- Herbicides, pesticides, and fertilizers

Does this backyard to-do list sound familiar to you? Water the lawn and garden; plant the flowers you bought in another state while on vacation; apply chemical fertilizers and pesticides to help the lawn grow and eliminate diseases, weeds, and insects.

Of course it does.

For years, this is what homeowners have been doing to take care of their property. Unfortunately, it's a hazardous to-do list that could be causing serious harm to your landscape, local wildlife, the environment, and the health of those who live on or visit your property.

For instance, applying chemical fertilizers might kill your weeds and unwanted insects, but the toxic remnants of these fertilizers might also kill the helpful creepy-crawlies, too. The toxins from the applied pesticides can also be carried off, through rainwater runoff, into streams, lakes, and oceans. And while watering the lawn might sound like the right thing to do, inefficient lawn-watering is a tremendous waste of a precious resource. Even mowing with a state-of-the-art mower—a simple way to care for your lawn—causes environmental damage by emitting toxic greenhouse gases into the environment.

Don't worry. We are not recommending that you ignore your weeds and let the grass grow to your knees. Instead, this chapter suggests some easier, and greener, changes in the way you take care of your yard—from designing it wisely to using nontoxic lawn care materials, and even choosing plants that are native to your area. After you start to make these changes, you'll wonder why you haven't been living like this all along.

Design Your Yard Wisely

Here's rule number one: don't tear out everything in your yard and start from scratch. Instead, take a sketchbook and spend some time in your yard or on your plot of land before you break ground. Take note of which types of flowers and plants are already there and where they are located. Are they in the shady areas or in direct sunlight all day long? Do they require a lot of maintenance and water, or do they do just fine on their own? Are these plants native to your region?

After you've done your homework, you can start designing your yard. What have you always wanted your yard to look like? Filled with color? With greenery that goes on for miles? Breathtaking water features? You can have all that and more and design it in the most eco-friendly way.

You can plant varieties that require minimal care and consider an irrigation system that collects and stores stormwater runoff to water your soil and plants. You might also want to dedicate a section of your yard to grow your favorite pesticide-free vegetables or herbs.

If you can't tell the difference between a perennial and an annual, consult with a landscape architect, who can walk you through a step-by-step landscaping plan of action.

Tips & Tools

Not sure what species of plants they are—perhaps they were planted by the previous homeowner? Take pictures with a digital camera and ask your local nursery to identify them and their place of origin. Then search the Internet to learn about the plants, where they are from, and their needs.

Invasive Plants

Introducing non-native plants into your yard can actually alter the genetic makeup of your native plants. It can also lead to the development of new plant diseases in your yard and cause a loss of food sources for wildlife. Studies have shown that invasive plants cause billions of dollars in damage each year.

So, what is an invasive plant? It depends on your region. For example, what might be an invasive plant in California might not be considered an invasive plant in Florida since soil and climate may be similar. Some examples

> ### Green Facts
>
> One of the most notorious examples of invasive plants is kudzu, a quick-growing vine from Asia that was introduced in the southeastern United States as a quick-growing groundcover for highway embankments. It has spread from East Texas to New England and has smothered 7 million acres of forest.

of invasive plants in the middle Atlantic states are purple loosestrife (also known as *Lythrum salicaria*), English ivy (*Hedera heliz*), and oriental bittersweet (*Celastrus orbiculatus*). Purple loosestrife was introduced to New England as an ornamental plant because of its beauty. Unfortunately, it can produce millions of seeds, which spread by wind or water, and grow to cover thousands of acres. It's a threat to open water habitat and costs the U.S. economy approximately $45 million each year.

Hard Hat Area

According to the Center for Plant Conservation (www.centerforplantconservation. org), an organization that maintains the National Collection of Endangered Plants, more than 200 native plant species in the United States have gone extinct, more than 730 plant species in the United States are federally listed as endangered or threatened, and 20 percent of our native plant species are in decline and on a conservation watch list.

In upstate New York, there has been concern over the Eurasian Watermilfoil, an invasive species of an aquatic plant that is native to Europe, Asia, and North Africa. According to the Lake George Association, the first documented sighting of Watermilfoil in North America was in 1942 in the District of Columbia, most likely brought here in the ballast of a ship. It has since spread to almost every continental state and throughout Canada. It's considered a danger because it spreads easily, grows quickly, and tends to crowd out native plants. This plant also reduces fish habitat and negatively impacts wetland habitats.

Hard Hat Area

Keep in mind that an invasive plant is not the same as a weed. A weed is any plant or grass that is growing where you don't want it to be growing, whether invasive or native.

Nursery staff, a gardener, or your landscape architect should be able to recommend native plants and grasses to choose from.

How do you stop the invasion if the plants are already calling your yard home? If possible, pull them out from the root to prevent them from spreading. If they have overtaken a large area or are difficult to remove, contact your local Cooperative Extension Center for assistance. They will also notify area residents.

Pesticides

A pesticide is a chemical used to kill or control pests such as insects and rodents. Homeowners regularly apply pesticides to their lawn and garden because bugs such as mosquitoes, fleas, ticks, spiders, chiggers, and others can become a serious nuisance to flowers, vegetables, humans, and pets.

According to the EPA, more than 1,055 active ingredients are registered as pesticides, which are formulated into thousands of pesticide products—such as bug sprays, baits, rat poison, and disinfectants. Here's a list of the most common forms of pesticides:

◆ **Traps and zappers**—Unfortunately, traps and zappers are an ineffective means of pest control because they trap or zap beneficial bugs as well as nuisance bugs.

Green Facts
In 1996, University of Delaware researchers Timothy Frick and Douglas Tallamy published a study in the journal *Entomological News*. They collected and identified the kills from six bug zappers at various sites throughout suburban Newark, Delaware, during the summer of 1994. Of the nearly 14,000 insects that were electrocuted and counted, only 31 percent were mosquitoes and biting gnats. Forty-eight percent were harmless, aquatic insects from nearby bodies of water. The researchers claimed that killing this number of harmless insects disturbs nearby ecosystems.

◆ **Botanical pesticides**—Although they are made from plants, these botanically derived pesticides can be more toxic than synthetic pesticides.

◆ **Synthetic pesticides**—These are pesticides that are made from chemical compounds. Some examples of synthetic pesticides are imidacloprid, otherwise known by its brand name Bayer Advanced, and fipronil, otherwise known as Termidor.

Synthetic pesticides have been around since World War II, and although advances have been made to decrease their toxicity and focus on particular groups of pests, they are still considered toxic to humans and the environment.

Unfortunately, exposure to pesticides can cause a host of side effects in humans and animals, from mild symptoms such as irritation of the skin or eyes, to serious side effects such as cancer and reproductive and developmental disorders. The side effects depend on the type of pesticide and the level of exposure.

Hard Hat Area

According to the Pesticide Action Network North America, each year homeowners apply at least 90 million pounds of pesticides to their lawns and gardens. Of the 30 commonly used lawn pesticides, 19 are carcinogens, 13 are linked to birth defects, 21 are linked to reproductive effects, 15 are linked to neurotoxicity, 26 are linked to liver or kidney damage, 27 are irritants, and 11 can disrupt the hormone system.

You can be exposed to pesticides through the air—for example, after you or a neighbor has applied them to the lawn. Pesticide particles can also make their way into your home through open windows or ventilation systems.

Pesticides can also be absorbed through the skin by such products as insect repellents, and you can ingest them by eating food that has been pretreated with pesticides. Pesticides can also make their way into our drinking water through stormwater runoff that goes into drains and makes its way into the water system.

Tips & Tools

When contracting with a company to take care of your lawns and gardens, make sure they follow the green techniques that we have talked about in this book, such as using noninvasive species of plants, using plants that require minimal irrigation, and applying nontoxic pesticides and herbicides as well as organic fertilizers.

The Good Bugs

Not all insects are bad for your lawn, and applying pesticides to your entire lawn can do more harm than good. As a matter of fact, many insects help to keep harmful insects away from your plants and grass. Take ladybugs, for example, which are not only the cutest insects in your yard, but which are very beneficial, too. Ladybugs feed on such harmful pests as aphids (known as plant lice) and scale insects (which also feed

Green Facts

According to Gardenstew.com, ladybugs have been valued by farmers since Medieval Times. Many believed that they were divinely sent to free crops of insect pests. The bug was dedicated to the Virgin Mary and named The Bug of Our Lady, eventually shortened to ladybug.

on plants). One ladybug can eat up to 60 aphids per day. If you apply a cure-all pesticide across your yard, you'll kill these wonderful ladybugs at the same time.

The praying mantis feeds on moths, mosquitoes, and flies, and is extremely fun to watch if you're lucky to have one (or more) in your yard. They don't bite or spread disease. Unfortunately, a single application of a noxious pesticide to your yard can wipe out its entire praying mantis population.

And what about bees? Homeowners are often quick on the pesticide trigger finger when it comes to eliminating buzzing bees, but the truth is that your garden needs bees. Bees distribute pollen so your veggies and plants can grow. Apply a pesticide and it could be bye, bye bees.

Green Facts

Did you know that honey bees are essential for the production of more than 90 crops? Unfortunately, the species is being threatened by what's called colony collapse disorder. The cause of the disorder is unknown, but it might be due to viruses, mites, or pesticides.

Integrated Pest Management

So, how do you go about getting rid of pesky pests without harming the beneficial bugs? After all, you might not want to use pesticides, but you don't want unwanted pests taking over your yard, garden, and pets. Don't fret. There are environmentally friendly ways to control the pest population.

First, before you do anything, look for the underlying or root cause to your problem and try to find a solution. Simply applying even natural remedies are not a good idea if you're still not sure what is causing the problem.

The EPA recommends creating an integrated pest management (IPM) program. Although originally used in agricultural and commercial settings, IPMs are also effective for dealing with pests in residential settings.

In an IPM program, you make a series of pest management evaluations, decisions, and controls. First, for example, you need to determine whether pest control action must actually be taken. Oftentimes, at the sight of one bee, ant, or gnat, homeowners believe that it's time to apply a pesticide to the yard to nip the problem in the bud and get rid of what they believe might be hundreds more out there. In reality, however, there might be just a few pests, and pest-control application might not even be necessary.

Second, determine whether the pest is beneficial or harmful to your plants and grass. Before deciding to get rid of the bugger, it's important to identify the bug and its job in nature. You can do this by taking a picture of the bug or bringing a sample to your local pest control company, who can identify it for you. After you know what it is, you can research the species and determine whether it's something you want to eliminate from your yard.

Finally, if you determine that the pest must be eliminated, it's important to do so by using environmentally friendly methods that do not harm the environment, other insects, and plants on your property, and that are little or no risk to humans. The EPA suggests effective, but less risky, pest control first, such as disrupting pest mating or trapping them. You can also use natural remedies that do not harm those who come in contact with them and that can be tailored to a certain bug's dislikes.

Natural and Organic Pest Remedies

You can make simple insect repellants with what's in your kitchen that will do the job just as nicely, and more affordably, than commercial pesticides. For example, did you know that vampires aren't the only ones that don't like garlic? Ants aren't too fond of the pungent smell, either, and will scatter when it's around. Placing a few cloves on an infested deck, for example, will send them crawling in another direction.

Another popular and safe way to repel insects and animals from your garden is to use hot pepper wax and powder. These contain capsaicin, which is the substance that makes hot peppers hot; in low doses capsaicin repels many insects and animals. It can also be used in much higher doses to kill bugs.

Green Fertilizers

Forget about using those smelly, toxic fertilizers. Organic fertilizers are made from plants, minerals, or animals and contain natural elements that are beneficial for plants to grow. There are numerous organic fertilizers available for conditioning the soil and feeding your lawns, vegetable gardens, and a variety of plants.

Tips & Tools _____

Before using organic fertilizers, test your soil to see what nutrients it is lacking.

According to planetnatural.com, organic lawn fertilizers such as bat guano, grass clippings, alfalfa meal, fish emulsion, and worm castings will not only keep your lawn green, but will also make it healthier and more equipped to defend itself against weeds and pests.

Compost

Yard and food waste make up 24 percent of the waste that ends up in landfills, waterways, and water treatment facilities. Compost is a combination of food waste, yard trimmings, and bulking agents, such as wood chips, and is used in soil to help plants grow. The EPA states that composting can, among other things:

◆ Suppress plant diseases and pests.

◆ Reduce or eliminate the need for chemical fertilizers.

◆ Facilitate reforestation, wetlands restoration, and habitat revitalization efforts by amending contaminated, compacted, and marginal soils.

Buying Bugs

To rid their yard of certain pests, some homeowners have been known to purchase helpful bugs, such as ladybugs, and release them in their yard. However, this is not a recommended practice. Ladybugs, for example, are known to nest together by the thousands. Unfortunately, harvesting these bugs during this dormant stage can cause serious side effects to the wild-harvested ladybugs' life. In addition, the ladybugs can pick up a parasite from their current garden and bring it to yours, leaving you with yet another pest to deal with.

Grow Your Own

Growing your own fruits and vegetables might sound like a lot of work, but it's not that difficult and provides you and your family with better-tasting, healthier foods than what you'll find in most grocery stores. In addition, growing your own fruits and vegetables costs substantially less than purchasing what others have grown. And with the rising costs of fuel and food, gardening is a terrific money-saving and eco-friendly alternative. Finally, growing your own fruits and vegetables actually provides you with a sense of accomplishment and is something you and your family can work on together.

All you need is a sunny place with good soil in which to plant your vegetables or fruits.

Green Facts

Think growing and eating just your own food can't be done? Read Barbara Kingsolver's book *Animal, Vegetable, Miracle* (Harper Collins, 2007), which recounts her family's efforts to grow as much of their own food as possible for a year. It's a fun yet educational read.

The Least You Need to Know

◆ Start taking care of your house and yard the new, environmentally friendly way.

◆ Design your yard to make the best use of its native plants and grasses.

◆ You can control pests and weeds without dumping a bunch of toxic pesticides on your lawn.

◆ Grow your own fruits and vegetables and enjoy a great, healthy, pesticide-free meal with your family. It's really easy to do!

Chapter 19

Shade and Sun

In This Chapter

♦ The pros and cons of the sun

♦ Take advantage of your climate zone

♦ Trees for warmth, shade, and protection

♦ Canopies, awnings, and shutters

Abiding by a green building philosophy means that your home becomes very dependent on the sun. The sun's rays provide free warmth, natural light, and help to charge solar panels to run various systems inside your home. All of this lowers your overall energy costs and energy use. The great thing is that everyone can do it.

However, as worthwhile as the sun is, it—and other harsh weather conditions such as snow, rain, and wind—can give the exterior of your home a serious beating. And just like anything that takes a regular beating over time, exterior building materials—siding, window frames and doors, and roofing—can begin to deteriorate, which can lead to extensive damage. The sun's harsh rays can even affect the interior of your home, damaging materials and causing colors to fade on your furniture, floors, and walls.

This chapter shows you how to let the sun in while minimizing its damaging effects by utilizing creative landscaping design, such as planting trees and shrubs; creating windbreaks; and installing exterior features such as canopies, shutters, and awnings.

Trees

The Environmental Protection Agency (EPA) estimates that you can reduce your home's cooling needs by up to 50 percent with just a little help from strategically placed trees. Even planting just a few trees can bring the temperature of your home down a few degrees.

Both deciduous and evergreen trees can provide significant shade to your home. Deciduous trees are full with leaves in the summer, during which time they can block out the blazing hot sun, and lose their leaves in the fall, which then allows the sun to penetrate in the winter. Evergreen trees keep their leaves or needles year-round.

Most trees require very little in the way of maintenance, perhaps just some pruning and mulching. Make sure you consider how tall the tree will be at its maximum growth. Avoid planting a tree that when grown will hit against the roof or gutters, especially during a storm.

Tips & Tools

Plant trees so they shade paved areas, too. Light energy striking dark pavement such as asphalt is absorbed by the pavement, causing the air above the pavement to rise in temperature. If the pavement is near your home, it can then reflect the heat toward your home, causing it to heat up as well. Trees reduce the amount of light hitting the pavement and thereby reduce the temperature of the air above the surface.

Deciduous Trees

There are many styles and sizes of deciduous trees to choose from, including oak, maple, ash, beech, birch, gum, pecan, and willow. Consult your landscape architect or the local nursery to determine which ones will be best for your yard.

Where you live determines on which side of the house you should plant your trees. For example, Minnesotans are told by the Minnesota Tree Care Advisors (www.mntca. org) that, contrary to popular belief, residents should not plant a tree on the south side of their homes. According to the MNTCA, "when the sun is high in the sky at midday, the shadow of a tree falls directly under the tree and entirely misses a home to its north. In winter, however, the shadow of the same tree will fall on the house throughout most of the day. To avoid shading south windows, any trees south of the home should be located at least twice their mature height away from the house." For other areas of the country, planting deciduous trees on the south-facing side of the home is a good way to block summer sun and warm the home in wintry weather.

Evergreens

Common evergreen varieties include cypress, fir, holly, juniper, pine, and spruce. Most evergreens grow best in sunny spots, although some can tolerate being in the shade. They aren't good for all climates and typically grow best in warmer areas. If your area is prone to drought, consider a backup irrigation system to keep the trees watered.

Tips & Tools _____

Ideally, your yard will have a combination of evergreen and deciduous trees. For instance, you might plant evergreens on the north side of your home to block out the chilly winter winds and plant deciduous trees on the south side of the house to help heat and cool your home.

Windbreaks

If your climate is prone to strong or cold winds, the wind might be leaking into your home and allowing warm air to escape. This increases your home heating costs, so it's important to take measures to prevent any incoming drafts.

A windbreak—also called a shelterbelt—is a carefully planted line of trees that prevents the wind from getting through to your home.

A windbreak helps block the cold winter wind and snow.

(National Resource Conservation Service)

Where you plant the windbreak depends on several factors, including:

- The position of the sun to your home

- The tree height at its maximum growth

- The position of power lines and poles

- The height of your roof

- The view you want through the window

The more rows of trees you plant, the greater the reduction in wind hitting your home. The trees should be planted close enough together so that at their maximum growth they are not overcrowding each other or the property.

Green Facts

Windbreaks are also effective in controlling drifting snow. By strategically locating windbreaks upwind of roads and highways, you can reduce blowing snow, resulting in less snow and ice on roads. This application, known as a living snow fence, can help the community save money on snow removal.

A state such as Minnesota, for example, where an average of $100 million per year is spent on snow removal, can save a great deal of money. Minnesota once performed a cost-benefit analysis of living snow fences and found that for every dollar spent on a living snow fence, there was a $17 return. This included not only the savings in fuel, but also less economic disruption resulting from closed roads. The living snow fences also can save lives by improving winter driving conditions.

Canopies, Shutters, and Awnings

Closing your blinds inside your home during the day is somewhat effective at decreasing the amount of heat and sun that enters your home, but outside window covering—canopies, awnings, and shutters—are far more effective. Canopies and awnings are architectural coverings that protect doorways or windows. Shutters are outside window coverings that can be opened and closed.

Canopies

Awnings and canopies extend the life of doors and windows by protecting them from harsh weather. The difference between them is that canopies tend to be permanently installed whereas awnings can be fixed or retractable—either manually or electronically—and even removed in winter or before potentially dangerous weather. Both can be made of metal or fabric. Metal units are highly durable, but can be limited in colors. Fabric units require cleaning, but they are available in a wide variety of shapes and sizes.

When an air conditioner is installed in a window with an awning, energy usage can be reduced by as much as 26 percent in warm climates and 33 percent in cool climates compared to homes with completely unshaded windows, according to a study by the Center for Sustainable Building Research at the University of Minnesota and the Professional Awning Manufacturers Association. This reduced energy usage occurs because awnings prevent solar radiation from penetrating through windows, which accounts for nearly 20 percent of the load on an air conditioner.

The size of the awning you choose will depend on its location. South-facing windows need smaller awnings than west- or east-facing windows to account for the angle of the rising and setting sun.

For maximum benefit, choose a light-colored, water repellent unit that has been treated to resist mildew and fading.

Green Facts

The U.S. Department of Energy states that awnings can reduce solar heat gain in the summer by up to 65 percent on south-facing windows and 77 percent on west-facing windows.

Tips & Tools

Insulated interior draperies and curtains prevent the penetration of heat, too. Venetian blinds can also cool your home, especially those coated with finishes that reflect the sun's heat.

Awnings can drastically reduce cooling costs.

(Professional Awning Manufacturers Association)

Shutters

Shutters are installed on the exterior of the window and are made of wood or metal; they are either solid or slatted. The shutters can be opened or closed to control the amount of sunlight entering the window. Consider plantation-style shutters, a shutter commonly used in the nineteenth-century American South, which feature wider, movable louvers.

Storm shutters are a great way of protecting your home from extremely high winds and their accompanying debris, especially if you live in an area prone to hurricanes. Permanent storm shutters are usually made of aluminum or steel and are attached to a building in a way in which they can be closed quickly in advance of a storm. Rolldown storm shutters are installed above the window and lowered when necessary, especially during a bad storm or hurricane season. Manually operated and motor-operated models are also available. They can withstand impacts from flying debris and winds up to 140 miles per hour or more.

Look for shutter models that meet the wind load and impact standards established for your area. These standards can be obtained from your local building department. If you have any questions about the strength of a specific model, check with the manufacturer.

Roof Gardens

As you already know, plants can be used to protect your home from the wind and sun, provide oxygen, and are the only natural things on the planet that filter and eliminate carbon dioxide. But not everyone is fortunate enough to have a lush, large piece of property to fill with plants. If you have a home in the city, you're probably severely limited on landscaping space, but you might still want to maximize your energy and cooling ability. To do so, consider a roof garden.

A roof garden is a unique way to create beauty in an unused space while also cooling your home, but there are several technicalities to consider before embarking on such an ambitious project.

While theoretically any roof surface can be greened—even sloped or curved roofs can support a layer of sod or wildflowers—it's important to use lightweight and recycled materials, lightweight soil that doesn't exert pressure on the roof of your home, and plants that won't root through the roof and eventually harm it. Also, because there is no such thing as a maintenance-free roof garden, you must have a method of draining excess water and the ability to add water during a dry spell. If your home isn't designed with a drainage system, one needs to be built, which could be costly. For a project of this nature, it's best to seek the help of a professional landscape architect, who will consider the roof's age, shape, and condition as well as your budget and wishes.

This green roof on a park building in Coralville, Iowa, also restores the aesthetic value of urban open space. This concept can be replicated on a private home.

(USDA)

What's Your Climate Zone?

Overall, the landscaping strategies you use to shade your home will depend on the area of the country in which you live. The U.S. Department of Energy divides the United States into four approximate climatic regions: temperate, hot-arid, hot-humid, and cool.

If you live in a hot-arid state, such as Florida, it is recommended that you do what you can to channel summer breezes toward your home, maximize summer shade with trees that still allows penetration of the sun at a lower angle in the winter time, and avoid planting flower beds that need frequent watering.

If you live in a climate area like New York, classified as a temperate region, you should install landscaping strategies that maximize the warming effects of the sun in the winter while deflecting winter winds and funneling summer breezes.

If you live in a hot-arid region such as Las Vegas, you should provide shading techniques for your home that cool roofs, walls, and windows while allowing summer winds in.

In cooler regions, such as Wisconsin, you should use dense windbreaks to protect the home from bitter winter winds while allowing the winter sun to reach your windows on the south side of your home. In the summer, you want to shade south and west windows and walls from the direct summer sun.

Regardless of your regional climate, you might have your own microclimate within your area. This means that, depending on the exact position of your home, you might have even more sun, shade, wind, rain, snow, moisture, and/or dryness than your neighbors and average local conditions. For instance, if your home was built on a sunny southern slope, it might have a warm microclimate even if you live in a cool region. Or, if you live in a hot-humid region, the ample number of trees that shade your home may provide a breezy, comfortable microclimate. A nearby lake or pond might increase your home's humidity or decrease its air temperature.

> **Green Facts**
>
> The net cooling effect of a young, healthy tree is equivalent to 10 room-sized air conditioners operating 20 hours a day.

The Least You Need to Know

- ◆ Start with smaller changes to keep the heat out—such as caulking windows—before investing in more costly landscaping changes.

- ◆ Watch how your property works—see how the sun hits it and how the snow drifts. There might be additional green landscaping measures you can take after you become more familiar with your property.

- ◆ Extra roofing space can be used to plant a roof garden that will cool your property.

- ◆ Your location will determine which trees and plants you use and where to plant them. What's good for New York might not be good for Tennessee. Know your region.

Chapter 20

Let It Rain!

In This Chapter

- ◆ Pollution-free watersheds
- ◆ Eco-friendly pavers
- ◆ How to xeriscape your lawn
- ◆ Green irrigation technique

All living things need water to survive, and rain brings that water. Unfortunately, the rain picks up toxins along the way, carrying them to storm drains and releasing them right into our *watersheds* and then into streams, rivers, and oceans.

Protecting the Watershed

One of the easiest ways to prevent pollutants from entering our waterways is to make some simple changes during the building, remodeling, and caring for your home, including the following:

def•i•ni•tion

A **watershed** is an area of land where all the water around it drains to one location—a nearby creek, stream, river, lake, or ocean.

Tips & Tools

Next time you mow, leave the grass clippings on the lawn. According to the EPA, the grass will decompose and feed your soil. This technique is recommended if you mow your lawn never more than 2 to 3 inches tall.

♦ Properly dispose of paints or oils. Don't pour them—or any other litter—down your drain.

♦ Be sure to use environmentally safe cleaning and household products.

♦ Pick up after Fido. Don't let his droppings go down the sewer. Dispose of them properly.

♦ Compost. According to www.recycleworks.org, yard and food waste make up 30 percent of the waste stream. Composting your kitchen and yard trimmings helps divert that waste from the landfill, waterways, and water treatment facilities. Composting is an effective way of reducing erosion, and recycling yard clippings and food scraps helps create a rich garden soil. For step-by-step information on composting, visit recycleworks.org.

Permeable Pavements

Streets, walkways, and driveways are typically made of asphalt or cement—materials that can prevent water from penetrating into the ground beneath. When rain hits pavement, it either evaporates, which is wasteful because the soil cannot benefit from the rain's nutrients, or it runs into the drainage system, dragging chemicals and other toxins with it. Installing permeable pavements is an effective means of controlling stormwater runoff and reducing the manmade effects of pollution.

Permeable paving, which is also called pervious paving or porous pavement, prevents the water from evaporating or being dragged down the sewer drain. Instead, the water moves through cracks in the pavement material and slides into the soil. Permeable pavements can be made from a variety of materials, including individual paving blocks or cobble stones, plastic systems that are filled with sand or gravel, clay bricks, or a more porous asphalt/cement mix. Clay brick is produced in many local regions, keeping local transportation costs—and greenhouse emissions—down. Grass pavers have large areas between the pavers where grass can grow. Gravel pavers use gravel between the pavers. Permeable pavers can be used in walkways and driveways.

Another advantage of permeable pavers is that they can be individually removed by hand and replaced without disturbing the entire walkway.

Permeable systems using interlocking concrete pavers have been used in Germany and elsewhere in Europe since the late 1980s and in North America since 1992, according to the Interlocking Concrete Pavement Institute. Pervious concrete pavement was first used in Florida in the early 1970s, and porous asphalt emerged at the same time. Permeable pavement systems have been successfully used in a variety of soils and climates, and research has demonstrated the ability of all permeable pavements to significantly reduce urban runoff.

> **Green Facts**
>
> To reduce stormwater runoff, some cities have limited the amount of impervious material that can be used in both residential and commercial settings.

If your home already has an asphalt driveway, do not dig it up just to install permeable pavement. Instead, wait until the driveway needs replacing and then upgrade. In the meantime, consider installing rain barrels, designing a rain garden, or xeriscaping.

What might look like an ordinary brick walkway is really a clay brick paver walkway. Look closely; you'll see spaces between the pavers that allow the water to seep through into the soil. This is the StormPave product from Pine Hall Brick.

(www.pinehallbrick.com).

Xeriscaping Made Simple

The term *xeriscape* means dry landscape. It was coined a little more than a quarter century ago, and the idea is simple: choose plants for your yard that have a low water tolerance, are well-suited to your local climate, and that require less maintenance. Such a landscape requires less irrigation and therefore produces less runoff, meaning that less pollution is added to our water supply.

According to the American Society of Landscape Architects (ASLA), the average American uses 200 gallons of water per day watering her lawn and plants. Just drive around any neighborhood on a given summer afternoon and count how many sprinklers are running! By reducing the amount of water you use to take care of your landscape and garden, you can lower your overall water consumption by at least 50 percent and help save the environment, and money.

Xeriscaping is not receiving quite the widespread acceptance that it deserves just yet, but it's a valuable green landscaping concept. It's an especially valuable idea for areas such as the Southwest that are prone to drought. Xeriscaping can be done on existing landscapes if you are remodeling or can be incorporated into your design plan when building a new home.

However, xeriscaping doesn't mean you'll eliminate watering your lawn completely. It means you water efficiently by determining exactly how much water each plant needs and grouping plants together according to these needs (also called *hydrozoning*).

Irrigation Information

Your lawn and garden are going to need water to survive, but the question is how much. Each part of a landscape—flowers, lawn, and gardens—requires different watering treatments for optimum growth. However, most homeowners simply drag out their garden hoses or run the sprinklers for hours. What they don't realize is that such practices are a waste of time and water.

Tips & Tools

Cut back on greenhouse emissions by using a manual mower, rather than an electric or gas-powered mower, to cut your grass. It will help to prevent water and air pollution.

If you already have an existing landscape that you either can't or don't want to convert to a xeriscape, you can install an irrigation system that harvests rainwater in a rain barrel and applies it to your lawn (for more on this, review Chapter 15). Rainwater is free. You can have an irrigation system installed that can be set to water your garden and lawn with the exact amount of water it needs.

Drip and bubbler systems are among the most popular irrigation systems:

- **Drip systems** are mainly used for flowers that can be harmed if sprayed directly, such as roses. The piping lays on top of the ground and drips moisture into the soil. With these systems, the homeowner programs which day to water and how much to water.

- **Bubbler systems** are primarily for vegetable gardens because they flood the area. You can get spray heads for these watering systems, too, such as a misty gentle sprayer for flowers and rotary shooters for large areas such as lawns. Manual and automatic systems with sensors and timers are available.

Other things to consider when installing an irrigation system are the soil condition, the elevation of the property, and which areas do and don't have shade. A low spot in the lawn might require less watering because the water drains down from the high spots. If your house has a narrow side yard that needs watering, it might require special directional heads so the water doesn't hit the house.

Irrigation systems can be installed by professionals with very little disruption to your lawn. Installers make a small cut in the lawn and insert the piping into the ground. If there are obstructions during the installation or you have difficult terrain, the process could take a little longer.

Wasteful Watering Habits

Don't just water your lawn out of habit. If Mother Nature has poured a few inches of rain onto your lawn, you might not need to water it at all this week. To determine how much rain has fallen, place a measuring cup in the yard and check it daily. If you have to water, do so with a slow sprinkle early in the morning so the midday sun doesn't evaporate the water before it has had a chance to soak into the soil.

Mulching helps your flower beds and gardens retain moisture and also helps prevent erosion. You can make mulch on your own by using chipped or shredded wood waste, grass clippings, or dry leaves. Distribute the mulch around the base of your plants to prevent weed growth. Mulch also helps regulate the temperature of the soil and feed the soil.

Hard Hat Area

Do you have a tendency to water your driveway, nearby sidewalks, and the side of the house and car while you're watering your lawn? That's a serious waste of resources. Be sure to set your sprinklers to point in the right direction.

Green Facts

The American Society of Landscape Architects (ASLA), The University of Texas at Austin's Lady Bird Johnson Wildflower Center, and the United States Botanic Garden are developing a rating system for sustainable landscape design called the Sustainable Sites Initiative. It will measure the sustainability of designed landscapes of all types, including residential landscapes.

Be sure you leave some space around the base of each plant and resist creating mulch mounds around plants and trees.

Go with the Flow

When designing your home and landscape, pay attention to the direction water will flow. It's important to keep water flowing away from your home into proper drainage systems to prevent damage to its foundation. However, you do not want the water to flow into areas that can lead to erosion. One ideal green landscaping solution is to redirect stormwater away from your property into rain barrels.

Water that flows out of the gutters and off the roof should flow down and away from your property. Water can take its toll on the outside of your home as much as the inside. Your backyard, driveway, and landscaping are susceptible to damage from heavy rain and snow runoff. Proper drainage can prevent your driveway or landscaping from washing away.

The number one thing to remember when planning for proper drainage is the law of gravity. Make sure all slopes lead away from the foundation of your house and driveway into a system where you can reuse the water.

Erosion

When something erodes, it breaks down—a process called denudation. Some erosion is part of nature's slow, natural landscaping change. For example, sea erosion occurs when waves crash against the rocks, loosening them and breaking them down. When it's windy, the wind can lift rocks, pebbles, and sand and move them to another location, changing the area's landscape. But other erosion can be caused by human activity.

Check with your state before breaking ground on your new home to determine your area's erosion and sedimentation control laws. These laws set standards for anyone conducting an activity that fills, displaces, or exposes earthen materials. Erosion control measures must be in place before breaking ground on a home.

Building a home contributes to erosion. In essence, you're breaking apart a plot of land, moving its contents around, and removing the excess from the property, oftentimes transporting it to another location. Smart green building calls for consideration of the land before you even break ground. It's important to review the property and note the existing landscape. Your goal is to keep it as close to its natural state as possible.

Tips & Tools

One great tip from www. wncgreenbuilding.com is to take a picture of the existing conditions before you begin excavating. Take note of the placement of trees and shrubs, etc. Strive to return cleared areas to their natural conditions. Talk to your builder about returning the soil that has been dug up back to the area. If that's not possible, avoid disposing of it near roads, streams, rivers, and storm drains.

The Least You Need to Know

♦ Do what you can to remove pollutants from the stormwater system.

♦ You have probably been watering your lawn and garden incorrectly for years. Provide proper irrigation and save water and energy.

♦ Consider landscaping with plants that need little to no water at all.

♦ Design your landscape to keep water flowing away from your house and its foundation.

Chapter 21

Pools, Hot Tubs, Fencing, and More

In This Chapter

- ◆ Environmentally friendlier pools and hot tubs
- ◆ Outdoor lighting
- ◆ Functional and eco-friendly fencing
- ◆ Green decking
- ◆ The ABCs of BBQs and other extras

Just a few more finishing touches and your Home Sweet Green Home will finally be complete! All you need to do is add eco-friendly versions of your favorite outdoor features—your pool, hot tub, barbecue, fencing, and decking. If you already own these items and they are in need of upgrading, go ahead and replace them with more sustainable, eco-friendly or energy-efficient models. And even though it might not appear that barbecues and hot tubs can be green, there are steps you can take to make them less harmful to the environment so you and your family can enjoy your outdoor space.

Pools and Hot Tubs

They take thousands of gallons of water to fill, hours of energy to run the pumps and filtration systems, and many bottles of chemicals to keep clean, but when summer heats up, taking a dip in a cool pool is a luxury many homeowners can't live without. And at the end of a long, hard day, sitting in the hot tub is a great way to relax your muscles and enjoy some time with family and friends.

Fortunately, today you have ways to make your pool and spa easier on your budget and the environment by using less water, saving electricity, and being practically chemical-free.

When it comes to owning an environmentally friendly pool or spa, it is more important to consider how water efficient the pool is than what it is made of.

Hard Hat Area

Find out your zoning laws from your local building department. These laws can determine the type and size of pool you can build on your property.

For a truly green pool, you can follow the lead of the Europeans and install a natural swimming pool. These chemical-free pools are built in the ground (looking a bit like a pond, with frogs, too!) and use a filtration system and plants around the edging to keep the water clean and safe for swimming.

Although it's a "very green" thing to do, building a natural pool isn't for everyone and can be very difficult to maintain, so you might consider opting for a more traditional approach—a regular aboveground or in-ground pool—and use chemical free cleaners and sanitizers to maintain it.

Because aboveground pools require minimal, if any, digging, they are more affordable than their in-ground counterparts. An aboveground swimming pool can start at $3,000, while an in-ground pool can start at $10,000 and run much higher. When considering the cost of a pool or hot tub, keep in mind that they will increase your electric and water bills.

Abovegrounds come in different shapes, depths, and sizes. They are assembled with a metal frame and a vinyl liner and can also be made of plastics and, sometimes, wood.

In-ground pools are a permanent fixture to your property and can improve your home's overall value. You can choose from a fiberglass, cement, or gunite pool, which is the most popular type of pool material in the United States. Gunite is a combination of cement and sand that is sprayed over a mesh grid. Like aboveground pools, in-grounds come in many shapes and can even be custom built.

A hot tub is like a huge bathtub with heated water and jets that create whirlpool action. Most are made of acrylic, fiberglass, or wood. Hot tubs can start at $3,000 depending on the size and run up to $10,000.

Eco-Friendly Pumping and Filtering

You really don't have a lot of choice on greening the structure of your pool or hot tub, but you can work on reducing your pool's impact on the environment. When installing a pool or spa, be sure to install energy-efficient filters and pumps. Make sure the spa is thoroughly insulated with full-foam, closed-cell insulation to hold the heat in and reduce the energy use.

When it comes to pumps, think smaller. A big pool doesn't necessarily need a big pump. The bigger the pump, the greater its energy use and, in turn, the bigger dent to your wallet. One study showed that using smaller and higher-efficiency pumps, and by operating the pumps for less time each day, pool owners saved as much as 75 percent on their energy bill. The right-size pump depends on what size pool you own, so ask your local pool retailer for advice.

Pools and spas lose water every day due to evaporation. How much water a pool loses depends on the humidity, the water temperature, and the wind. To reduce evaporation, you can add a smaller windbreak with trees or shrubs near the pool or spa. Be sure, however, that these trees or shrubs do not block the sun.

Heating and Filtering

Use the sun's warmth and energy—with solar covers, pool heaters, and pumps—to run the pool and spa more efficiently and for much less money.

Solar pool and spa systems use a small solar, or photovoltaic (PV), cell to charge a battery. After being charged all day by the sun, the battery provides the electricity to heat the system for approximately 8 to 10 hours in the summer and sometimes less in the winter, when the sun goes down. Solar covers sit on top of the pool when it's not in use and keep the water at a warmer temperature. Solar pool heaters heat the water from the filter in an energy collector and then send it back to the pool.

Tips & Tools

If you have already installed solar panels on your roof, you can coordinate these panels to heat your pool water as well.

Traditionally, hot tubs have been heated using a natural gas or electric heater, but solar hot water heaters are available for hot tubs, too. Spa covers can also reduce much of the water lost from evaporation.

To keep a pool running or a spa clean and filtered around the clock takes quite a bit of energy—for example, many pool owners are told to run the pool filter from 8 to 12 hours per day. However, studies have shown that running the filter for only 6 hours per day really doesn't change the quality of the water and can shave 60 percent off the electric bill.

To save more money and energy, set the pool and spa systems to run during nonpeak hours, when the electricity is typically cheaper.

More Energy- and Water-Saving Tips

The Association of Pool and Spa Professionals offer more tips to keeping your pool and/or spa water healthy and pristine:

- **Cover up**—A properly maintained spa or pool cover can reduce evaporation and water waste by 95 percent. A floating cover under the spa cover will prevent additional evaporation and retain heat. For maximum effectiveness, replace spa covers every three years.

- **Be vigilant**—Fix any leaks or service problems as they occur. Don't waste water by letting it leak away.

- **Maintain your spa**—Proper spa maintenance will greatly increase the time between draining and refilling. Cleaning and replacing filters according to the manufacturer's directions will extend spa cleanliness.

- **Use a battery-operated automatic pool cleaner regularly to clean the water.**

- **Replace your aging sand or DE filtering system**—Instead, use a cartridge filter that does not need to be removed to be cleaned on a regular basis.

- **Remove debris that blows in from trees and landscaping**—Scoop it out immediately so it doesn't get into your filter or other systems.

- **Rinse bathing suits out with clear water, rather than washing them with soap**—Soap powder residue is a major contributor to poor water quality in pools and spas.

- **If it's clean, don't drain it**—Drain spas and pools only when you have a water quality problem. Water needs to be changed in a spa only two to three times a year if you maintain your spa properly and it incorporates new water-cleaning technology. Pools need to be completely drained only if repairs require it.

◆ **Reuse**—When you do drain your spa, let it sit open for 48 to 72 hours with no new chemicals added, and then use the water on garden plants or ask your retailer about products that neutralize chemicals. To prevent unsupervised use, ensure that proper safety barriers are in place any time the spa safety cover is removed.

◆ **Recycle**—Use captured rainwater to replace water lost to evaporation in spas and pools.

◆ **Upgrade**—Spas manufactured in the last five years have new-technology cleaning systems that keep the water clean much longer—up to six months without refilling. This new technology is also available for some older models. Your spa dealer can advise you whether you can add this technology to your spa.

◆ **Use a dark-colored liner**—It will heat up the water and maintain the temperature longer.

Chemical-Free Zone

Spas and pools use many chemicals—especially chlorine and algeacides—to keep the water sparkling clean and algae-free and to prevent the corrosion or staining of the pool's equipment. However, these chemicals can have an adverse effect on your health and on the environment. Chlorine, for example, can irritate your eyes, skin, and lungs. When the chemically treated water splashes onto the grass, it can taint your landscape and become part of stormwater runoff.

But there are ways to make your pool and spa chemical-free. One method, electronic ionization technology, sanitizes pools without using chlorine and other chemicals. Created by NASA in the 1960s, today's electronic ionization technology systems release copper and silver ions in the water. These ions destroy bacteria and algae, and then the pool filter takes over and removes them from the pool. Other manufacturers have developed chemical-free cleaners as well.

Your hot tub has the ability to plug in an ozonator, an electrical device that produces ozone, which is then used as a water sanitizer. An ozonator eliminates the need for chlorine and other chemicals. They are also more powerful than regular sanitizers and last longer than regular chemicals. There is a question, however, as to the negative health effects of bromate, a chemical the ozonator produces in its place.

Pool and Spa Living featured an efficient hot tub that meets green guidelines from the National Association of Home Builders. Featured in the National Homebuilder Mainstream GreenHome in Raleigh, North Carolina, it was installed with insulation that reduces energy use by 50 percent compared to other typical spas. It uses unheated rainwater from a rainwater collection system to fill it; and the jets, pumps, heater, and other equipment are run using solar electricity generated by photovoltaic roofing tiles that resemble slate shingles. The spa is chemical-free, using chlorine-free sanitizers to keep the water crystal clear.

Also, becoming more popular are saltwater pools, equipped with a special filtering system. The salt is at levels that are hardly noticeable. Talk to a pool expert if you are interested.

Fencing

Robert Frost once said, "Good fences make good neighbors," but the right fence also makes a positive environmental statement, so it's important to choose eco-friendly materials. Fences are usually built from aluminum, vinyl, cement, bamboo, brick, stone, but by far the most popular type of fencing material is wood, which can be both renewable and sustainable.

According to the American Fence Association, whitewood—pine, spruce, and fir—is the most popular type of fencing wood in the United States and Canada. In the West, it's western red cedar and redwood. In the upper border, it's northern white cedar; in the Midwest and Southeast, it's southern yellow pine.

If you use pressure-treated wood—which preserves the wood and prevents rotting—make sure you know what it's been treated with. At one time, the most common chemical used in pressure-treated wood was chromated copper arsenate (CCA); this chemical contains arsenic, which can be toxic to the environment and to the user when the wood is burned. The EPA worked with pesticide manufacturers to voluntarily phase out CCA use for wood products around homes and in children's play areas.

Today, many new chemicals for treating wood are less toxic to the environment and to the user, including alkaline copper quaternary (ACQ), copper azole (CA), and micronized copper quaternary (MCQ). However, it is recommended that when handling any kind of treated wood products, you should cover your nose, mouth, and hands. Also ACQ needs to use special fasteners and hardware because the chemicals can deteriorate the standard fasteners. Although it contains chemicals, the ACQ product is low-toxicity, very durable, and resists rot.

As we mentioned earlier in the book, items made with vinyl have become popular because of their affordability and durability. Vinyl fencing comes in a variety of styles and colors and doesn't show scratches. It is treated to protect from ultraviolet rays and is one of the most popular types of fencing used today. However, there is a serious health concern regarding traditional vinyl. Even though some vinyl fencing contains recycled materials and can be recycled, it is best to avoid vinyl products; non-pressure-treated wood is the better choice.

Living Walls

Another fencing option to keep unwanted intruders off your property and provide some privacy is a living wall fence, which is a "fence" made of shrubbery, plants, or trees. The difference between a living wall fence and a windbreak is that you have more tree options to choose from for your living wall fence since they are not being used to protect your property against winds.

You can still use evergreen trees, which are tall enough to provide adequate privacy for larger yards. Hedges can work well in smaller yards, or a combination of both is suitable. However, avoid deciduous plants whose leaves can fall off each season and leave you with visible gaps in your fencing.

Bamboo is another great material for fencing and it's become more popular. Many colors, thickness, and styles of bamboo fencing are available, For example, Tonkin, a creamy white bamboo, is imported from China, while Taiwan bamboo actually grows in the United States and is very common fencing material. Tam Vong is a Vietnamese bamboo that resists splitting and holds up well to the forces of Mother Nature. Black bamboo is also a strong bamboo with a rich dark color, but it is in high demand and a bit pricier. Although some bamboo is not grown in the United States, you need to weigh the economic cost of transporting the wood versus the fact that bamboo is a healthier choice for the environment.

Before proceeding with any fencing project, check your community's building and zoning codes. Many codes specify a maximum fence height, the distance that you can build from your property line and the street, and even limit the materials you can use.

Hard Hat Area

Call before you dig! For safety purposes, call your local utilities office before you dig to prevent power outages or service interruption!

Step Up to Your Deck

Decks are great places for you and your family and friends to relax, enjoy a barbecue, and take in the great outdoors. But you should consider several things when building a green deck. Most importantly, decks must be constructed with proper sustainable wood that is impervious to moisture and insects, so they don't rot or decay. They should also be constructed properly so they do not cause water or structural damage to your home.

If you like the beautiful, rich look of a wood deck, select wood that has been certified by the Forest Stewardship Council (FSC), which means it has been harvested from sustainable managed forests. The Council also suggests engineered wood products that use smaller trees. Traditionally, redwood (especially Brazilian found in South America and Brazil) and cedar wood were popular choices for their durability and resistance to insects, but they aren't as abundant as they once were.

Other new tropical wood choices include the following:

◆ **Ipe** (pronounced *ee-pay*) is known by many names, including Brazilian Walnut and Ironwood. It is a dense, hard wood that is very resistant to insects. It doesn't need treatment, but be forewarned that the color changes with time. Ipe wood has been given the highest, Class A fire rating, the same rating given to concrete and steel.

◆ **Cambara** is wood found in Central and South America and has good resistance to both decay and dry wood insects. Meranti, which comes from the Philippines and Southeast Asia, is as strong as Ipe but not as bug-resistant.

If you are looking for a wood alternative, try composite decking—a combination of plastic and wood fibers. It requires less maintenance than wood, has a longer life span, can be painted and stained, and is impermeable to rot and insects. Recycled plastic decking can be used as well, but make sure the decking is made completely of recycled plastic.

Green Facts

Trex is one such brand of wood-alternative decking. The company turns millions of pounds of recycled and reclaimed plastic and waste—mostly from recovered plastic grocery bags, plastic film, and waste wood fiber—into decking. Trex says it purchases approximately 300 million pounds of used polyethylene and an equal amount of hard-wood sawdust each year, materials that would normally end up in a landfill. It also claims to recycle more than 1.3 billion grocery bags annually.

The construction of the deck is just as important as the decking materials. Without attaching the deck to the home properly, water can leak into the home and cause damage from mold and decay. Discuss this with your builder.

Light the Way: Outdoor Lighting

Good outdoor lighting can achieve several goals. It can …

♦ Deter intruders.

♦ Prevent falls and accidents.

♦ Create beautiful aesthetic value on your property.

A variety of outdoor lighting techniques can soften, highlight, and create curb appeal. For example, pathway lights can serve as architectural accents during the day and create a charming ambience at night. Uplighting highlights certain aspects of the landscape, perhaps your property's trees or architectural highlights. Accent lighting shows off flowers or shrubs. Spotlighting shows off particular features, such as a statue or flag.

You do not need underground wires or electricity to light up your landscape. Instead, install solar lighting fixtures that provide sufficient light to mark entrances and accent your walkways and steps. Using solar lighting saves energy and money.

The key to good solar lighting depends on where you put the panel. The panel must be in a place where it will receive adequate sunlight during the day. Keep all lighting away from awnings, fencing, and trees.

Another outdoor lighting option is infrared motion detectors (IMDs), which turn on the lights when they detect movement. They are programmed to react to a person's body heat, and switch on when motion is detected (up to 70 feet away) in a monitored area. This makes them far more energy efficient than lights that stay on all night.

The ABCs of BBQs

Grilling is one of our most treasured outdoor activities. A 2007 study conducted by the Hearth, Patio & Barbecue Association (HPBA) showed that 77 percent of all U.S. households own a grill or smoker.

Grilling with charcoal briquettes or lump charcoal adds great flavor, but burning charcoal releases toxins into the air. Although lump charcoal produces far less ash than the briquettes, it still isn't the best grilling option.

Tips & Tools _____

The Rainforest Alliance Smartwood program evaluates forest product operations that reclaim or use reclaimed, recycled, and/or salvaged wood materials. They have certified Char-Broil products, an additive-free briquette. You can find more information on this at www.originalcharcoal.com.

Using natural gas is probably the cheapest and most energy-efficient way to barbecue. Electric grills are safe—no open flames, no charcoal, no starter fluids to use—but they use energy. Pellet grills, which use small wood pellets in a variety of flavors, are becoming increasingly more popular. They require electricity to run, but the wood pellet fuel is made from recycled sawdust, making it a green fuel.

If you use a charcoal grill, you can still be a greener griller by forgoing the use of lighter fluid. Instead, use a chimney starter to light your charcoal. These handy devices eliminate the need for lighter fluid and actually heat the coals more quickly, which reduces their burn.

A chimney starter.

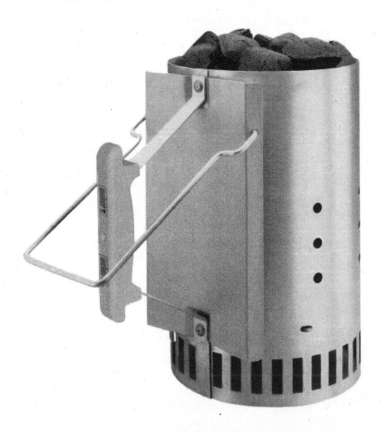

Play Structures

Don't forget about the kids! Having an open grassy area for children to run and play in is a must for any family. And play structures—swings, slides, ropes, and so on—are a great way to keep them exercising and occupied. Until 2001, most playground equipment included toxic CCA preservatives. Fortunately, wood treated with CCA is banned for use in children's play structures, and companies now make playground equipment that uses 100 percent recycled plastic or recycled wood.

A Few Extras: Keeping Warm

Want to stay warm while you're outside on a nice cool night? Hold off roasting chestnuts on an open fire. Although wood-burning pits are becoming more and more popular with homeowners, it's important to know that some are rated for burning standard firewood only, while others can also burn pressed wood or firelogs (such as Duraflame), which are made from recycled sawdust and petroleum wax. Not all fire pits are rated to burn firelogs.

A better way to keep your tootsies warm is to use an outdoor heater. A tabletop or freestanding propane heater emits carbon dioxide and other gases, but it is not as harsh on the air as a wood-burning pit.

The Least You Need to Know

- To help keep your spa heated, place it in a part of the backyard that gets direct sunlight for most of the day.

- Choose the smallest pump and the largest filter for the pool to maximize its efficiency.

- Fencing offers privacy and can also act as a wind barrier. Fences should be made of certified sustainable wood.

- You can still grill, just weigh the pros and cons of each style of grill and its environmental impact.

- Outdoor firepits are a great way to stay warm, but be sure to use firelogs that are made of recyclable materials.

Chapter 22

It Can Be Done

In This Chapter

- ◆ Follow the leader
- ◆ It can be done
- ◆ Sustainable communities
- ◆ Ed Begley Jr.'s green building philosophy

Green living isn't a trend, it's a way of life.

Throughout this book you've seen examples of people who have built or remodeled green homes.

We couldn't end this book without showing you even more examples of great green building concepts and homes. There are so many that this chapter could be a book in itself, but we've chosen a few we hope will inspire you and demonstrate that no matter where you live, you, too, can have a beautiful, healthy green home.

This chapter features builders who are determined to build with the future of the environment and the health of their residents in mind.

Green Communities

You already know how much of an impact you and your family can have by going green. Just imagine what can happen when an entire community of homeowners works together to help save precious resources! Many builders have developed sustainable communities, which are planned, built, or modified to promote sustainable living.

Want to get an idea of what it's like to live in a green community? Take a trip to Findhom Foundation community, an eco-village located on the west coast of Scotland. It has 300 residents and 90 ecological structures, including gardens, wind turbines, and more (www.findhom.org). For a green community a little closer to home, visit The Milkweed Mercantile, located at Dancing Rabbit Ecovillage in Rutledge, Missouri. It is housed in a spacious two-story straw bale, solar- and wind-powered building.

This section highlights some other green communities that are worth a visit.

Raleigh's Chavis Heights Community

Advanced Energy, a Raleigh-based nonprofit, completed a large-scale, multifamily, mixed-income community in North Carolina to achieve ENERGY STAR certification. The Chavis Heights development, located in downtown Raleigh, is 168 units of affordable housing including town homes, condominiums (half of which are handicapped-accessible), and a senior center.

These homes are at least 15 percent more energy efficient than homes built to the 2004 International Residential Code (IRC) and include additional energy-saving features that typically make them 20 to 30 percent more efficient than standard homes. Energy-saving features at Chavis Heights include tight and properly insulated building shells, sealed and tested duct systems, high-efficiency windows, fresh-air ventilation, compact fluorescent lighting, and on-demand water heaters in the senior center. Residents can expect to save up to 15 percent on their energy bills.

DC's Jefferson at Half Street

JPI East, a division of JPI in Irving, Texas, is developing a multifamily rental community in Washington, D.C., to have the LEED silver certification for new construction. Known as Jefferson at Half Street, the development will be a 419-unit luxury multifamily community that will include 12,000 square feet of retail space facing Half Street, a popular retail destination in the city.

To achieve the U.S. Green Building Council's LEED silver certification, JPI met a number of requirements, including low-flow bathroom fixtures, ENERGY STAR appliances and programmable thermostats, energy-efficient heating and cooling systems (40 to 50 percent energy savings), low-E glass windows, air filters, eco-friendly paints and carpets, and a green roof. The project is part of Capitol Yards, JPI's master-planned development situated between the U.S. Capitol and the new Washington Nationals' ballpark.

Oakland Park, Florida

Located near Orlando, Florida, Oakland Park has been certified as "green" by the Florida Green Building Coalition (FGBC), an independent, third-party authority. All 750 homes will be certified green. Oakland Park is being developed on a bluff overlooking the shore of Lake Apopka, Florida's fourth-largest lake. Lake Apopka was polluted by decades of agricultural runoff, but it is now being restored. Oakland Park is participating in that project with a shoreline restoration project.

Oakland Park is a traditional neighborhood design community with walkable streets. The West Orange Trail, a 22-mile trail, runs through the property. Downtown Winter Garden, where many buildings date back to the early 1900s, is a short bike ride away. For more information, visit www.oaklandpark1844.com.

From Tragedy to Triumph: Greensburg, Kansas

On May 4, 2007, the community of Greensburg, Kansas, was hit by a massive 2-mile-wide EF5 tornado at speeds of 205 mph. The tornado killed 12 residents and destroyed more than 95 percent of the homes and businesses in the town. Instead of letting this tragedy destroy them, townspeople used it as an opportunity to rebuild. The Greensburg City Council approved a resolution that all city building projects will be rebuilt to LEED platinum level standards.

The city arranged for the trees that didn't survive the storm to be removed and made into useful lumber. One portable sawmill company brought in equipment to process the tree trunks into lumber that was reused in buildings, benches, and more.

The Discovery Channel filmed a series about Greensburg that aired on its new network, Planet Green.

> **Green Facts**
>
> Levittown, New York, set a goal to become America's most energy-efficient suburb. Track its progress on its website: www.greenlevittown.com.

Cherry Hill, New Jersey

The town of Cherry Hill rolled out a 10-point environmental plan that includes switching municipality vehicles to hybrid, placing solar panels on city buildings, switching to energy-saving lightbulbs, and implementing the RecycleBank rewards program throughout the city.

Green Facts

RecycleBank is a rewards program that motivates households and communities to recycle by rewarding recycling participation with RecycleBank Points that are redeemable with more than 400 national and local RecycleBank reward partners (such as Coca-Cola, Kraft Foods, CVS Pharmacy, Target, and IKEA). RecycleBank's main goal is to keep recyclables out of landfills, and so far, in the 75 communities in New York, New Jersey, Connecticut, Delaware, Pennsylvania, Massachusetts, and Nebraska where the program has been implemented, it has been a great success. In one week, they saw a 134 percent increase in recycling rates.

RecycleBank motivates households and communities to recycle by rewarding RecycleBank Points to households for their recycling efforts. Every household receives a cart embedded with a radio frequency identification (RFID) chip. Through the single-stream recycling process (no need to separate recyclables), all materials are placed into a cart for curbside pick-up. Recycling trucks retrofitted with RecycleBank technology read the RFID chip and record the amount of household recycles. The weight and participation is then translated into RecycleBank Points, which households can view and redeem at www.recyclebank.com. These RecycleBank Points can be used with more than 400 national and local RecycleBank reward partners.

Each week a household can see how much it has recycled compared to its neighborhood and city. But more uniquely, each household can view its carbon footprint in terms of how many trees and gallons of oil it has saved because of its recycling efforts. RecycleBank also tracks the carbon footprint of every RecycleBank household on its home page. RecycleBank households have saved more than 300,000 trees and more than 21 million gallons of oil by recycling. (Check its website for up-to-the-minute numbers.)

RecycleBank is market-driven, proven, and simple to implement. Cities with the RecycleBank program save hundreds of thousands of dollars each year in landfill fees because waste is recycled instead of being sent to the landfill. RecycleBank reward partners are associated with environmental incentives, achieve brand differentiation, keep their packaging out of landfills, and reward citizens for doing what's good for the earth.

Ed Begley Jr. and the $100 Thermostat

Actor and environmentalist Ed Begley Jr.

Probably the most well-known celebrity environmentalist, Ed Begley Jr. has been an environmentalist since the 1970s and can often be seen riding his *hybrid* electric bicycle or electric vehicle around Hollywood. His home is the focus of HGTV's *Living with Ed*, and he was named one of the top three environmentalists in the world.

In interviews, Begley has been quoted as saying that although some green building technologies might not be affordable to everyone, everyone can start the ball rolling by investing in a $100 energy-saving thermostat. "You know, you put it down to a lower temperature, it gets into the low 60s perhaps as the house cools down over the night, and you save all this energy. You put an energy-saving thermostat in every home, and you have enough natural gas left over so everybody can drive a natural gas vehicle with no net gain, tomorrow."

def•i•ni•tion

Hybrid vehicles have a fuel-efficient gas engine and a battery-powered electric motor.

The successful actor also runs his modestly sized two-bedroom home off solar panels, and he did so to prove that it could be done. He started the process by retrofitting the existing structure. What was his first step? Blow in R-30 insulation to his attic. The investment of a few hundred dollars immediately began to pay off. One step at a time, he continued to make changes: installing energy-saving thermostats, energy-saving lightbulbs, energy-saving appliances, double-pane windows, and more. Eventually, he invested in solar and wind power, and his natural gas bill was never more than $30 in the winter or more than a total of $300 per year.

Today, Begley is the spokesperson for MyGreenCottage, a national builder that builds custom green homes. Partial proceeds of every home sold by MyGreenCottage go to Habitat for Humanity and Adventures for Wish Kids, and the company builds one home for a deserving family for every 500 homes it sells.

Matthew Linden, ConsciousBuild

Matthew Linden is a luxury green home builder and the owner of ConsciousBuild in San Luis Obispo, California. He built his own home as green as possible and uses it as an educational tool for others. He even filmed the entire construction process and posted it on his website so homeowners and builders can learn about the process (www.consciousbuild.com).

When most people reflect on their childhoods, the simple, yet wonderfully mastered all-American images of Norman Rockwell usually come to mind. However, from a very early age, Matthew Linden envisioned a different set of images.

"Early on in my life I was exposed to exquisitely designed and built homes in and around Southern California," said Linden. "I recall my mother bringing me to various design home tours year after year where I would marvel at these beautiful places that people called their home; to me they were works of art. I owe a great deal of my taste and love of architecture to those experiences."

Combining his love of design with his concern for the planet, Linden has been an advocate of responsible building practices throughout his career. He has been incorporating environmentally sustainable products and techniques into his luxury custom homes for close to a decade; he believes it's his mission to educate his clients on the importance of making responsible choices and thereby contributing to the health of the planet.

His current project, a 6,000-square-foot home, ConsciousBuildOne (CB1), will be used as an educational model for the latest in environmentally sustainable products, techniques, and technologies. Some of the unique green materials and green/sustainable practices include the following:

♦ Onsite buildings were dismantled and have been used in the construction process of the new building.

♦ Passive solar principals and technology have been employed.

- High-volume fly ash, 40 percent, is used for all the footings and foundation work.

- All framing lumber is FSC-certified, and insulation is made of recycled denim material.

- Loewen dual-glazed, low-E, gray glass windows have been installed.

- Formaldehyde-free, wheat-board kitchen cabinets, countertops, and tiles are made from recycled materials such as paper.

- Whirlpool ENERGY STAR appliances are used throughout the home.

- No-VOC paint has been used.

- Pre-stained concrete exterior siding was chosen.

- A greywater system was installed for irrigating the landscape.

- Seventy Coastal Live Oak trees have been planted.

A Green Interior and Exterior in Louisville, KY

A home remodeled into a "green home" by Décor&You.

(Christopher Sims, CID, Décor&You)

Interior designer Christopher Sims, CID, who operates a Décor&You franchise in Louisville, Kentucky, was delighted when one of his customers wanted to "go green." However, the remodel expanded far beyond the original proposal. The clients, who are airline pilots, wanted to compensate for the large carbon footprint their careers leave on the world. The original proposal to redo the flooring and provide a few other minor green upgrades kept expanding as the clients added more features. The final project included …

- ◆ Reclaimed white oak flooring that was salvaged from barns and warehouses in the Pennsylvania area dating back 95 to 115 years.

- ◆ Converting to compact fluorescent lights (ceiling fans, pendants, and chandeliers all were updated to compact fluorescent models).

- ◆ Zero-VOC Sherwin Williams Harmony Paint.

- ◆ ENERGY STAR or better appliances.

- ◆ A geothermal HVAC system; the couple had five wells dug in their yard to harness the geothermal energy.

- ◆ Solar roof panels.

- ◆ A stormwater runoff system that included an underground storage tank that fed an organic vegetable garden and native plants. In addition, the couple installed a composting tank.

Bryan Roberts's Florida Earthship

An earthship is a home made of truly earthy materials (see Chapter 7 for more information). Bryan Roberts, who builds earthships, tells about the project:

> This home is to be completely off-the-grid using solar for power and capturing rainwater for all of the home's water needs. The home is constructed using many recycled items, including over 1,500 used tires; 35,000 bottles; and more than 30,000 aluminum cans. The home has greywater recycling systems in a solarium within the home, which not only filters the water for reuse, but also grows produce for use by its inhabitants. The effluent from the toilets passes through a constructed wetlands outside to remove contaminants before being returned to the earth.

> It has been a struggle to say the least; but we feel it is worth it as this home treads so lightly on the environment. Using no fossil fuels for power, reusing greywater to produce food, and treating blackwater before it is returned to the earth, this home works in harmony with its surroundings rather than starkly against it. It will be using solar air conditioning to condition the indoor temperature in conjunction with the thermal mass of the earthen walls.

Bryan Roberts of Eco-Tech Construction is in the middle of building an earthship in Manatee County, Florida.

Roberts is opening his project up for others to see and learn. For more information, visit www.eco-techconstruction.com.

Platinum Living

Green living can be beautiful, and this loft in an abandoned commercial building is a perfect example of that. Richard Renner Architects in Sherborn, Massachusetts, was awarded the Platinum Certification in the LEED for Homes Pilot Program—the highest that can be achieved—for converting the second floor of a brick commercial building into a residential loft in Portland, Maine.

The two-bedroom loft conversion is part of a project that converts a derelict neighborhood into a flexible, modern, and environmentally responsible live/work combination. The open plan includes high levels of insulation and triple-glazed windows that reduce energy use. Other features include radiant heating, a heat-recovery ventilation system, a grid solar PV system, FSC-certified wood framing and floors, bamboo cabinets, low-VOC materials, a vegetated roof, and so much more.

A great example of adaptive reuse, this home is located in a former commercial building in Portland, Maine.

(Peter Vanderwarker, photographer)

Take the Next Steps

Obviously, you purchased this book because you are interested in making your home as energy efficient as possible while also minimizing your impact on the environment and keeping you and your family as healthy as possible. So, now that you are accomplishing that, consider taking the next step and greening another aspect of your life. Perhaps you can take a closer look at the clothes you wear, the cleaning supplies you use, or the car you drive.

That's Not All Folks!

Well, that's almost it for this edition of *Green Building and Remodeling Your Home*. As you begin your own green project, keep in mind that there are new products and services coming on the market every day. So it's important to keep up-to-date with what's happening by reading magazine articles and books and visiting websites like the ones we've mentioned throughout this book. Eco-friendly products that you use today can be improved with another more energy-efficient or safer product that saves homeowners even more money.

We don't expect you to jump on the bandwagon for every new product as soon as it's released, but it's important to know when it pays to upgrade.

The industry is moving fast! There are so many companies now that offer green building products and services. Just take it one step at a time and you will leave a positive imprint on the environment for future generations to come.

Green Facts
Every year, Americans throw away 50 billion food and drink cans, 27 billion glass bottles and jars, and 65 million plastic and metal jar and can covers. More than 30 percent of our waste is packaging materials. It can take from 100 to 400 years for things like cloth and aluminum to decompose. Glass has been found in perfect condition after 4,000 years in the earth! Minimize your impact on the earth by reducing the amount you consume and reusing and recycling what you do use.

The Least You Need to Know

- Look to other projects for inspiration. Visit green homes and communities.

- Follow the lead of activists like Ed Begley Jr. and start small—with just a $100 thermostat—then go from there.

- The community-based RecycleBank program can save your community hundreds of thousands of dollars each year in landfill fees.

- Green building is not a trend. It's a way of life. Incorporate green living into all aspects of your life.

Glossary

active solar   A system using mechanical devices (pumps, fans, and so on) that transfers collected heat to the storage medium and/or the end use.

adaptability   Designing a space now to meet your future needs. This prevents the need for additional remodeling down the road.

advanced framing techniques   A cost-saving method of construction that uses alternative framing methods to conserve building materials.

agricultural waste   Materials left over from agricultural processes (for example, wheat stalks and shell hulls) that are used as building materials.

air changes per hour (ACH)   How often the air in your home is replaced in a given period of time. One air change means the air is replaced in a one-hour period.

air exchange rate   The rate at which outside air replaces indoor air in a given space.

alternative energy   Energy from sources other than fossil fuels such as oil, natural gas, and coal. For example, wind power and solar energy.

annual fuel utilization efficiency (AFUE)   The higher the percentage, the greater the efficiency of the appliance.

asbestos   A mineral fiber that can pollute air or water and cause cancer or asbestosis when inhaled. It's use has been restricted by the EPA.

ASHRAE American Society of Heating, Refrigeration & Air-Conditioning Engineers.

biodegradable A material that decomposes into natural components when exposed to the air, sunlight, or moisture.

blackwater Water that contains animal, human, or food waste.

British thermal unit (BTU) The quantity of heat required to raise the temperature of 1 pound of water 1°F.

brownfields Industrial or commercial facilities that have been expanded or not used because there is a threat of contamination. Some developers have fixed the potential problems on brownfields and developed the properties for residential or commercial use.

carbon footprint The total amount of carbon dioxide and other greenhouse gases emitted over the life cycle of a product or service.

carbon monoxide (CO) A colorless, odorless, poisonous gas, produced by the incomplete burning of carbon-based fuels, including gasoline, oil, and wood.

carcinogen A substance that can cause cancer in animals or humans.

cellulose insulation Insulation alternative to glass fiber.

certified lumber Lumber that has been certified sustainable harvest by an independent certification authority, such as the Forest Stewardship Council.

CFLs Stands for compact fluorescent lightbulbs, which are more energy efficient and last longer than standard incandescent lightbulbs.

cistern A small tank used to store rainwater.

compost A mixture of decaying organic matter, such as leaves and manure, used as fertilizer. The process of creating compost is called composting.

construction waste Waste from building, remodeling, repairing, or demolishing any structure.

cool roof A roof designed to reflect the heat of the sun away from the home.

cradle-to-cradle Term used to describe a material or product that is recycled into a new product at the end of its life.

cradle-to-grave Term used to describe the life of a material or product up to the point of disposal.

daylighting   Using natural light in an interior space to substitute for artificial light.

deconstruction   Taking apart or removing some home components with the primary goal of reusing them in mind.

dual-flush toilet   Water-saving toilets that have two settings for liquid and for full-flush solid removal.

durability   The ability of a product to exist for a long time.

embodied energy   The amount of energy used to create a product.

energy-efficient mortgage   Mortgages that are specifically designed to encourage homeowners or homebuyers to upgrade their homes with energy-efficient features.

Energy Policy Act   The Energy Policy Act of 1992 addresses a variety of energy issues and created new legislation and some tax breaks.

ENERGY STAR   The Environmental Protection Agency's (EPA's) program for identifying and promoting energy-efficient products to help reduce greenhouse emissions.

engineered lumber/wood   Composite wood products made from lumber, fiber or veneer, and glue.

erosion   The wearing away of land surface by wind or water. Erosion is often sped up by farming, residential development, and other types of development.

flow reducer   A device attached to a fixture that reduces the amount of water flow.

fly ash   Noncombustible residual particles expelled by flue gas and used to make concrete. It reduces the amount of CO_2-producing cement in the mix.

Forest Stewardship Council (FSC)   A third-party certification organization that evaluates the sustainability of forest products. FSC-certified wood products have met specific criteria in areas such as forest management, labor, and fair trade.

formaldehyde   A colorless, flammable gas or liquid that can be found in lacquers, paints, wood products, foam insulation, and more. Exposure has been linked to various forms of cancer, allergic reactions, respiratory problems (including asthma), and even death.

geothermal heat   An energy-saving pump with an underground coil that transfers heat from the ground to the inside of a building.

global warming   An increase in the near surface temperature of the earth.

granny flat   An accessory dwelling unit (also known as a mother-in-law unit).

green design   Architectural designs that conform to the principles of green building, including solar panels, recycling, energy-efficient systems, and more.

green label   A certification program by the Carpet and Rug Institute for carpet and adhesives meeting specified criteria for the release of volatile organic compounds.

green roof   A contained green space on, or integrated with, a building roof. Green roofs maintain living plants in a growing medium on top of a membrane and drainage system. They are considered a sustainable building strategy in that they have the capacity to reduce stormwater runoff from a site, modulate temperatures in and around the building, have thermal insulating properties, can provide habitat for wildlife and open space for humans, and provide other benefits.

greenhouse effect   The warming of Earth's atmosphere attributed to a buildup of carbon dioxide or other gases.

greenhouse gas   A gas, such as carbon dioxide or methane, which contributes to potential climate change.

greenwash   False claims by a company that its produce or service is "eco-friendly."

greywater   Residential wastewater composed of wash water from kitchen, bathroom, and laundry sinks, tubs, and washers. The water can be stored and used again to water lawns or gardens.

halogen   A type of incandescent lamp with higher energy efficiency than standard lamps.

heat pump   An electric device with capabilities for heating and cooling air.

high efficiency   Something that requires less energy or water to run.

home equity line of credit   A source of credit that uses your home as collateral. You can borrow from the line of credit to make green upgrades and repairs until you have reached your maximum credit limit.

home equity loan   A loan obtained for a variety of reasons and secured by the equity in your home. The interest you pay is usually tax-deductible.

HVAC   General term for the heating, ventilation, and air conditioning system.

hydrocarbons (HCs)   Chemical compounds that consist entirely of carbon and hydrogen.

hydronic radiant heating   A heating system that uses a boiler to heat hot water and a pump to circulate the hot water in plastic pipes installed in a concrete slab in the floor.

IAQ   Indoor air quality.

impervious surface   A surface that rejects the precipitation falling on it, rather than allowing it in (infiltration).

indigenous planting   Using plants that are native to the area in landscaping.

indoor air pollution   Chemical, physical, or biological contaminants in indoor air.

infiltration   When water penetrates the ground into the soil below or when air leaks through the building to the outside.

insulated concrete form (ICF)   Forms for poured concrete walls that stay in place as a permanent part of the wall.

integrated pest management (IPM)   A mixture of chemical and other nonpesticide methods to control pests.

kilowatt hours   One watt hour is the amount of energy (usually electrical or natural gas) expended by a 1-watt load (for example, a lightbulb) drawing power for one hour.

lead   A metal that is hazardous to your health if breathed or swallowed. Used previously in paints, it must be removed by professionals when remodeling.

LEED   A green building rating system developed by the U.S. Green Building Council. LEED stands for Leadership in Energy and Environmental Design.

Life Cycle Analysis (LCA)   The assessment of a product's full environmental costs, from raw material to final disposal, in terms of consumption of resources, energy, and waste.

linoleum   A natural flooring product made from cork flour, linseed oil, oak dust, and jute.

low emissivity (low-E) windows   Technology that lowers the amount of energy loss through windows; it lets light in while keeping heat or cold out.

medium-density fiberboard   A composite wood fiberboard used for cabinetry and other interior applications. MDF containing urea formaldehyde can contribute to poor indoor air quality.

mercury   A toxic, odorless liquid at room temperature that converts to an odorless, colorless gas when heated. Fluorescent lights contain significant amounts of mercury. Newer lights are available with reduced amounts of the substance.

methane   A potent greenhouse gas emitted from landfills, natural gas, and petroleum systems; stationary and mobile combustion; wastewater treatment; and certain industrial processes.

mulch   Any material—usually wood chips, leaves, and so on—placed over the soil to keep it from eroding.

nonrenewable energy   Energy derived from sources that are depletable or exhaustible, such as oil, coal, and natural gas.

offgassing   When volatile chemicals are released into the air.

ozone depletion   The destruction of the earth's ozone layer.

passive solar   Using the sun's energy to heat or cool your home.

permeable (or porous) paving   Pavement that allows the passage of water into the ground.

photovoltaic (PV) cell   A device that converts solar energy into electricity.

Portland cement   A type of cement made by burning limestone and clay. It is a basic ingredient in concrete.

post-consumer recycling   Use of materials generated from residential and consumer waste.

post-industrial material   Industrial manufacturing scrap or waste; also called pre-consumer material.

R-value   A measure of the insulating quality of a substance; the higher the R-value, the greater the insulating quality.

radiant barrier roof sheathing   Material installed to reduce summer heat gain and winter heat loss.

radiant heat   A heating system that uses hot water, steam pipes, or electric resistance coils to heat the floors of your home.

radon   A colorless, naturally occurring, radioactive gas found in soil and rock. Breathing in too much is unhealthy and can cause illness.

rainwater harvest   The gathering of rainwater for use in or around your house.

reclaimed lumber   Lumber reclaimed by the "deconstruction" of a building or structure.

recycled content   The amount of pre- and post-consumer recovered material in building materials.

recycled-content aggregate   Reused concrete salvaged from demolition projects.

recycled-content material   Products manufactured using post-consumer materials.

recycling   Reusing materials and objects in original or changed forms rather than discarding them as waste.

refurbished   Fixing a product so it can be used again in some form.

renewable resources   A resource, such as trees or grass, that can be replenished.

reuse   Using a product in its original form more than once.

salvage   Materials saved from damage or destruction.

SEER (or EER)   Stands for seasonal energy efficiency ratio; it's the amount of cooling produced (BTU) by air conditioning divided by the amount of electricity (watts) used. The higher the SEER number, the greater the efficiency.

solar panels   Devices that convert light from the sun into electricity.

solar water heating   Heating water by allowing ground- or rooftop-mounted panels to collect solar rays.

straw bale construction   Using straw bales as insulation in a home structure.

structural bamboo construction   Using bamboo as a home construction material.

structural insulated panel (SIP)   A composite building material consisting of two layers of structural board with an insulating layer of foam between. SIPs can be used as walls, roofs, or flooring.

sustainability   Practices that would ensure the continued viability of a product or practice well into the future.

sustainable development   Developing residences or commercial buildings that meet the needs of the present owners without compromising the ability of future generations to meet their needs as well.

tankless water heaters   Water heaters that store water and heat it extremely quickly instead of using energy to keep the water consistently warm. These water heaters take up less space than storage tank types.

ventilation rate   The rate at which indoor air enters and leaves a building.

volatile organic compound (VOC)   Products—such as particle board, plywood, adhesives, paints, varnishes, carpets, and more—that are made with materials that offgas, usually in the form of formaldehyde gas, a byproduct of hydrocarbon-based materials. Exposure to VOCs can cause a myriad of health problems. Many low-VOC alternatives are available for green builders and remodelers.

water-source heat pump   A heat pump that uses wells or heat exchangers to transfer heat from water to the inside of a home.

weather stripping   Putting thin strips of metal, rubber, vinyl, or foam around doors and windows to prevent air or moisture from infiltrating and causing energy loss.

whole-house fan   A large fan that draws hot air out of a home and replaces it with cooler outside air.

wind turbine   A device for generating electricity from wind; a windmill.

xeriscape   Water-efficient landscaping design and implementation; it uses native or natural plans that are drought or heat resistant.

B

Green Building Resources

Nonprofit Organizations

Alliance for Healthy Homes: afhh.org

Organization working to prevent and eliminate hazards in the home that are harmful to the health of children and families.

Alliance to Save Energy: ase.org

Supports energy efficiency and advocates policies to reduce consumer costs and lessen greenhouse gas emissions.

American Concrete Institute: aci-int.org

Provides concrete knowledge and information necessary to utilize its full potential.

American Council for an Energy-Efficient Economy: aceee.org

Dedicated to advancing energy efficiency.

American Lung Association Health House: healthhouse.org

Source for consumers and builders wanting to know how to build and maintain healthier homes.

American National Standards Institute: ansi.org

Voice of the U.S. Standards and Conformity Assessment System.

American Planning Association: planning.org

Public interest and research organization committed to urban, suburban, regional, and rural planning.

American Solar Energy Society: ases.org

Organization working to increase the use of solar energy and energy efficiency in the United States.

American Wood Protection Association: awpa.org

Organization promulgating voluntary wood preservation standards, ensuring that treated wood products perform satisfactorily.

ATHENA Institute International: athenasmi.ca

Helps architects and engineers to evaluate new and existing buildings' environmental impact through life cycle analysis (LCA).

Build It Green: builditgreen.org

Promotes healthy, energy- and resource-efficient buildings in California.

Building Materials Reuse Association: buildingreuse.org

Education and research organization of building deconstruction and reuse/recycling of recovered materials.

Cool Roof Rating Council: coolroofs.org

Implements and communicates an energy performance rating system for roof surfaces, supports research, and provides education.

Ecological Design Institute: ecodesign.org

Dedicated to research and the education of ecological design.

Ecology Action: ecoact.org

Provides educational services and technical assistance for maximum environmental quality.

Environmental Working Group: ewg.org

Uses public information to protect public health and the environment.

Freecycle.org: freecycle.org

Nonprofit movement of giving or getting materials for free to keep out of landfills.

Global Environment & Technology foundation: getf.org

Promotes the development and use of innovative technology to achieve sustainable development.

Global Environmental Options: globalenvironmentaloptions.org

Encourages sustainable solutions to global environmental problems.

Global Green USA: globalgreen.org

Addresses environmental issues.

Green Seal: greenseal.org

Provides science-based environment certification standards.

Greenguard Environmental Institute: greenguard.org

Oversees the institute's certification program.

National Pest Control Association: pestworld.org

Provides information on pest management.

National Rural Water Association: nrwa.org

Provides support with water and wastewater systems. They help set up proper testing methods.

Northwest Energy Efficiency Alliance: nwalliance.org

Encourages the development and adoption of energy-efficient products and services.

Pacific Northwest Pollution Prevention Resource Center: pprc.org

Source of high-quality, unbiased pollution prevention information in the Northwest.

Pew Charitable Trusts: pewtrusts.org

Educates the public and policymakers about the causes, consequences, and solutions to environmental problems.

Soil and Water Conservation Society: swcs.org

Serves as an advocate for conservation professionals and science-based conservation practices, programs, and policy.

Solar Living Institute: solarliving.org

Promotes promoting sustainable living through environmental education.

Steel Door Institute: steeldoor.org

Promotes the use of steel doors in the construction industry.

Timber Framers Guild of North America: tfguild.org

Trade association dedicated to the craft of timber framing.

United States Green Building Council: usgbc.org

Committed to expanding sustainable building practices.

Wild Ones: for-wild.org

Nonprofit environmental education and advocacy organization.

Professional, Trade, and Industry Organization

American Chemistry Council: americanchemistry.com

Works to improve the quality of materials used in the building industry and serves as a resource for new ideas in energy conservation, etc.

American Indoor Air Quality Council: iaqcouncil.org

Promotes awareness, education, and certification in the field of indoor air quality.

American Institute of Architects: aia.org

Professional association representing the interests of architects.

American Institute of Steel Construction: aisc.org

Dedicated to keeping the steel and construction communities informed.

American Institute of Timber Construction: aitc-glulam.org

National trade association of structural glued laminated (glulam) timber industry.

American Lighting Association: americanlightingassoc.com

Trade association representing the lighting industry.

American Plastics Council: plastics.org

Division of American Chemistry Council representing manufacturers of plastic resins.

American Society of Heating, Refrigerating & Air-Conditioning Engineers: ashrae.org

The society advances technology to serve the populace and promote sustainability.

American Society of Landscape Architects: asla.org

National professional association representing landscape architects.

American Wind Energy Association: awea.org

National trade association promoting wind energy around the world.

Association of Home Appliance Manufacturers: aham.org

U.S. trade association of the home appliance industry.

Building Green, Inc.: buildinggreen.com

Independent company providing information to building industry professionals.

Building Stone Institute: buildingstoneinstitute.org

Nonprofit trade association educates consumers on the uses and benefits of natural stone.

Business for Social Responsibility: bsr.org

Helps companies integrate sustainability into business strategy and operations through research, consulting, and so on.

Cali Bamboo: calibamboo.com

Promotes the use of bamboo for everyday products.

Carpet America Recovery Effort: carpetrecovery.org

A joint industry/government effort to increase the amount of carpet recycling and reduce the amount of carpet waste in landfills.

Construction Materials Recycling Association: cdrecycling.org

Association that promotes the recycling of materials from construction or demolition.

Ebuild: ebuild.com

Part of *Building Products Magazine* and an online directory of materials, tools, and products.

Energy Efficient Building Association: eeba.org

Provides education and resources for resident design, development, and construction industries.

Enertia Building Systems: enertia.com

Designers and manufacturers of geo-solar homes.

Forest Stewardship Council: fscus.org

Coordinates the development of forest management standards throughout the United States.

Geothermal Energy Association: geo-energy.org

Trade association of U.S. companies supporting the expanded use of geothermal energy.

Hardwood Council: hardwoodcouncil.com

Provides practical information about American hardwoods in sustainable design and building.

International Code Council: worldbc.org

Membership association that develops codes used to construct residential and commercial buildings, homes, and schools.

International Electrotechnical Commission: iec.ch

Global organization that prepares and publishes international standards for electrical and electronic technologies.

International Log Builders' Association: logassociation.org

Worldwide organization dedicated to furthering the craft of handcrafted log building.

International Organization for Standardization: iso.org

World's largest developer and publisher of international standards.

International Society of Arboriculture: isa-arbor.com

Worldwide professional organization dedicated to fostering an appreciation for trees.

International Solar Energy Society: ises.org

UN–accredited society that supports the advancement of renewable energy technology implementation and education throughout the world.

National Fire Protection Association: nfpa.org

Fire, electrical, and building safety information.

National Hardwood Lumber Association: natlhardwood.org

Association dedicated to maintaining order, ethics, and structure in the hardwood marketplace.

National Oak Flooring Manufacturers Association: nofma.org

Establishes and enforces grade rules for most domestic species of wood flooring.

National Tile Contractors Association: tile-assn.com

Nonprofit trade association serving the tile industry.

National Wood Flooring Association: woodfloors.org

Provides resources for flooring.

National Wood Window and Door Association: nwwda.org

Trade association with information on windows, doors, and skylights.

North American Insulation Manufacturers Association: naima.org

Trade association of North America concentrating on energy efficiency and environmental preservation through insulation products.

North American Steel Framing Alliance: steelframingalliance.com

Encourages the widespread, practical, and economical use of cold-formed steel framing.

Northeast Sustainable Energy Association: nesea.org

Member organization promoting the understanding, development, and adoption of energy conservation and nonpolluting renewable energy technology.

Plumbing, Heating, Cooling Contractors National Association: naphcc.org

Trade association in the construction industry.

Reflective Insulation Manufacturers Association: rima.net

Educates the marketplace on the benefits of reflective technology.

Renewable Energy Policy Project: crest.org

Works to accelerate the use of renewable energy.

Scientific Certified Systems: scscertified.com

Third-party provider of certification, auditing, and testing services and standards.

Sierra Green Building Association: sigba.org

Promotes effective environmental design in communities.

Solar Energy: solarenergy.com

Support team providing information about products and services.

Solatube Innovation in Daylighting: solatube.com

Innovation in lighting through natural light.

Solutions for Remodeling: solutionsforremodeling.com

Information on remodeling, green building, and certifications.

Southern Forest Products Association: sfpa.org

Trade organization for the forest products industry.

Southern Pine Council: southernpine.com

Joint promotional body supported by manufacturers of southern pine lumber.

Sustainable Buildings Industry Council: sbicouncil.org

Promotes a whole building approach in design.

Sustainable Energy Coalition: sustainableenergycoalition.org

Advocates federal energy policies that lead to a cleaner environment and safe energy technology.

Vinyl Siding Institute: vinylsiding.org

Trade association for manufacturers of vinyl; it furthers the development and growth of the vinyl siding industry.

Western Red Cedar Lumber Association: wwpa.org

Trade association representing softwood lumber manufacturers in Western states.

Whole Building Design Guide: wbdg.org

Helps users create a high-performance building by applying integrated design and team approach.

Government Organizations

Building Concerns: buildingconcerns.com

Works to give the northern California community a better understanding of the principles and standards in ecologically appropriate building and development.

California Integrated Waste Management Board Green Building Program: ciwmb.ca.gov/greenbuilding

State agency of California designated to oversee, manage, and track waste.

Center for Disease Control & Prevention: cdc.gov/nceh/publications

Promotes health and quality of life that result from interactions between people and their environment.

City of Austin Green Building Program: austinenergy.com

Power source for Austin, Texas; it has energy-savings information.

Maryland Environmental Design Program: dnr.state.md.us

State of Maryland program that provides the business community, local governments, and interested citizens with information they need to enhance and restore natural resources.

National Council for Science & The Environment: ncse.org

Regional economic development marketing organization for southeastern North Carolina.

National Institute of Standards and Technology: nist.gov

Provides technology, measurement, and standards that products and services rely on.

National Invasive Species Information Center: invasivespeciesinfo.gov

Provides information on invasive species.

Natural Resources Conservation Service: nrcs.usda.gov

Provides leadership to American landowners and managers to conserve soil, water, and other natural resources.

New York State Energy Research & Development Authority: nyserda.org

Public benefit corporation that focuses on research and development, including the environmental effects of energy consumption.

New York State Environmental Conservation: dec.ny.gov

Conserves, protects, and improves New York State's natural resources and environment.

NYC Waste Less: nyc.gov

New York City resource for waste prevention and recycling information.

Occupational Safety and Health Administration: osha.gov

Works to ensure the safety and health of America's workers.

Oregon Office of Energy: oregon.gov

State of Oregon's official site.

Recycle Works: recycleworks.org

Recycling program of San Mateo County, California.

United States Department of Energy: eia.doe.gov

Energy statistics from the U.S. government.

United States Environmental Protection Agency: epa.gov

Protects human health and the environment.

Watersense, U.S. Environmental Protection Agency: epa.gov/watersense

Partnership program sponsored by the EPA showing how to save water and protect the environment.

WNC Green Building: wncgreenbuilding.com

Online version of the WNC Green Building Directory. This guide explains "green" or environmentally conscious building and offers guidelines and resources.

General Resources

California Redwood Association: calredwood.org

Information on redwood trees.

Center for Plant Conservation: centerforplantconservation.org

Conserves and restores rare native plants of the United States.

Community Greenhouse Foundation: communitygreenhouse.org

Facilitates the development of sustainable green construction in the United States.

Composting 101: composting101.com

An online guide for composting.

Concrete Exchange: concreteexchange.com

Website for learning about concrete countertops; it has a do-it-yourself session.

Dan Vandervort's Home Tips: hometips.com

Online tips for homeowners.

Do-It-Yourself: doityourself.com

Home improvements and home repair information.

Earth911.com: earth911.com

Delivers local information on recycling and product stewardship.

Earth Easy: eartheasy.com

Strives to help reduce the impact on the earth's resources and our contribution to global warming.

Earth Island Institute: earthisland.org

Develops and supports projects that sustain the environment.

The Electronic Product Environmental Assessment Tool: epeat.net

Helps purchasers in the public and private sector evaluate and compare products.

The Energy Foundation: ef.org

Organization advancing energy efficiency and renewable energy.

Fireman's Fund Insurance: firemansfund.com

Insurance fund that offers green building coverage.

Fireplaces.com: fireplaces.com

Information on planning for a fireplace.

Forecast Earth: climate.weather.com

Provides information on green living.

Green Builder Sourcebook: greenbuilder.com

A source for sustainability.

Green Building Alliance: greenbuildingalliance.org

Canadian organizations working together to provide leadership and support for the development of sustainable building practices.

Green Building Solutions: greenbuildingsolutions.org

Endorses the practice of conserving resources and minimizing environment and health issues in buildings.

Green Electronics Council: greenelectronicscouncil.org

Inspires and supports the design and manufacture of electronic products that contribute to a healthy, fair, and prosperous world.

Green Living Ideas: greenlivingideas.com

Provides ideas, tips, and information that help improve environmental sustainability.

Green Living Journal: greenlivingjournal.com

Online publication that educates readers on environmental issues.

Green Living Online: greenlivingonline.com

Provides resources for protecting the environment for future generations.

Green Map System: greenmap.org

Map system that charts communities' natural, cultural, and green living resources.

Green Roofs for Healthy Cities: greenroofs.org

Increases awareness of the economic, social, and environmental benefits of green roof infrastructure.

GreenBuilding: GreenBuilding.com

Resources for green building.

Greenpeace: greenpeace.org

Independent global campaigning organization working to protect and conserve the environment.

Home Depot Foundation: homedepotfoundation.org

Provides resources to assist nonprofit organizations to build affordable homes.

Hot Tub & Spa Annual: poolspaliving.com

Information on spas and hot tub manufacturers.

Housing Zone: housingzone.com

Website for residential construction industry.

Hub Pages: hubpages.com

Resources for information on various topics, including the environment.

Ideal Bite: idealbite.com

Free site for eco-living tips.

Institute for Sustainable Forestry: treesfoundation.org

Provides free information to increase the effectiveness of community-based conservation efforts in California.

Insulating Concrete Form Association: forms.org

Information on insulating concrete forms.

Jetson Green: jetsongreen.com

Web magazine featuring news and trends on green building, green design, sustainable development, and clean technology.

Live Green Live Smart: livegreenlivesmart.org

Strives to influence builders and homeowners to be green and sustainable.

Natural Resource Defense Council: nrdc.org

Environmental action organization looking to protect the planet's wildlife and wild places and to ensure a safe and healthy environment for all living things.

Natural Stone Council Committee on Sustainability: genuinestone.com

Information on genuine stone and the environmental impact of stone products.

The Nature Conservancy: nature.org

Protects ecologically important lands and waters for nature and people.

On Line Tips: onlinetips.org

Provides tips to consumers for home improvements.

Smart Growth Resource Library: smartgrowth.org

Works to serve the economy, communities, and the environment.

Timber Frame Home: timberframehome.com

Source for timber frame information.

Tree Care Information: treesaregood.com

Tree care information for the public.

Tree Hugger: treehugger.com

Provides green news, solutions, and product information.

Underwriters Laboratories, Inc.: ul.com

Tests products to meet compliance for public safety.

Wind Energy Works: windenergyworks.org

A national alliance that supports wind energy development across the country.

The NAHB National Green Building Program

The NAHB National Green Building Program helps any builder, any-where build a green home. When builders attend the NAHB National Green Building Conference, they work toward their Certified Green Professional™ educational designation or plan the green features in their next project using the online scoring tool at nahbgreen.org.

You can score your home using the NAHB Model Green Home Building Guidelines, the first national rating system for green, single-family homes. The online scoring tool, an explanation of the point system, shows you how to score your project to the Bronze, Silver, or Gold level; a list of accred-ited verifiers is available at nahbgreen.org.

This score sheet introduces you to the rating system.

There's More to NAHB Green

Using the online version of this scoring tool at nahbgreen.org as a guide, a builder can request the home receive National Green Building Certification from the NAHB Research Center. The home must be inspected at close-in and when it is finished to verify that the green features chosen are in place.

The Research Center provides local verifier training and accreditation to ensure that certification is consistent, accurate, neutral, and technically rigorous throughout the country.

NAHB Green also includes marketing and advocacy guidance for members and local home building associations to communicate the benefits of green building and the importance of keeping these innovative practices voluntary.

Learn more at www.nahbgreen.org. It's green building, priced right.

Section 1: Lot Design, Preparation, and Development

Guidelines	Points
1.1 Select a site to minimize environmental impact.	
1.1.1 Avoid environmentally sensitive areas identified through the site footprinting process	7 ____
1.1.2 Choose an infill site	9 ____
1.1.3 Choose a greyfield site	7 ____
1.1.4 Choose an EPA-recognized brownfield site	7 ____
1.2 Identify goals with your team.	
1.2.1 Establish a knowledgeable team by identifying team member roles and writing a mission statement that includes project goals and objectives	6 ____
1.3 Design the site to minimize environmental impact and protect, restore, and enhance the natural features and environmental qualities of the site.	
1.3.1 Conserve natural resources	6 ____
1.3.2 Site the home and other built features to optimize solar resource	6 ____
1.3.3 Minimize slope disturbance	5 ____
1.3.4 Minimize soil disturbance and erosion	6 ____
1.3.5 Manage storm water using low impact development	8 ____
1.3.6 Devise landscape plans to limit water and energy demand	8 ____
1.3.7 Maintain wildlife habitat	5 ____

1.4 Develop the site to minimize environmental intrusion during onsite construction.

1.4.1 Provide onsite supervision and coordination during clearing, grading, trenching, paving, to ensure targeted green development practices are implemented   5 ____

1.4.2 Conserve existing onsite vegetation   5 ____

1.4.3 Minimize onsite soil disturbance and erosion   6 ____

Your Section Total ____

Section 2: Resource Efficiency

<u>Guidelines</u>   <u>Points</u>

2.1 Reduce the quantity of materials used and waste generated.

2.1.1 Create an efficient floor plan that maintains home's functionality   1–9 ____

2.1.2 Employ advanced framing techniques   4–8 ____

2.1.3 Use building layouts that maximize resources and minimize material cuts   6 ____

2.1.4 Create a detailed framing plan and material takeoffs   7 ____

2.1.5 Use materials requiring no additional finish resources to complete application onsite   4 ____

2.1.6 Use precut or preassembled building systems or methods as outlined below:

     A. Provide precut joist or premanufactured floor truss   3–9 ____

     B. Provide panelized wall framing system   6 ____

     C. Provide panelized roof framing system   6 ____

     D. Provide modular construction for entire house   7 ____

2.1.7 Use a frost-protected shallow foundation   4 ____

Guidelines	Points

2.2 Enhance durability and reduce maintenance.

2.2.1 Provide covered entry (awning, covered porch) at exterior doors — 6 ____

2.2.2 Use recommended-sized roof overhangs for the climate — 7 ____

2.2.3 Install perimeter drain for all basement footings sloped to discharge to daylight, sump pit — 7 ____

2.2.4 Install drip edge at eave and gable roof edges — 6 ____

2.2.5 Install gutter and downspout system to divert water 5 feet away from foundation — 6 ____

2.2.6 Divert surface water from all sides of building — 7 ____

2.2.7 Install continuous and physical foundation termite barrier where necessary — 7 ____

2.2.8 Use termite-resistant materials for walls, floor joists, trusses, exterior decks, etc. — 7 ____

2.2.9 Provide a water-resistant barrier behind the exterior veneer or siding — 8 ____

2.2.10 Install ice flashing at roof edge — 5 ____

2.2.11 Install enhanced foundation waterproofing — 7 ____

2.2.12 Employ and show on plans all flashing details — 9 ____

2.3 Reuse materials.

2.3.1 Disassemble existing buildings instead of demolishing — 6 ____

2.3.2 Reuse salvaged materials — 5 ____

2.3.3 Provide onsite bins or space to sort, store scrap materials — 6 ____

2.4 Use recycled-content materials.

2.4.1 Use recycled-content building materials; list components used — 3–6 ____

Guidelines	Points

2.5 Recycle waste materials during construction.

2.5.1 Develop and implement a construction and demolition waste management plan — 7 ____

2.5.2 Conduct onsite recycling efforts — 5 ____

2.5.3 Recycle construction waste offsite — 6–12 ____

2.6 Use renewable materials.

2.6.1 Use materials manufactured from renewable resources — 3–5 ____

2.6.2 Use certified wood and use wood-based materials from certified sources — 4/per ____

2.7 Use resource-efficient materials.

2.7.1 Use products that are composed of fewer resources — 3 ____

Your Section Total ____

Section 3: Energy Efficiency

Guidelines	Points

3.1 Minimum Energy Efficiency Requirements

3.1.1 Mandatory Home is equivalent to the IECC 2003 or local energy code, whichever is more stringent — Req.

3.1.2 Mandatory Size space heating and cooling system and equipment according to building heating and cooling loads calculated using ANSI/ACCA Manual J 8th edition or equivalent — Req.

3.1.3 Mandatory Conduct third party plan review to verify design/compliance with Energy Efficiency section — Req.

Guidelines	**Points**

3.2 Performance Path

3.2.1 Home is X% above IECC 2003

    A. 15% (Bronze)   37 ____

    B. 30% (Silver)   62 ____

    C. 40% (Gold)   100 ____

3.3 Prescriptive Path

An energy efficiency practice identified with a "PP" in Section 3.3 is a Performance Path practice likely to be used to calculate X% above ICC IECC in Section 3.2. If Section 3.3 is used to obtain points in addition to points from 3.2, those practices from Section 3.3 used to comply with Section 3.2 shall not be awarded any additional points.

3.3.1 Building Envelope

    (PP)A. Increase effective R-value of building envelope using advanced framing techniques, continuous insulation, and/or integrated structural insulating system. Measures may include but are not limited to:

        SIPS   8 ____

        ICFS   8 ____

        Advanced framing or insulated corners, intersections and headers   6 ____

        Raised heel trusses   2 ____

        Continuous insulation on exterior wall   4 ____

        Continuous insulation on cathedral ceiling   4 ____

    (PP)B. Air sealing package is implemented to reduce infiltration   10 ____

    (PP)C. ENERGY STAR–rated windows appropriate for local climate   8 ____

Guidelines	Points

3.3.2 HVAC design, equipment, and installation

A. Size, design, and install duct system using ANSI/ACCA Manual D® or equivalent — 8 ____

B. Design radiant/hydronic space heating systems using industry approved guidelines — 8 ____

C. Use ANSI/ACCA Manual S® or equivalent to select heating and cooling equipment — 8 ____

D. Verify performance of the heating and cooling system — 8 ____

E. Use HVAC installer or technician certified by national or regionally recognized program — 6 ____

(PP)F. Fuel-fired space heating equipment efficiency (AFUE)

Gas furnace greater than or equal to 81% — 4 ____

Gas furnace greater than or equal to 88% (ENERGY STAR) — 6 ____

Gas furnace greater than or equal to 94% — 8 ____

Oil furnace greater than or equal to 83% — 2 ____

Gas or oil boiler greater than or equal to 85% (ENERGY STAR) — 2 ____

Gas or oil boiler greater than or equal to 90% — 6 ____

(PP)G. Heat pump efficiency (cooling mode)

9 SEER 13–14 — 6 ____

9 SEER 15–18 — 6 ____

9 SEER 19+ — 7 ____

9 Staged air conditioning equipment — 9 ____

Guidelines	Points

(PP)H. Heat pump efficiency (heating mode)

    7.2–7.9 HSPF   6 ____

    8.0–8.9 HSPF   7 ____

    9.0–10.5 HSPF   9 ____

    >10.5 HSPF   10 ____

(PP)I. Ground source heat pump installed by a certified geothermal service contractor (cooling mode)

    EER = 13–14   5 ____

    EER = 15–18   6 ____

    EER = 19–24   8 ____

    EER = >25   10 ____

(PP)J. Ground source heat pump installed by a certified geothermal service contractor (heating mode)

    COP 2.4–2.6   6 ____

    COP 2.7–2.9   8 ____

    COP = 3.0   10 ____

K. Seal ducts, plenums, equipment to reduce leakage. Use UL 181 foil tapes and/or mastic.   6 ____

L. When installing ductwork: 8 ____

    1. Do not use building cavities used as ductwork, e.g., panning joist or stud cavities

    2. Install all heating and cooling ducts and mechanical equipment within conditioned envelope

    3. Do not install ductwork in exterior walls

M. Install return ducts/transfer grilles in rooms with doors (except baths, kitchen, closets, laundry)   6 ____

Guidelines	Points
N. Install ENERGY STAR–rated ceiling fans	1/per ____
O. Install whole-house fan with insulated louvers	4 ____
P. Install ENERGY STAR–labeled mechanical exhaust for every bathroom ducted to outside	8 ____
3.3.3 Water heating design, equipment, and installation	
A. Water heater Energy Factor equal to or greater than those listed:	4 ____
Natural Gas: Energy Factor in Gallons	
0.64	30 ____
0.62	40 ____
0.60	50 ____
0.58	65 ____
0.56	75 ____
Electric: Energy Factor in Gallons	
0.95	30 ____
0.94	40 ____
0.92	50 ____
0.90	65 ____
0.88	80 ____
0.86	100 ____
B. Install whole house instantaneous (tankless) water heater	4 ____
C. Insulate all hot water lines with a minimum of 1" insulation	4 ____
D. Install heat trap on cold and hot water lines to and from the water heater	3 ____
E. Install manifold plumbing system (parallel piping configuration, stacking plumbing)	5 ____

Guidelines	Points

3.3.4 Lighting and appliances

A. Use an ENERGY STAR Advanced Lighting Package .... 7 ____

B. Install all recessed fixtures within the
conditioned envelope .... 7 ____

C. Install motion sensors on outdoor lighting .... 7 ____

D. Install tubular skylights in rooms
without windows .... 2 ____

E. Install ENERGY STAR–labeled appliance:

Refrigerator .... 3 ____

Dishwasher .... 3 ____

Washing machine .... 5 ____

3.3.5 Renewable energy/solar heating and cooling

3.3.5.1 Solar space heating and cooling

A. Use sun-tempered design: building orientation,
sizing of glazing, design of overhangs to provide
shading .... 10 ____

B. Use passive solar design: sun-tempered design
as above plus additional south-facing glazing,
appropriately designed thermal mass to
prevent overheating .... 10 ____

C. Use passive cooling, including shading,
overhangs, window cross ventilation .... 8 ____

3.3.5.2 Solar water heating

A. Install SRCC-rated solar water heating system

Solar fraction: 0.3 .... 8 ____

Solar fraction: 0.5 .... 10 ____

Guidelines	Points

3.3.5.3 Additional renewable energy options

A. Supply electricity needs by onsite renewable energy source whereby the system is estimated to produce the following kWh per year:

2,000–3,999	8 ____
4,000–5,999	10 ____
6,000+	12 ____

B. Provide clear and unshaded roof area (+/- 30 degrees of south or flat) for future solar collector or photovoltaics; provide rough-in piping from the roof to the utility area

Conduit	3 ____
Insulated piping	5 ____

C. Provide homeowner with information and enrollment materials about options to purchase green power from the local electric utility — 2 ____

3.3.6 Verification

3.3.6.1 Conduct onsite third-party inspection to verify installation of energy-related features — 8 ____

3.3.6.2 Conduct third-party testing to verify performance: blower door, duct leakage, flow rates — 8/per ____

Your Section Total ____

Section 4: Water Efficiency

Guidelines	Points

4.1 Water Use

4.1.1 Hot water delivery to remote locations aided by installation of: — 6/per ____

A. On-demand water heater at point of use served by cold water only

B. Control-activated recirculation system

Guidelines	Points
4.1.2 Water heater located within 30 feet pipe run of all bathrooms and kitchen	9 ____
4.1.3 ENERGY STAR water-conserving dishwasher, washing machine, etc.	7/per ____
4.1.4 Water-efficient showerhead using aerator/venturi with flow rate < 2.5 gpm	2/per ____
4.1.5 Water-efficient sink faucets/aerators < 2.2 gpm	2/per ____
4.1.6 Ultra low-flow (<1.6 gpm/flush) toilets: (power-assist: 4 pts; dual flush: 6 pts)	4–6 ____
4.1.7 Low-volume, non-spray irrigation system installed such as drip irrigation, bubblers	7 ____
4.1.8 Irrigation system zoned separately for turf and bedding areas	6 ____
4.1.9 Weather-based irrigation controllers such as computer-based weather record	7 ____
4.1.10 Collect and use rainwater, as permitted by local code	9 ____
4.1.11 Innovative wastewater technology as permitted by local code	7 ____
Your Section Total	____

Section 5: Indoor Environmental Quality

Guidelines	Points
5.1 Minimize potential sources of pollutants.	
5.1.1 For vented space heating and water heating equipment:	8 ____
A. Install direct vent equipment	
B. Install induced/mechanical draft combustion equipment	

Guidelines	Points

5.1.2 Install space heating and water heating equipment in isolated mechanical room or closet with an outdoor source of combustion and ventilation air ..... 6 ____

5.1.3 Install direct-vent, sealed-combustion gas fireplace, sealed wood fireplace, or sealed woodstove; install no fireplace or woodstove ..... 6 ____

5.1.4 Ensure a tightly-sealed door between the garage and living area and provide continuous air barrier between garage and living areas including air sealing penetrations ..... 9 ____

5.1.5 Ensure particleboard, medium density fiberboard (MDF), and hardwood plywood substrates are certified to low formaldehyde emission standards ..... 6 ____

5.1.6 Install carpet, carpet pad, and floor covering adhesives that hold "Green Label" from Carpet and Rug Institute's indoor air quality testing program or equivalent ..... 6 ____

5.1.7 Mask HVAC outlets during construction and vacuum all ducts, boots, and grills ..... 5 ____

5.1.8 Use low-VOC emitting wallpaper ..... 3 ____

5.2 Manage potential pollutants generated in the home.

5.2.1 Vent kitchen range exhaust to the outside ..... 7 ____

5.2.2 Provide mechanical ventilation at a rate of 7.5 cfm per bedroom +7.5 cfm and controlled automatically or continuous with manual override
Choose:

    A. Exhaust or supply fan(s) ..... 7 ____

    B. Balanced exhaust and supply fans ..... 9 ____

    C. Heat-recovery ventilator ..... 10 ____

    D. Energy-recovery ventilator ..... 10 ____

Guidelines	Points

5.2.3 Install MERV 9 filters on central air or
ventilation systems   3 ____

5.2.4 Install humidistat to control whole-house
humidification system   4 ____

5.2.5 Install sub-slab depressurization system
to facilitate future radon mitigation system   6 ____

5.2.6 Verify all exhaust flows meet design
specifications   9 ____

5.3 Manage moisture (vapor, rainwater, plumbing, HVAC).

5.3.1 Control bathroom exhaust fan with a timer or
humidistat   6 ____

5.3.2 Install moisture-resistant backerboard under
tiled surfaces in wet areas   6 ____

5.3.3 Install vapor retarder directly under slab
(6-mil) or on crawl space floor (8-mil)   9 ____

5.3.4 Protect unused moisture-sensitive materials
by just-in-time delivery, storing in dry area, or
tenting and storing on raised platform   6 ____

5.3.5 Keep plumbing supply lines out of exterior walls   5 ____

5.3.6 Insulate cold water pipes in unconditioned spaces   4 ____

5.3.7 Insulate HVAC ducts, plenums, and trunks
in unconditioned basements and crawl spaces   4 ____

5.3.8 Check moisture content of wood before it
is enclosed on both sides   4 ____

Your Section Total ____

Section 6: Operation, Maintenance, and Homeowner Education

Guidelines	Points

6.1 Provide Home Manual to owners/occupants on the use and care of the home, including: 9 ____

    A. Narrative detailing importance of maintenance and operation to keep a green-built home green

    B. Local Green Building Program certificate

    C. Warranty, operation, and maintenance instructions for equipment and appliances

    D. Household recycling opportunities

    E. Information on how to enroll in program where home receives energy from renewable energy provider

    F. Explanation of the benefits of using compact fluorescent lightbulbs in high-usage areas

    G. A list of actions to optimize water and energy use

    H. Local public transportation options (if applicable)

    I. Clearly labeled diagram showing safety valves and controls for major house systems

6.2 Optional information to include in the Home Manual (see User Guide)   2 ____

6.3 Provide education to owners/occupants in the use and care of their dwellings: instruct homeowners/occupants about the building's goals and strategies and occupant's impact on costs of operating the building; provide training to owners/occupants for all control systems in the house   7 ____

6.4 Solid waste: Encourage homeowners/occupants to recycle by providing built-in space in the home's design (kitchen, garage, covered outdoor space) for recycling containers   1 ____

Your Section Total ____

Section 7: Global Impact

Guidelines	Points

7.1 Products

7.1.1 Note product manufacturer's operations
and practices (environmental management system)   3 ____

7.1.2 Choose low- or no-VOC indoor paints   6 ____

7.1.3 Use low-VOC sealants   5 ____

7.2 Innovative Options

7.2.1 Demonstrate that builder's operations and
business practices include environmental
management concepts   4 ____

Your Section Total ____

Points Required for Green Building Certification

Section	Bronze	Silver	Gold
1. Lot Design, Preparation, and Development	8	10	12
2. Resource Efficiency	44	60	77
3. Energy Efficiency	37	62	100
4. Water Efficiency	6	13	19
5. Indoor Environmental Quality	32	54	72
6. Operation, Maintenance, and Homeowner Education	7	7	9
7. Global Impact	3	5	6
Additional Points from Sections of Your Choice	100	100	100
TOTALS	**237**	**311**	**395**

Appendix D

LEED Rating System List

The LEED for New Construction Rating System is designed to guide and distinguish not only residential homes, but high-performance commercial and institutional projects, including office buildings, high-rise residential buildings, government buildings, recreational facilities, manufacturing plants, and laboratories.

Following is a partial list for new construction. For an extensive list for LEED certification, please visit usgbc.org.

LEED for New Construction v 2.2 Registered Project Checklist

Project Name: _____

Project Address: _____

Project Totals (Pre-Certification Estimates)—69 Points

Certified: 26–32 points

Silver: 33–38 points

Gold: 39–51 points

Platinum: 52–69 points

Sustainable Sites—14 Possible Points

Prereq 1: Construction Activity Pollution Prevention, Required

Credit 1: Site Selection (1 pt)

Credit 2: Development Density and Community Connectivity (1 pt)

Credit 3: Brownfield Redevelopment (1 pt)

Credit 4.1: Alternative Transportation, Public Transportation (1 pt)

Credit 4.2: Alternative Transportation, Bicycle Storage and Changing Rooms (1 pt)

Credit 4.3: Alternative Transportation, Low-Emitting and Fuel-Efficient Vehicles (1 pt)

Credit 4.4: Alternative Transportation, Parking Capacity (1 pt)

Credit 5.1: Site Development, Protect or Restore Habitat (1 pt)

Credit 5.2: Site Development, Maximize Open Space (1 pt)

Credit 6.1: Stormwater Design, Quantity Control (1 pt)

Credit 6.2: Stormwater Design, Quality Control (1 pt)

Credit 7.1: Heat Island Effect, Nonroof (1 pt)

Credit 7.2: Heat Island Effect, Roof (1 pt)

Credit 8: Light Pollution Reduction (1 pt)

Water Efficiency—5 Possible Points

Credit 1.1: Water-Efficient Landscaping, Reduce by 50% (1 pt)

Credit 1.2: Water-Efficient Landscaping, No Potable Use or No Irrigation (1 pt)

Credit 2: Innovative Wastewater Technologies (1 pt)

Credit 3.1: Water Use Reduction, 20% Reduction (1 pt)

Credit 3.2: Water Use Reduction, 30% Reduction (1 pt)

Energy and Atmosphere—17 Possible Points

Prereq 1: Fundamental Commissioning of the Building Energy Systems, Required

Prereq 1: Minimum Energy Performance, Required

Prereq 1: Fundamental Refrigerant Management, Required

Credit 1: Optimize Energy Performance—1–10 points

    Credit 1.1: 10.5% New Buildings/3.5% Existing Building Renovations (1 pt)

    Credit 1.2: 14% New Buildings/7% Existing Building Renovations (2 pts)

    Credit 1.3: 17.5% New Buildings/10.5% Existing Building Renovations (3 pts)

    Credit 1.4: 21% New Buildings/14% Existing Building Renovations (4 pts)

    Credit 1.5: 24.5% New Buildings/17.5% Existing Building Renovations (5 pts)

    Credit 1.6: 28% New Buildings/21% Existing Building Renovations (6 pts)

    Credit 1.7: 31.5% New Buildings/24.5% Existing Building Renovations (7 pts)

    Credit 1.8: 35% New Buildings/28% Existing Building Renovations (8 pts)

    Credit 1.9: 38.5% New Buildings/31.5% Existing Building Renovations (9 pts)

    Credit 1.10: 42% New Buildings/35% Existing Building Renovations (10 pts)

Credit 2: On-Site Renewable Energy—1–3 points

    Credit 2.1: 2.5% Renewable Energy (1 pt)

    Credit 2.2: 7.5% Renewable Energy (2 pts)

    Credits 2.3: 12.5% Renewable Energy (3 pts)

Credit 3: Enhanced Commissioning (1 pt)

Credit 4: Enhanced Refrigerant Management (1 pt)

Credit 5: Measurement and Verification (1 pt)

Credit 6: Green Power (1 pt)

Materials and Resources—13 Possible Points

Prereq 1: Storage and Collection of Recyclables, Required

Credit 1.1: Building Reuse; Maintain 75% of Existing Walls, Floors, and Roof (1 pt)

Credit 1.2: Building Reuse; Maintain 95% of Existing Walls, Floors, and Roof (1 pt)

Credit 1.3: Building Reuse; Maintain 50% of Interior Nonstructural Elements (1 pt)

Credit 2.1: Construction Waste Management, Divert 50% from Disposal (1 pt)

Credit 2.2: Construction Waste Management, Divert 75% from Disposal (1 pt)

Credit 3.1: Materials Reuse, 5% (1 pt)

Credit 3.2: Materials Reuse, 10% (1 pt)

Credit 4.1: Recycled Content, 10% (post-consumer + 1/2 pre-consumer) (1 pt)

Credit 4.2: Recycled Content, 20% (post-consumer + 1/2 pre-consumer) (1 pt)

Credit 5.1: Regional Materials, 10% Extracted, Processed & Manufactured (1 pt)

Credit 5.2: Regional Materials, 20% Extracted, Processed & Manufactured (1 pt)

Credit 6: Rapidly Renewable Materials (1 pt)

Credit 7: Certified Wood (1 pt)

Indoor Environmental Quality—15 Possible Points

Prereq 1: Minimum IAQ Performance, Required

Prereq 2: Environmental Tobacco Smoke (ETS) Control, Required

Credit 1: Outdoor Air Delivery Monitoring (1 pt)

Credit 2: Increased Ventilation (1 pt)

Credit 3.1: Construction IAQ Management Plan, During Construction (1 pt)

Credit 3.2: Construction IAQ Management Plan, Before Occupancy (1 pt)

Credit 4.1: Low-Emitting Materials, Adhesives and Sealants (1 pt)

Credit 4.2: Low-Emitting Materials, Paints and Coatings (1 pt)

Credit 4.3: Low-Emitting Materials, Carpet Systems (1 pt)

Credit 4.4: Low-Emitting Materials, Composite Wood and Agrifiber Products (1 pt)

Credit 5: Indoor Chemical and Pollutant Source Control (1 pt)

Credit 6.1: Controllability of Systems, Lighting (1 pt)

Credit 6.2: Controllability of Systems, Thermal Comfort (1 pt)

Credit 7.1: Thermal Comfort, Design (1 pt)

Credit 7.2: Thermal Comfort, Verification (1 pt)

Credit 8.1: Daylight and Views, Daylight 75% of Spaces (1 pt)

Credit 8.2: Daylight and Views, Views for 90% of Spaces (1 pt)

Innovation and Design Process—5 Possible Points

Credit 1.1: Innovation in Design (1 pt)

Credit 1.2: Innovation in Design (1 pt)

Credit 1.3: Innovation in Design (1 pt)

Credit 1.4: Innovation in Design (1 pt)

Credit 2: LEED Accredited Professional (1 pt)

LEED® is a registered trademark owned by the U.S. Green Building Council and is used by permission.

Index

A

AAMA (American Architectural Manufacturers Association), 94
accent lighting, 169
acid staining, 123
active solar heating, 137
adaptability of homes, 13
adaptive reusability of land, 69
adhesive-free flooring, 118
adobe roofing, 111
advanced framing technique, 58, 82
aerators
   defined, 189
   faucets, 193
   showerheads, 192
aerogel, 87
affordability
   myth, 22-23
   resale homes, 32
AFUE (annual fuel utilization efficiency), 139
AIA (American Institute of Architects), 51
air pollution, 5
air quality. *See* IAQ
ALA (American Lung Association), 195
Alliance to Save Energy website, 47
aluminum
   siding, 114
   windows, 99
Alys Beach, Florida, 115-116
ambient lighting, 169
American Architectural Manufacturers Association (AAMA), 94
American Institute of Architects (AIA), 51
American Institute of Architects Committee on the Environment, 14
American Lung Association (ALA), 195
American Society of Heating, Refrigeration & Air-Conditioning Engineers (ASHRAE), 201
American Society of Home Inspectors, 35
American Society of Landscape Architects, 52
annual fuel utilization efficiency (AFUE) rating, 139
appearance myths of green building, 21
appliances
   dishwashers, 157
   disposing of old, 158
   ENERGY STAR certifications, 152-153
   gas versus electric, 154
   refrigerators/freezers, 155-156
   size, 154
   stoves/ovens, 154-155
   upgrading, 152
   washers/dryers, 156-157
architects, 50
artificial lighting, 170
asbestos, 11
ASHRAE (American Society of Heating, Refrigeration, & Air-Conditioning Engineers), 201
awareness, 13-15, 21
awnings, 222

B

backdrafting, 201
bamboo
   countertops, 162
   flooring, 120
bathrooms
   cabinets, 162-163
   countertops, 158
      bamboo, 162
      ceramic tiles, 160
      concrete, 160
      Corian, 158
      glass tiles, 161
      paper composite, 159
      recycled glass, 159
      recycled plastic, 161
      stainless steel, 162
      terrazzo, 161
      wood, 162
batt insulation, 91
Begley, Ed Jr., 251-252
benefits
   EEMs, 46
   green building
      energy efficiency, 8-9
      health, 10-11
      increasing home values, 12
      indoor air quality, 11
      local economy stimulation, 12
      reducing carbon footprints, 6-8
      saving money, 9-10
      social responsibility, 13
      sustainability, 12
benzene, 197
bioretention systems, 184
botanical pesticides, 212

brainstorming wants/needs, 30
brick siding, 113
Brooks, Colette, 42
brownfields, 69-70
bubbler irrigation systems, 231
budgets for remodeling jobs, 37
builders
   cooperation myth, 23
   researching, 52-53
building
   dream team members
     architects, 50
     contractor certifications, 49-50
     finding, 49
     landscapers, 51
     researching, 52-53
   new homes
     evaluating/prioritizing, 39
     land, 39
     McMansions, 40
     smaller homes, 40-41
bulk moisture, 86
buying resale homes for remodeling, 31-34

C

cabinets for kitchens and bathrooms, 162-163
Cadora, Eric, 42
California tax credits, 48
Cambara, 242
canopies, 222-223
carbon footprints
   McMansions, 40
   measuring, 6
   primary, 8
   reducing, 6-8
   secondary, 8
   smaller homes, 40-41
carbon monoxide, 197

CARE (Carpet America Recovery Effort), 119
Carpet & Rug Institute (CRI), 125
carpets, 125
caulking windows, 102
CCA (chromated copper arsenate), 80
cedar shake shingles, 108
cellulose insulation, 90
cement siding, 113
Center for Plant Conservation website, 211
central air conditioners, 140
ceramic tile
   countertops, 160
   flooring, 122
certifications, 43-44
   contractors, 49-50
   energy-efficient windows, 94
   ENERGY STAR appliances, 152-153
CFLs (compact florescent lights), 167-168
CGPs (Certified Green Professionals), 50
chain of custody, 58
Chavis Heights in Raleigh, North Carolina, 248
chemicals. *See also* VOCs
   benzene, 197
   chromated copper arsenate (CCA), 80
   formaldehyde, 11, 88, 197
   methylene chloride, 197
   pools/hot tubs, 239-240
Cheng, Fu-Tang, 160
Cherry Hill, New Jersey, 250
choosing
   exterior paint, 114
   insulation, 88-89
chromated copper arsenate (CCA), 80
clay roofing tiles, 109

climate
   considerations, 36
   zones, 225
Clinton, Bill, 15
closed-loop geothermal systems, 138
CMRA (Concrete Materials Recycling Association), 57
coconut palm flooring, 124
combustion venting, 203
comfort flooring, 118
Committee on the Environment formed by American Institute of Architects, 14
communities, 248-250
compact florescent lights (CFLs), 167-168
compost, 216
computer-aided design programs, 30
concrete
   countertops, 160
   flooring, 123
   insulated concrete forms (ICF), 80
   roofing tiles, 109
Concrete Exchange, 160
Concrete Materials Recycling Association (CMRA), 57
condensation, 96
conduction, 84
Connecticut tax credits, 48
ConsciousBuild in California, 252-254
consequences of global warming, 4
conservation easements, 72
conserving water
   faucets, 192-193
   greywater reuse, 182-183
   pools/hot tubs, 237
     heating, 237-238
     pumps/filters, 237
     tips, 238-239
   rain gardens, 184

rainwater harvesting, 180-182

showerheads, 191-192

toilets, 188
  gallons per flush, 188
  leaks, 188
  low-flow, 189-191
  ULFT, 188

construction waste, 5, 63-64

consumer awareness, 13-15, 21

contractors
  certifications, 49-50
  researching, 52-53

controlling lighting, 171

convection, 84

convection ovens, 154

cool roofing, 112

cooling systems, 139
  central air conditioners, 140
  duct cleaning, 205-206
  fans, 141
  passive, 141
  room air conditioners, 140
  size, 135-136

Corian countertops, 158

cork flooring, 122

costs
  affordability myth, 22-23
  budgets for remodeling jobs, 37
  green homes, 9-10
  solar heating, 137

cotton insulation, 92

countertops, 158-162

Craigslist website, 59

credit ratings, 33

credit reports, 33

CRI (Carpet & Rug Institute), 125

cross-linked polyethylene (PEX) piping, 147

cumaru, 119

curb appeal, 106

D

daylight lighting, 170

deciduous trees, 220

decks, 242

deconstruction, 9, 62-63

denim insulation, 92

designs
  lighting, 169-170
  windows, 95-96
    glazing, 97
    low-E coatings, 97
    solar heat gain coefficient, 98
    U-values, 98
  yards, 210

diffusion, 85

dimmer switches, 171

dishwashers, 157

disposing of old appliances, 158

dollar bill refrigerator test, 156

doors, 103-104

drain water recovery systems, 146

dream team members, 49-53

drip irrigation systems, 231

dryers, 156-157

dual-flush toilets, 190

duct cleaning, 205-206

durability
  flooring, 118
  materials, 24

E

earthships, 83, 254

eBay website, 59-60

economy, 12

EEMs (Energy Efficient Mortgages), 10, 46-47

efficiency
  energy
    auditing, 22

EEMs, 10, 46-47
EIMs, 10
energy loss, 8-9
ENERGY STAR, 14
fuel heating systems, 139

EIMs (Energy Improvement Mortgages), 10

electric appliances, 154

electricity
  overview, 166
  sources, 171-172

electronic filters, 204

Elmwood Reclaimed Timber in Kansas City, Missouri, 120

embodied energy, 57

energy
  efficiency
    audits, 22
    EEMs, 10, 46-47
    EIMs, 10
    energy loss, 8-9
    ENERGY STAR, 14
  electricity
    overview, 166
    sources, 171-172
  Home Energy Rating Systems (HERS), 46
  loss, 8-9
  pools/hot tubs, 238-239
  sources, 171-172

Energy Efficient Mortgages (EEMs), 10, 46-47

Energy Improvement Mortgages (EIMs), 10

Energy Policy Act, 47

energy recovery ventilators (ERVs), 202

ENERGY STAR, 14
  appliances, 152-153
  water heater criteria, 144

environmental stewardship, 16

EPA (Environmental Protection Agency), 5, 16

erosion, 232

ERVs (energy recovery ventilators), 202

evergreens, 221
examples
  Alys Beach, Florida,
    115-116
  Begley, Ed Jr., 251-252
  Cherry Hill, New Jersey,
    250
  Findhom Foundation com-
    munity, 248
  Greensburg, Kansas, 249
  Homes Pilot Program, 255
  JPI East, 248
  Kaufmann brownfield/
    infill, 73
  Linden, Matthew, 252-254
  LivingHomes model home,
    42-43
  National Homebuilder
    Mainstream GreenHome,
    26-27
  Oakland Park, Florida, 249
  Paterson, Sharon, 17-18
  Raleigh Chavis Heights,
    248
  Roberts, Bryan's Florida
    earthship, 254
exterior paint, 114

F

fans, 141
farmland, 72
faucets, 192-193
fences, 240-241
fertilizers, 215-216
fiberglass, 90, 99
filtration, 203-204
Findhom Foundation commu-
  nity website, 248
finding
  dream team members, 49
    architects, 50
    contractor certifications,
      49-50

landscapers, 51
  researching, 52-53
HERS evaluators, 46
home inspectors, 35
materials, 58
  construction waste,
    63-64
  deconstruction sites,
    62-63
  locally, 58
  reducing needs, 58
  reusable, 59-62
  toilet leaks, 188
fire pits, 245
Fireman's Fund, 53
fixed skylights, 100
flashing, 86
flat roofs, 106
floodplains, 72
flooring, 118-125, 133
flow of water, 232
forced air heating, 133
forced hot water heating, 132
foreclosures, 33-34
*Forever Green; The History and
  Hope of the American Forest*,
  73
formaldehyde, 11, 88, 197
foundations, 80-81
framed openings, 41
frames for windows, 99
framing techniques, 81-84
Freecycle website, 59-60
freezers, 155-156
fuel-efficient heating systems,
  139

G

gallons per flush (GPF), 188
garages
  doors, 104
  exhaust, 204-205
gardening, 216
gas appliances, 154

GCP (Green Certified
  Professional) training course,
  50
geothermal heating, 138-139
glass tile countertops, 161
glazing windows, 97
global warming
  consequences, 4
  defined, 3
good bugs, 213
Gore, Al, 13
GPF (gallons per flush), 188
granny flats, 41
gravity-assisted toilets, 190
Greater World subdivision, 83
green building
  benefits, 6-12
  construction waste, 5
  movement, 13-15
Green Certified Professional
  (GCP) training course, 50
green communities, 41, 248
  Cherry Hill, New Jersey,
    250
  Findhom Foundation, 248
  Greensburg, Kansas, 249
  JPI East, 248
  Oakland Park, Florida, 249
  Raleigh Chavis Heights,
    248
Green Label Plus, 125
green materials. *See* materials
Green Pyramid, 38
green roofing, 111-112
Green Seal standards, 25
GREENGUARD
  Environmental Institute, 197
"The Greening of the White
  House," 15
Greensburg, Kansas, 249
greenwashing, 25
greyfields, 71
greywater reuse, 182-183
grills, 243-244

H

halogens, 169
handyman specials, 34
Harrington, Sir John, 189
health advantages, 10-11
Hearth, Patio, and Barbecue
   Association, 135
heat
   effects on homes, 84-85
   roofing, 107
heat pumps, 134
heat recovery ventilators
   (HRVs), 202
heating systems
   AFUE ratings, 139
   duct cleaning, 205-206
   geothermal, 138-139
   outdoors, 245
   pools/hot tubs, 237-238
   size, 135-136
   solar, 137-138
   types, 132
      forced air, 133
      forced hot water, 132
      heat pumps, 134
      pellet stoves, 135
      radiant floor heating,
         133
      wood stoves, 135
   water heaters, 144
      drain water recovery sys-
         tems, 146
      ENERGY STAR crite-
         ria, 144
      indirect, 145
      insulation, 148
      on-demand, 144
      piping, 146-147
      solar, 145-146
      water temperature, 149
HEPA (high efficiency particulate air) filters, 204
HERS (Home Energy Rating
   System), 46

HETs (high-efficiency toilets),
   190
Historic Albany Foundation in
   Albany, New York, 61
historical home renovations,
   25-26
Home Energy Rating Systems
   (HERS), 46
home equity loans, 46
home equity lines of credit, 46
home inspectors, 35
home values, 12
homebuilding techniques
   foundations, 80-81
   framing, 81-84
   heat effects, 84-85
   insulation, 87-92
   moisture, 85-87
   steel, 81
homeowners insurance, 53-54
Homes Pilot Program, 255
hot tubs, 236-237
   chemicals, 239-240
   energy/water saving tips,
      238-239
   heating, 237-238
   pumps/filters, 237
HRVs (heat recovery ventilators), 202
humidifiers, 203
hybrids, 251
hydrozoning, 230

I

IAQ (indoor air quality), 196
   duct cleaning, 205-206
   filtration, 203-204
   garage exhaust, 204-205
   green home advantages, 11
   moisture, 198-200
   pollutants, 196
   radon, 198
   ventilation, 200-202
      combustion, 203
      ERVs, 202

   HRVs, 202
   humidifiers, 203
   stop, 201
   testing, 202
   whole house, 201
   VOCs, 197
IceStone, 159
ICF (insulated concrete
   forms), 80
An Inconvenient Truth, 13
increasing home values, 12
indirect water heaters, 145
indoor air pollution
   green home advantages, 11
   non-green homes, 5
indoor air quality. *See* IAQ
induction cooktops, 154
infill development, 67-68
infrastructure, 39
inspectors, 35
insulated concrete forms
   (ICF), 80
insulation, 87-88
   batt, 91
   choosing, 88-89
   denim and cotton, 92
   loose-fill, 89-90
   open-cell foam, 91
   soy, 92
   water heaters, 148
insurance, 53-54
integrated pest management,
   214-215
integration of elements/
   components, 35-36
interior doors, 104
invasive plants, 211-212
Ipe, 242
irrigation systems, 230-231

J-K

JPI East in Washington, D.C.,
   248
jute, 123

Kaufmann, Mike and Juli, 73
kitchens
  cabinets, 162-163
  countertops, 158
    bamboo, 162
    ceramic tiles, 160
    concrete, 160
    Corian, 158
    glass tiles, 161
    paper composite, 159
    recycled glass, 159
    recycled plastic, 161
    stainless steel, 162
    terrazzo, 161
    wood, 162

L

laminar-flow showerheads, 192
laminated wood, 120
lamination, 120
land
  Leavell, Chuck tree farm, 73
  new homes, 39
  site planning, 67
    adaptive reusability, 69
    brownfields, 69-70
    greyfields, 71
    infill development, 67-68
  sites to avoid, 71
    farmland, 72
    floodplains, 72
    wetlands, 71
  smart growth, 66-67
landscapers, 51
landscaping
  design, 210
  fertilizers, 215-216
  invasive plants, 211-212
  pesticides, 212-213
    good bugs, 213
    integrated pest manage-
      ment, 214-215

natural/organic, 215
  types, 212-213
roof gardens, 224
shading homes
  awnings and canopies, 222-223
  climate zones, 225
  shutters, 224
  trees, 220-221
  windbreaks, 221-222
watering
  flow, 232
  irrigation systems, 230-231
  wasteful watering habits, 231-232
  xeriscaping, 230
latex paints, 126
laundry appliances, 156-157
lead paints, 126-127
lead-based paint, 10
leather flooring, 124
Leavell, Chuck, 73
LEDs (light-emitting diodes), 169
LEED (Leadership in Energy
  and Environmental Design), 14
  green material standards, 56
  Professional Accreditation
    program, 49
life-cycle analysis, 56
lighting, 166
  artificial versus daylight, 170
  compact florescent lights, 167-168
  controls, 171
  designs, 169-170
  halogens, 169
  LEDs, 169
  outdoors, 243
lime washes, 114
limestone, 121
Linden, Matthew, 252-254

linoleum flooring, 123
living walls, 241
LivingHomes model home, 42-43
local building requirements, 37
local economic stimulation, 12
local suppliers, 58
locations. *See also* land
  new homes, 39
  resale homes, 32
loose-fill insulation, 89-90
low-E (low-emissivity), 97
low-flow showerheads, 192
low-flow toilets, 189-191
low-sloped roofs, 106

M

marble, 121
materials
  aerogel, 87
  adobe roofing, 111
  aluminum
    siding, 114
    windows, 99
  bamboo
    countertops, 162
    flooring, 120
  batt insulation, 91
  brick siding, 113
  cedar shake shingles, 108
  cellulose insulation, 90
  cement siding, 113
  ceramic tile
    countertops, 160
    flooring, 122
  chain of custody, 58
  concrete
    countertops, 160
    flooring, 123
    insulated concrete forms
      (ICF), 80
    roofing tiles, 109
  Corian, 158
  cork flooring, 122

cotton insulation, 92
denim insulation, 92
durability, 24
exchanges, 62
fiberglass, 90, 99
finding, 58
    construction waste,
        63-64
    deconstruction sites,
        62-63
    local businesses, 58
    reducing needs, 58
    reusable, 59-62
glass tile countertops, 161
Ipe, 242
laminated wood, 120
leather flooring, 124
LEED standards, 56
limestone, 121
linoleum flooring, 123
marble, 121
metal roofing, 111
mineral wool, 90
paints
    exterior, 114
    lead, 126-127
    lead-based, 10
    types, 126
    VOCs, 126
PaperStone countertops,
    159
piping, 146-147
plantation-grown wood,
    120
pressure-treated wood, 80
reclaimed wood, 120
recycled glass countertops,
    159
recycled plastic counter-
    tops, 161
reducing, 58
reusable, 59
    online communities,
        59-61
    salvage yards, 61-62
rock wool, 90

sandstone, 121
slag, 69
slag wool, 90
slate, 110, 121
soy insulation, 92
stone flooring, 121-122
sustainable, 56-57
straw bale homes, 84
terrazzo, 122, 161
vinyl
    siding, 114
    window frames, 99
wood
    Cambara, 242
    countertops, 162
    flooring, 119-120
    Ipe, 242
    pressure-treated, 80
    siding, 113
    stoves, 135
    windows, 99
McMansions, 40
measuring
    carbon footprints, 6
    energy efficiency, 22
MEFs (modified energy fac-
    tors), 157
megawatts, 48
MERV (Minimum Efficiency
    Reporting Value), 204
metal roofing, 111
methylene chloride, 197
mineral wool, 90
Minnesota Tree Care
    Advisors, 220
modified energy factors
    (MEFs), 157
moisture
    controlling, 86-87
    indoor air quality, 198-200
    movement, 85-86
mortgages
    EEMs, 10, 46-47
    EIMs, 10
mosquitoes, 184
motion detectors for lights,
    171

MyGreenCottage, 252
myths
    affordability, 22-23
    appearance of buildings, 21
    builder cooperation, 23
    durability of materials, 24
    green advertising, 25
    green technology, 24
    historical home renova-
        tions, 25-26
    replacing everything in the
        house, 24

N

NADCA (National Air Duct
    Cleaners Association), 205
NAHB (National Association
    of Home Builders), 10, 50
NARI (National Association
    of the Remodeling Industry),
    50
National Fenestration Rating
    Council (NFRC), 94
National Homebuilder
    Mainstream GreenHome,
    26-27
National Lead Information
    Center website, 127
National Terrazzo & Mosaic
    Association (NTMA), 161
National Wetlands Research
    Center, 71
natural flooring, 118
natural pest remedies, 215
Natural Resources Defense
    Council, 16
new home planning
    evaluating/prioritizing, 39
    land, 39
    McMansions, 40
    smaller homes, 40-41
New Jersey tax credits, 48
New York tax credits, 48
NFRC (National Fenestration
    Rating Council), 94

non-green homes
  indoor air pollution, 5
  remodeling
    brainstorming wants/
      needs, 30
    integration of elements/
      components, 35-36
    prioritizing, 36-38
    resale home purchases,
      31-34
  VOCs, 6
  water consumption, 5
non-petroleum-based flooring,
  118
Not So Big House, The, 40
NTMA (National Terrazzo &
  Mosaic Association), 161

O

Oakland Park, Florida, 249
on-demand water heaters, 144
online communities for materials, 59-61
open space, 66
open-cell foam insulation, 91
open-loop geothermal sys-
  tems, 138
optimum value engineering
  (OVE), 58
organic pest remedies, 215
Original Charcoal Company
  website, 244
outdoors
  decks, 242
  erosion, 232
  fences, 240-241
  fertilizers, 215-216
  framework building tech-
    niques
    earthships, 83, 254
    foundations, 80-81
    framing, 81-84
    heat effects, 84-85
    insulation. *See* insulation
    moisture, 85-87

    steel, 81
  gardens, 216
  grills, 243-244
  heating, 245
  invasive plants, 211-212
  lighting, 243
  pesticides, 212-213
    good bugs, 213
    integrated pest manage-
      ment, 214-215
    natural/organic, 215
    types, 212-213
  play structures, 245
  pools and hot tubs, 236-237
    chemicals, 239-240
    energy/water saving tips,
      238-239
    heating, 237-238
    pumps/filters, 237
  shading homes
    awnings and canopies,
      222-223
    climate zones, 225
    roof gardens, 224
    shutters, 224
    trees, 220-221
    windbreaks, 221-222
  stormwater pollutants,
    228-229
  water flow, 232
  watering
    irrigation systems,
      230-231
    wasteful watering habits,
      231-232
    xeriscaping, 230
  yard design, 210
OVE (optimum value engi-
  neering), 58, 82
ovens, 154-155

P

Pacific Yurts, 83
paints
  exterior, 114

  lead, 126-127
  lead-based, 10
  types, 126
  VOCs, 126
panel filters, 203
paper composite countertops,
  159
PaperStone countertops, 159
passive cooling techniques,
  141
passive solar heating, 137
Patterson, Sharon, 17-18
pellet stoves, 135
permeable pavements,
  228-229
Pesticide Action Network
  North America, 213
pesticides, 212-213
  good bugs, 213
  integrated pest manage-
    ment, 214-215
  natural/organic, 215
  types, 212-213
PEX (cross-linked polyethylene) piping, 147
piping, 146-147
placement of windows, 99-100
Planet Green, 23
planning
  new homes
    evaluating/prioritizing,
      39
    land, 39
    McMansions, 40
    smaller homes, 40-41
  remodels, 31
    brainstorming wants/
      needs, 30
    buying resale homes,
      31-34
    integration of elements/
      components, 35-36
plantation-grown wood, 120
play structures outdoors, 245
pleated filters, 204

pollutants
    indoor air, 5, 196
    stormwater, 228-229
polyvinyl chloride (PVC), 11,
    146-147
pools, 236-237
    chemicals, 239-240
    energy/water saving tips,
        238-239
    heating, 237-238
    pumps/filters, 237
prefab homes, 42
pressure-assisted toilets, 190
pressure-treated wood, 80
primary carbon footprints, 8
prioritizing
    green pyramid, 38
    new homes, 39
    remodels, 36
        budgets, 37
        climate, 36
        local requirements, 37
        small differences, 38
programmable thermostats,
    136
purple loosestrife, 211
PVC (polyvinyl chloride), 11,
    146-147

Q

quality
    indoor air, 196
        duct cleaning, 205-206
        filtration, 203-204
        garage exhaust, 204-205
        green home advantages,
            11
        moisture, 198-200
        pollutants, 196
        radon, 198
        ventilation, 200-203
        VOCs, 197
    water, 178-179

R

R-values, 87
radiant floor heating, 118, 133
radiation, 85
radon, 198
rain gardens, 184
Rain Gardens of Michigan
    website, 184
rainwater harvesting, 180-182
Raleigh Chavis Heights, 248
rammed earth construction,
    80
reclaimed wood, 120
recyclable flooring, 118
RecycleBank technology, 250
recycled glass countertops,
    159
recycled plastic countertops,
    161
reducing
    carbon footprints, 6-8
    materials, 58
refrigerators, 155-156
remodels, 31
    brainstorming wants/needs,
        30
    integration of elements/
        components, 35-36
    prioritizing, 36
        budgets, 37
        climate, 36
        local requirements, 37
        small differences, 38
    resale home purchases, 31
        affordability, 32
        foreclosures, 33-34
        handyman specials, 34
        location, 32
        resale values, 32
Renner, Richard, 255
renovating historical homes,
    25-26
replacement windows, 94
resale values, 32

researching companies, 52-53
Residential Energy Services
    Network website, 46
resources, 5, 16
reuse stores, 62
reusing
    greywater, 182-183
    materials, 59
        online communities,
            59-61
        salvage yards, 61-62
Reynolds, Michael, 83
Roberts, Bryan's Florida
    earthship, 254
rock wool, 90
roof gardens, 224
roofing
    climate control, 107
    styles, 106-107
    types, 107
        adobe, 111
        concrete, 109
        cool, 112
        green, 111-112
        metal, 111
        shingles/shakes, 108
        slate, 110
        tiles, 109
room air conditioners, 140

S

safety of flooring, 118
salvage yards, 61-62
sandstone, 121
sashes, 99
Seattle, Washington, tax cred-
    its, 48
Second Use Building
    Materials in Seattle,
    Washington, 61
secondary carbon footprints, 8
SEER (Seasonal Energy
    Efficiency Ratio), 140
self-cleaning ovens, 155
sensors for faucets, 193

SFI (Sustainable Forestry Initiative), 56
shading homes
    awnings and canopies, 222-223
    climate zones, 225
    shutters, 224
    trees, 220
        deciduous, 220-222
        evergreens, 221
    windbreaks, 221-222
shakes, 108
SHGC (solar heat gain coefficient), 98
shingles, 108
showerheads, 191-192
shutters, 224
siding
    aluminum, 114
    brick, 113
    cement, 113
    vinyl, 114
    wood, 113
SIP (Structural Insulated Panels), 81
site planning, 67
    adaptive reusability, 69
    avoiding, 71-72
    brownfields, 69-70
    greyfields, 71
    infill development, 67-68
size
    appliances, 154
    heating and cooling systems, 135-136
skylights, 100-101
slag, 69
slag wool, 90
slate, 110, 121
sliding glass doors, 104
smart growth, 66-67
smart windows, 103
social responsibility, 13,16
solar
    gain, 97

heat gain coefficient (SHGC), 98
heating, 137-138
power, 172
protection film, 101-102
reflectance, 107
water heaters, 145-146
solid waste reduction programs, 62
sources of power, 171-172
South Carolina tax credits, 48
soy insulation, 92
spatial layering, 41
stainless steel countertops, 162
standby heat loss, 144
state radon contacts, 198
steel framing, 81
steep-sloped roofs, 106
stone flooring, 121-122
stop ventilation, 201
storm windows, 101
stormwater pollutants, 228-229
stoves, 154-155
straw bale homes, 84
Structural Insulated Panels (SIP), 81
styles of roofing, 106-107
subsidence, 71
suppliers, 58
    construction waste, 63-64
    deconstruction sites, 62-63
    locally, 58
    reduce materials, 58
    reusable, 59-62
Susanka, Sarah, 40
sustainability
    defined, 12
    green home advantages, 12
    materials, 56-57
Sustainable Forestry Initiative (SFI), 56
synthetic pesticides, 212

T

tankless heaters, 144
task lighting, 169
tax credits, 47-48
techniques for homebuilding
    foundations, 80-81
    framing, 81
        advanced framing technique, 82
        earthships, 83
        SIP, 81
        steel, 81
        straw bale, 84
        yurts, 83
    heat effects, 84-85
    insulation, 87-88
        batt, 91
        choosing, 88-89
        denim and cotton, 92
        loose-fill, 89-90
        open-cell foam, 91
        soy, 92
    moisture
        controlling, 86-87
        movement, 85-86
    steel, 81
    straw bale, 84
    yurts, 83
technologies
    computer-aided design programs, 30
    myths, 24
    RecycleBank, 250
terrazzo, 122, 161
testing IAQ, 202
thermal emittance, 107
toilets, 188
    gallons per flush, 188
    HETs, 190
    inventor, 189
    leaks, 188
    low-flow, 189-191
    ULFT, 188
traps, 212

trees, 220-221
tubular skylights, 100
types
    cooling systems, 140-141
    countertops, 158
        bamboo, 162
        ceramic tiles, 160
        concrete, 160
        Corian, 158
        glass tiles, 161
        paper composite, 159
        recycled glass, 159
        recycled plastic, 161
        stainless steel, 162
        terrazzo, 161
        wood, 162
    flooring
        carpeting, 125
        ceramic tile, 122
        coconut palms, 124
        concrete, 123
        cork, 122
        leather, 124
        linoleum, 123
        stone, 121-122
        wood, 119-120
    heating systems, 132
        forced air, 133
        forced hot water, 132
        geothermal, 138-139
        heat pumps, 134
        pellet stoves, 135
        radiant, 133
        solar, 137-138
        wood stoves, 135
    low-flow showerheads, 192
    low-flow toilets, 190
    paints, 126
    pesticides, 212-213
    roofing, 107
        adobe, 111
        concrete, 109
        cool, 112
        green, 111-112
        metal, 111
        shingles/shakes, 108
        slate, 110
        tiles, 109
    siding
        aluminum, 114
        brick, 113
        cement, 113
        vinyl, 114
        wood, 113
    water heaters
        indirect, 145
        on-demand, 144
        solar, 145-146
    windows, 99

U

U-values for windows, 98
ULFT (ultra-low flush toilets), 188
ultraviolet rays (UV), 101
UNICEF website, 178
upgrading
    appliances, 152
    windows
        caulking, 102
        smart windows, 103
        solar protection film, 101-102
        storm windows, 101
Urban Land Institute, 68
USGBC (U.S. Green Building Council), 14, 49
UV (ultraviolet rays), 101

V

vacuum-assisted toilets, 190
values of homes, 12
vapor moisture, 86
ventilating skylights, 100
ventilation, 200-202
    backdrafting, 201
    combustion, 203
    ERVs, 202
    HRVs, 202
    humidifiers, 203
    stop, 201
    testing, 202
    whole house, 201
Vetrazzo, 159
vinyl
    siding, 114
    window frames, 99
visual weight, 41
VOCs (volatile organic compounds), 6
    defined, 6
    health concerns, 11
    indoor air quality, 197
    non-green homes, 6
    paints, 126

W

wallpaper, 127
walls
    paints, 125-127
    wallpaper, 127
wants/needs brainstorming, 30
washing machines, 156-157
WashWise Rebate Program, 48
waste
    construction, 63-64
    watering habits, 231-232
water
    conserving
        faucets, 192-193
        greywater reuse, 182-183
        pools/hot tubs, 237-239
        rain gardens, 184
        rainwater harvesting, 180-182
    consumption, 5
    landscaping
        irrigation systems, 230-231
        wasteful watering habits, 231-232

water flow, 232
xeriscaping, 230
pools and hot tubs, 236-237
chemicals, 239-240
energy/water saving tips, 238-239
heating, 237-238
pumps/filters, 237
quality, 178-179
showerheads, 191-192
stormwater pollutants, 228-229
toilets, 188
gallons per flush, 188
HETs, 190
inventor, 189
leaks, 188
low-flow, 189-191
ULFT, 188
water factor (WF), 157
water heaters, 144
drain water recovery systems, 146
ENERGY STAR criteria, 144
indirect, 145
insulation, 148
on-demand, 144
piping, 146-147
solar, 145-146
water temperature, 149
water temperature on water heaters, 149
WaterSense, 189
watersheds, 228
WDMA (Window & Door Manufacturers Association), 94
websites
acid staining concrete, 123
Alliance to Save Energy, 47
American Institute of Architects, 14
American Society of Home Inspectors, 35

American Society of Landscape Architects, 52
carbon footprint scores, 6
CARE, 119
Center for Plant Conservation, 211
ConsciousBuild, 252
Craigslist, 59
credit reports, 33
eBay, 59
ENERGY STAR, 14
EPA, 16
Findhom Foundation community, 248
Fireman's Fund, 53
Freecycle, 59
Green Seal standards, 25
GREENGUARD Environmental Institute, 197
Hearth, Patio, and Barbecue Association, 135
LivingHomes, 42
Minnesota Tree Care Advisors, 220
National Lead Information Center, 127
Natural Resources Defense Council, 16
Oakland Park, Florida, 249
Original Charcoal Company, 244
Rain Gardens of Michigan, 184
RecycleBank technology, 250
refrigerator efficiency, 155
Residential Energy Services Network, 46
state radon contacts, 198
tax credits, 47
UNICEF, 178
USGBC, 14
wetlands, 71
WF (water factor), 157

white roofs, 113
WHO (World Health Organization), 5
whole house ventilation, 201
wind power, 172
windbreaks, 221-222
Window & Door Manufacturers Association (WDMA), 94
windows, 94
condensation, 96
designs, 95-98
energy-efficient certifications, 94
frames/sashes, 99
placement, 99-100
replacement, 94
skylights, 100-101
types, 99
upgrading, 101-103
wood
Cambara, 242
countertops, 162
flooring, 119-120
Ipe, 242
pressure-treated, 80
siding, 113
stoves, 135
windows, 99
World Health Organization (WHO), 5

X – Z

xeriscaping, 51, 230

yards, 210-216
shading homes, 220-225
watering, 230-232
yurts, 83

zappers, 212